RANDY CHARLES EPPING

THE 21ST-CENTURY ECONOMY

A Beginner's Guide

Randy Charles Epping, based in Nyon, Switzerland, and São Paulo, Brazil, has worked in International Finance for over twenty-five years, holding management positions in European and American investment banks in London, Geneva, and Zurich. He has a master's degree in International Relations from Yale University, in addition to degrees from the University of Notre Dame and the University of Paris–Sorbonne. He is currently the manager of IFS Project Management AG, a Switzerland-based international consulting company. He is also the president of the Central Europe Foundation, a Zurich-based charity providing assistance to students and economic organizations in Central and Eastern Europe. In addition to several other books and articles on the world economy, he has written a novel, *Trust*, a financial thriller based in Budapest, Zurich, New York, and São Paulo.

ALSO BY RANDY CHARLES EPPING

The Beginner's Guide to the World Economy

Novels

Trust

THE 21ST-CENTURY ECONOMY

A BEGINNER'S GUIDE

With 101 Easy-to-Learn Tools
for Surviving and Thriving
in the New Global Marketplace

RANDY CHARLES EPPING

VINTAGE BOOKS
A DIVISION OF RANDOM HOUSE, INC.
NEW YORK

FIRST VINTAGE BOOKS EDITION, APRIL 2009

Copyright © 2009 by Randy Charles Epping

All rights reserved. Published in the United States by Vintage Books,
a division of Random House, Inc., New York, and in Canada by
Random House of Canada Limited, Toronto.

Vintage and colophon are registered trademarks of Random House, Inc.

Library of Congress Cataloging-in-Publication Data

Epping, Randy Charles.
The 21st-century economy : a beginner's guide : with 101
easy-to-learn tools for surviving and thriving in the new global
marketplace / Randy Charles Epping.
p. cm.
ISBN: 978-0-307-38790-5
1. International finance.   2. Economic history—21st century.
3. Globalization.   4. International trade.   I. Title.   II. Title:
Twenty-first-century economy.

HG3881.E568 2010
330.9—dc22
2008041554

Book design by R. Bull

Maps © copyright 2006 SASI Group (University of Sheffield) and
Mark Newman (University of Michigan): http://www.worldmapper.org

www.vintagebooks.com

Printed in the United States of America

10   9   8   7   6   5   4

To Thalia Zepatos, thank you for your inspiration. To Richard Lupoff and Frank Robinson, thank you for your example. To János Faragó, thank you for your ideas. And to Jerrod, Shawn, and Chas Engelberg, thank you for your corrections.

In Memoriam: Tracy Lawrence Epping

I would also like to thank my agent, Kirsten Manges, and my editors at Vintage Books, Edward Kastenmeier, Tim O'Connell, and Marty Asher, for their vision and ongoing efforts to create an economically literate world. As the *Economist* once said, "Politicians care about what voters think, especially voters in blocks, and not a shred about what economists think. Talking to politicians about economics is therefore a waste of time. The only way to make governments behave as if they were economically literate is to confront them with electorates that are."

TABLE OF CONTENTS

Never before has it been so important for us to become economically literate. The idea of this book is not only to give you a thorough understanding of what's happening in the world economy today, but to provide you with the tools to be able to make sense of future economic events—good or bad. These days, the front pages of our newspapers are flooded with business- and economics-related articles. Web sites are increasingly devoted to economic issues. And the news we see and hear on TV and radio is increasingly economic in content.

Even the water-cooler conversations have become economic in nature. How's your 401(k) surviving the crash? Will Congress be able to get us out of the mess we're in? What about those foreign investors, are they going to pull out their investments and bring down the economic house of cards? How are we going to be able to pay for our children's education, our retirement, our fuel this winter? Will there be enough money around to ensure our economic survival in the years to come?

Faced with the enormous complexity of the new global economy, many of us tend to shrug our shoulders and say, "It's all too difficult. Let the economists figure it all out." But if we're going to survive and thrive in this strange new world, we're going to have to understand the basics. Unfortunately, most economists today are not able to explain things simply.

I remember how my first economics professor at Yale, a brilliant man by all accounts, thought that any question needed to be answered with a complicated graph or a formula. No question could be answered with a simple yes or no. Always with a "Let me draw you an equation," or "Let's look at this graph." I would sit there and stare at the complex array of numbers and Greek letters he was writing on the blackboard and wonder, *Is this really the only way to understand economics?*

I had the impression that if someone had asked the ques-

INTRODUCTION

UNDERSTANDING THE WORLD economy has never been more important than it is today. What happens in one corner of the globe can affect us and our families in ways that would have been unimaginable in previous years.

In today's interconnected fusion economy, almost anything can happen. A downturn in one part of the world can turn into a global financial meltdown within days—if not hours. When a housing crisis in a few American states grew into a full-fledged financial crisis in 2008, for example, it sparked one of the biggest stock-market meltdowns in modern history. And when countries, companies, and banks around the world began tumbling like dominoes, the so-called credit crisis became an economic inferno. Money dried up and companies were forced to lay off employees and cut back production. Even the developing world was impacted, when investors from rich countries pulled funds from the four corners of the globe to cover losses at home.

It was just a matter of time before the economic crisis became a political and social crisis as well. When people lose their jobs or their retirement savings—or worse, when food runs out, as it already has in some countries around the world—it doesn't take much to bring down governments or engender social chaos.

tion "What's the weather like today?" the brilliant economist would begin his answer by writing out a complex formula or matrix equation. Sometimes, all you have to do is look out the window. The answers are often right there, staring at us in the face.

What is a stock index? Think of checking the cost of a few items in a store to see how the "market" as a whole is priced. Or what is a leveraged buyout? Think of a seesaw, lifting a heavy weight at one end with a small amount of force at the other. The same concept allows investors who borrow money to finance their acquisitions to get more "bang for their buck."

We are all citizens of this increasingly interconnected world, and we're going to have to understand the economic forces shaping our daily lives if we're going to profit from them or intelligently oppose them. Student, farmer, businessperson, criminal, lawyer, politician, homemaker, or environmental activist—whoever we are, we all have a role to play. And without a basic understanding of the world economy and its effect on our daily lives, we're never going to be effective members of society.

The intent of this book is to provide an easy-to-understand survey of the 21st-century economy, so that whoever we are—consumers, voters, businesspeople, or students—we'll be able to survive, and thrive, in the new global marketplace. All we need is a basic understanding of how this new 21st-century economy works.

Although this isn't meant to be a "get-rich-quick" book, it's obvious that any successful foray into the global marketplace needs to be accompanied by a thorough understanding of the principles on which global finance and economics are based. Imagine trying to invest in an Internet-based IPO without knowing your way around the Web-based economy. Or trying to convince your government to increase spending on biofuels without knowing the underlying fundamentals of the "green" economy and the effect these policies will have on global food production. Or how to bail out failed banks without bankrupting the government in the process.

I hope this book helps you on your journey through this perilous new century. If you have any questions or suggestions, please feel free to contact me at RCEpping@aya.yale.edu, through the publisher of this book, Vintage Books, or through the fusion economics Web site: www.fusioneconomics.com. I'm always happy to receive readers' comments and hear how they are using their newfound knowledge.

You can read this book from front to back, from back to front—however you'd like. And don't worry, you'll find no graphs and no equations. By the time you finish, you should be able to understand every one of the major economic forces that are shaping our daily lives.

Along the way you'll find occasional informational sidebars that explain various economic concepts that are important for understanding the 21st-century economy. "What is subprime debt?" "What is a derivative?" "What is a carbon footprint?" "What is the G8?" At the end, you'll find an extensive glossary with definitions of all the major economic terms—credit default swaps, Fed funds, current accounts, hedge funds, etc.—that you can refer to whenever you encounter them in the news, at work, in class, on the Web, or on TV. Eventually, the complex fusion economy of the 21st century won't be so difficult to comprehend.

Then it's up to you to go out and change the world. In whatever way you choose.

MAPS

Map of the World According to Population

Map of the World According to National Income

THE
21ST-CENTURY
ECONOMY

A BEGINNER'S GUIDE

CHAPTER I

WHAT IS THE FUSION ECONOMY?

THE CONVERGING WORLD economy has created a whole new paradigm for the 21st century. Global warming, credit crunches, currency meltdowns, food crises, and trade wars are just a few examples of how our everyday lives are being altered by a myriad of forces, many of which are economic in nature. And like nuclear fusion, which joins together hydrogen molecules and releases enormous amounts of energy in the process, the converging global economy is releasing a lot of new energy—we just need to figure out how to use it.

This new _fusion economy_ brings together forces and reactions in ways that are impossible to understand using normal linear forms of approach. It used to be that we could follow a fairly simple path to arrive at an economic conclusion. A better product or a more efficient company meant more productivity, which meant a higher standard of living for all. But today, things aren't so simple. How can we say that economic growth in China or India is a good thing if it increases global pollution or leads to food scarcity? How can we say that increased access to mortgage financing is a good thing if it entices subprime borrowers to buy houses they can't afford to pay for, leading to failing banks in Europe and the United States, stock market crashes in Asia, and a worldwide credit crisis?

population increase

3

• •

INFORMATIONAL TOOL:

What are subprime mortgages?

During the housing boom at the beginning of the 21st century, many mortgage companies and banks in the United States began providing loans to home buyers who normally wouldn't have been given credit. These "subprime" borrowers were allowed to buy homes by paying slightly more than normal rates, often with floating interest rates that rise and fall with the general market. Most of these subprime mortgages were repackaged and sold as bonds to investors throughout the world economy, mainly to banks and financial institutions—from Frankfurt to Tokyo to Zurich. Many were given AAA ratings, implying that the chances of not being paid back were minimal. Unfortunately, many ended up being classified as "junk" and brought down banks, investment funds, and insurance companies around the world.

• •

With hundreds of billions of dollars worth of mortgage-backed securities being traded annually, the market for subprime debt became, at one point, bigger than the entire market for U.S. Treasury bonds—the biggest bond market in the world. When banks and mortgage companies realized they could pass on the risk of the mortgages they were issuing, they became more concerned about increasing volume and less concerned about whether the borrowers could pay back their loans. Consequently, credit standards were relaxed and many poor and low-income borrowers were given mortgages to buy homes—leading to ever-increasing home prices. Many borrowers bought homes they knew they couldn't afford, but assumed that rising home prices would cover their loan commitments, allowing them to refinance at a later date, once the house's value had gone up.

Thats not good

When the housing market began to cool, many subprime borrowers were unable to refinance their loans and were unable to make the interest payments on their original loans. Delinquencies—borrowers' failure to make their mortgage payments—began to rise, and the value of the bonds that were based on subprime mortgages began to decline. When large numbers of these subprime borrowers started going bankrupt, the subprime mortgage securities had to be revalued downward.

In the end, the banks and investment houses around the world that had bought these mortgage-backed securities were forced to write off large portions of their debt—up to 80 percent of their original value in some cases—leading to a credit crisis that spread around the world as other banks and investment houses refused to provide the cash that the world's companies and financial institutions need to keep running. Banks around the world had to be rescued by cash-strapped governments. In the United States, Lehman Brothers, one of the largest investment banks in the country, was forced into bankruptcy, and another investment bank, Bear Stearns, had to be sold off with help from the U.S. Federal Reserve—for a fraction of its previous value. AIG, the largest insurance company in the world, also had to be bailed out by the Federal Reserve. Once the financial meltdown had started it was impossible to stop.

• •

INFORMATIONAL TOOL:

What is a **mortgage-backed security**?

Think of an IOU backed by a deed to a house. A mortgage-backed security is a type of collateralized debt obligation, a bond or other security that is backed by assets such as loans or mortgages. During the first years of the 21st century, many subprime mortgages were repackaged and sold as bonds to investors, with the understanding that the loans would be sufficient to pay back the bonds at one point in the future. When property prices tumbled beyond anyone's expectations, the crash of the mortgage-backed securities market led to a global financial meltdown. Many central banks and monetary authorities around the world were forced to take over vast portfolios of "toxic" mortgage-backed securities.

• •

In addition to financial meltdowns, even cataclysmic events such as hurricanes and global warming are influenced by the expanding 21st-century economy, which is bringing forces to bear that are making it impossible to predict what will happen in the future. For example, the destruction of the Amazon rain forest, primarily for economic reasons, has led to a sharp increase in the release of carbon dioxide into the atmosphere. And industrial pollution in the United States, Europe, and China has contributed to the shrinking of the Arctic ice cap and an unprecedented melting of the permafrost, releasing even more carbon dioxide and methane gas into the atmosphere, leading to even more global warming. This greenhouse effect has led to ever higher temperatures—literally a "meltdown" in some parts of the world. And no one seems to know where it will all end.

Even efforts to reduce global warming, such as the promotion of biofuels, have led to unintended and unforeseen consequences. In addition to the use of massive amounts of water to produce sugar- or corn-based biofuels, the reduction of farmland for the production of food for human consumption led to rising shortages of rice, corn, and wheat on the world markets, resulting in riots in some countries and calls for increased protectionism in others.

The converging global economy is also shaking up traditional patterns of trade and investing. Before the 21st century, for example, people tended to limit their investments to purchases of domestic stocks and bonds. They then waited patiently for their investments to increase in value or provide a safe, fixed income over time. But in today's fusion economy, our money is being invested—whether we're aware of it or not—in pension funds, governments, and banks that buy an increasingly complex array of securities and investment vehicles.

The 21st-century economy has brought strange new correlations between investors and between markets. And the results can be catastrophic. Investors who are losing money in one sector tend to sell investments in another sector—or another part of the world—to pay their debts. When stocks fall sharply in the United States and Europe, for example, emerging-market funds from Brazil to Bangladesh can decline sharply as investors sell their shares abroad in order to raise cash to pay for losses at home. Currencies in previously healthy economies around the world often crash as speculators rush to safe haven currencies such as dollars and yen.

It has been said that a butterfly flapping its wings over Tokyo could cause a rainstorm over New York's Central Park several days later. The 21st-century economy has taken this linear correlation to another level. Causes and effects are converging, fusing together in a complex web that no one—not even the experts—are able to fully understand. Just as Metcalfe's Law, which says that the value of a network is proportional to the square of the number of its users, the expanding global economy is growing and expanding in ways we are unable to control.

And the speed of change is increasing exponentially. In today's modern economy, events have an almost immediate effect. If stocks fall sharply in China, markets around the world plunge instantly. Political events, such as an assassination or an unexpected election result—or even random events such as earthquakes or terrorist attacks—can cause the "invisible hand" of the marketplace to buy or sell precipitiously.

• •

INFORMATIONAL TOOL:

What is the *invisible hand* of the marketplace?

The idea that there is an "invisible hand" of the marketplace, guiding consumers and businesses to make the right economic decisions, was developed by the economic philosopher Adam Smith in the 18th century. His theory was that markets, if left to themselves, would find the most efficient way of doing things. The invisible hand is, in fact, the result of millions of profit-seeking consumers and producers making rational economic decisions. This invisible hand is thought to steer the market in the most logical direction and keep all economic forces in balance.

• •

Like the aforementioned butterfly flapping its wings over Tokyo, even small investment decisions can affect the global marketplace. With China holding more than a trillion dollars of U.S. government securities, any sign that the dollar could lose value in the years ahead—a decision by the U.S. Federal Reserve to lower interest rates, for example, or a move in Congress to force China to revalue its currency—may set in motion political and economic changes that could end up dethroning the dollar as the world's preferred reserve currency.

At the beginning of the 21st century, the euro had already begun supplanting the dollar as the world's currency of choice—there are now more euro notes and coins in circulation than dollars. And the international bond markets have begun issuing more euro-denominated securities than dollar-denominated securities. Many countries are now accounting for their purchases and sales of commodities and other goods on the international marketplace in euros instead of the almighty greenback—leading to an eventual decline in value of the dollar as countries sell the U.S. currency to buy others to use in the global marketplace.

In many ways, old paradigms have become obsolete and a new world order has been established. Asia's export boom at the beginning of the 21st century, for example, was mainly based on sales of products to U.S. consumers. Without them, it was assumed, the booming Asian economies would slow, engendering economic and political turmoil. In order to keep the U.S. economy afloat—and in part to ensure the safety of the foreign reserves sitting in Asian central banks' vaults—Asian nations became the United States' biggest creditor.

Trillions of dollars of U.S. government securities have been sold to mercantilist Asian and oil-rich Middle East nations, allowing the United States to fund its huge budget and trade deficits. The decision by foreign investment funds and central banks to subsidize the U.S. economy—providing the credit to fuel the U.S. housing bubble, leading eventually to a worldwide financial meltdown affecting even the cash-rich economies in Asia and the Middle East—shows how much the balance of power has shifted and how interconnected the world has become.

• •

INFORMATIONAL TOOL:

What is the difference between a budget deficit and a trade deficit?

When a government overspends—paying out more for guns and butter than it gets from tax revenue, for example—it is said to run a budget deficit. A trade deficit occurs when a country "spends" more than it "earns" on the international marketplace. A country runs a trade deficit when it imports more than it exports—more foreign oil and foreign-made toys coming in, for example, than wheat and computer software going out. The excess in imports means more money has to be spent to pay for the foreign purchases.

• •

In one of the biggest economic revolutions in history, the expanding 21st-century economy has begun shifting power from the developed world to the developing world—with Brazil, Russia, India, and China, the so-called *BRIC* countries, leading the way. Adjusting for purchasing power, the economies of the emerging markets have surpassed the economic output of the developed world. Their economic machine is already consuming over half of the world's energy, and they have been responsible for 80 percent of the increase in oil consumption during the first years of the 21st century. The export-oriented powerhouses of the developing world have been able to acquire more than three-quarters of the world's foreign currency reserves and increase the stock market valuations of their companies enormously. This led fund managers to invest even more money in the emerging markets, leading to even more growth and even more consumption of the world's resources.

• •

INFORMATIONAL TOOL:

What are the **BRIC** countries?

Think of a brick being used to build developing-country factories. The BRIC term is an acronym used to describe the four largest developing countries of the 21st-century economy: Brazil, Russia, India, and China. Coined by Goldman Sachs in 2003, the term has been expanded at times to include

Mexico (BRIMC) and Korea (BRICK). The Next Eleven or N11 countries have also been singled out for strong economic growth during the 21st century. They are: Bangladesh, Egypt, Indonesia, Iran, Mexico, Nigeria, Pakistan, the Philippines, South Korea, Turkey, and Vietnam.

• •

Where will it all end? With economic and political events occurring around the world at a dizzying pace—from credit meltdowns to terrorist attacks—the ability of any one country to control or significantly influence the maelstrom of forces buffeting the economic landscape will be increasingly limited in the years to come.

CHAPTER 2

WHAT IS MACROECONOMICS?

ECONOMICS IS AN art as much as it is a science. And economics in the 21st century, the art form *and* the science, is being transformed significantly. It used to be that economists limited themselves to looking at the behavior of governments, firms, and individuals in a carefully defined framework. Inflation, unemployment, and interest rates—the traditional components of macroeconomics—were the main areas of interest, with very little else occupying the limelight.

Now there is a whole new horde of players clamoring to be center stage. Hedge funds, subprime mortgage securities, black markets, outsourcing, pollution rights, and carbon footprints are just as much a part of the world economy as the behavior of firms and individuals when interest rates rise or fall or when taxes are slashed.

• •

INFORMATIONAL TOOL:

What is the difference between **macroeconomics** and **microeconomics**?

Think of using the Web to look at a map of your country and then zooming in to a view of your home. Macroeconomics looks at the "big-picture" aspects of an economy, such as inflation, unemployment, and *economic growth. Microeconomics looks at the economic behavior of individuals and how firms make decisions under various economic conditions.*

• •

The study of the global economy is essentially a macroeconomic survey, but there is a constant interplay between the world at large and the role we all play in it. When we go to the store and buy foreign-grown bananas, fill up our gas tank with imported oil, or watch a foreign-made music video on TV or on the Web, we're participating in the world economy. And it is not only as consumers of imported goods or services that we are part of the world economy. The money that our pension funds or college endowments invest in foreign markets helps pay for our retirement or for a new dormitory on campus. In fact, foreign investment in our home economy—and foreign purchases of our government debt—provide needed capital and jobs, making our lives better.

Unfortunately, it's not just the legal activities that make up the new 21st-century global economy. If we buy drugs—or if we join in the fight against illegal drugs by helping Latin American farmers substitute food crops for coca—we are also participating in the world of international trade and finance. Even economic sanctions against foreign regimes that abuse human rights or destroy the environment make us part of the world economy. Basically, buying anything that crosses an international border, from an illegal music download to imported hashish, integrates us into the ever-expanding global economy.

How do we size up a country's economy? Mainly, by putting a value on every good and service produced in an economy. *Gross domestic product (GDP)* and *gross national product*

(GNP) are the terms economists use to describe the total amount of goods and services produced by a country in any given year.

• •

INFORMATIONAL TOOL:

*What is the difference between **gross domestic product** and **gross national product**?*

Think of the word domestic *implying a more locally oriented viewpoint. While gross domestic product (GDP) concentrates on the economic activity taking place within the country's borders, gross national product (GNP) includes international income and expenses—those coming from foreign operations, for example, or income from foreign stocks or interest payments on bonds that one country's government has sold to another— an important consideration in the 21st-century economy, where countries like China and Korea hold hundreds of billions of dollars of U.S. Treasury bonds. Whatever figure is used, always remember to verify whether it applies to the quarter or to the entire year. GDP growth of 1 percent, if it's for only the first quarter, indicates an annual GDP of more than 4 percent, once compounded growth is factored in.*

• •

Sometimes GNP is bigger than GDP and sometimes it's the other way around. Countries like Ireland, which have a large portion of domestic companies in foreigners' hands, have a smaller GNP than GDP because the payments to foreign stock-holders are deducted from the GDP figures. On the other hand, British, U.S., and Swiss residents own a lot of companies abroad, so their GNP is usually larger than their GDP because it includes income from foreign production that is not included in the "domestic" summary.

How do you compare GDP among countries with different currencies? One way is to translate the various figures into a common currency, such as the U.S. dollar.

Country	Currency	GDP In Local Currency	GDP In U.S. Dollars
European Union	euros	12,279,000,000,000	$16,830,000,000,000
United States	U.S. dollars	14,839,000,000,000	$14,859,000,000,000
Japan	yen	488,000,000,000,000	$5,388,000,000,000
China	yuan	33,017,000,000,000	$4,818,000,000,000
Germany	euros	2,517,000,000,000	$3,440,000,000,000
France	euros	2,000,000,000,000	$2,734,000,000,000
United Kingdom	pounds	1,600,000,000,000	$2,442,000,000,000
Russia	rubles	46,449,000,000,000	$1,680,000,000,000
Spain	euros	1,156,000,000,000	$1,581,000,000,000
Canada	Can. dollars	1,817,000,000	$1,468,000,000,000
India	rupees	64,865,000,000,000	$1,362,000,000,000
Brazil	reals	3,082,000,000,000	$1,308,000,000,000
Mexico	pesos	12,793,000,000,000	$959,000,000,000
Indonesia	rupiahs	5,618,000,000,000	$505,000,000,000
Switzerland	francs	527,000,000,000	$454,000,000,000
Israel	shekels	805,000,000,000	$209,000,000,000
Singapore	dollars	309,000,000,000	$209,000,000,000
Kenya	shillings	2,711,000,000	$35,000,000,000

Source: *Economist, The world in 2009*, CIA

Unfortunately, official exchange rates give a skewed view of the size of a country's economy if the cost of goods and services isn't the same in every country. In India and China, for example, everything from meat to movie tickets is much cheaper than in wealthier countries like the United States and France—so the GDP often ends up looking much smaller than it really is. That is why economists have come up with a "real-world" exchange rate called *purchasing power parity*, or PPP. This is arrived at by using a basket of goods and services in each country that allows GDP to be compared across borders.

The way it works is simple: One country, such as the
United States, is chosen as the base country. The GDP of the
other countries is adjusted to take into account the comparable
"real" value of the goods and services that make up the country's economy and not what the exchange rates provide. The
cheap cost of haircuts or shoes in China, for example, would be
adjusted upward to give them equivalent value to the haircuts
and shoes in the United States. The "basket" of goods and services that is used to determine purchasing power parity includes
a wide variety of everyday items such as rent, food, and transportation.

• •

INFORMATIONAL TOOL:

What is the **Big Mac index?**

*Think of walking into McDonald's in different countries around the world
and comparing the price of a Big Mac to one at home. One of the best
ways to calculate purchasing power parity (PPP), the "real-world"
exchange rate of currencies around the world, is to look at the price of a
single product that's sold in almost every country in an identical form. The
Economist magazine calculates PPP by using the price of Big Macs
around the world. If it costs twice as much, for example, to buy a Big
Mac in London than in Miami, it means that the current exchange rates
don't really give us a true picture of the size of the British economy. By
using the Big Mac's price to calculate a real-world exchange rate, we are
better able to compare the size of one country's economy to the others.*

• •

Using the Big Mac index or some other form of purchasing
power parity to translate gross domestic product gives us a more
transparent—and, hopefully, more realistic—view of the size of

each country in the global economy. Many developing countries, where official exchange rates usually undervalue the total amount of goods and services produced, would have much bigger GDPs if purchasing power parity were used to calculate their relative size. For example, official exchange rates show that the Chinese economy grew from 12 percent to 20 percent of the U.S. economy at the beginning of the 21st century. By using purchasing power parity to compare them, however, we see that China actually grew from 45 percent of the U.S. economy to approximately 100 percent in "real" terms during the first years of the 21st century.

COUNTRY	NOMINAL GDP IN U.S. DOLLARS	GDP ADJUSTED FOR PURCHASING POWER PARITY
United States	$14,400,000,000,000	$14,400,000,000,000
China	$4,818,000,000,000	$9,128,000,000,000
Japan	$5,322,000,000,000	$4,546,000,000,000
India	$1,362,000,000,000	$3,728,000,000,000
Germany	$3,444,000,000,000	$2,989,000,000,000
Russia	$1,680,000,000,000	$2,310,000,000,000
United Kingdom	$2,840,000,000,000	$2,277,000,000,000
France	$2,734,000,000,000	$2,226,000,000,000
Brazil	$1,308,000,000,000	$2,114,000,000,000
Mexico	$959,000,000,000	$1,624,000,000,000
Spain	$1,581,000,000,000	$1,470,000,000,000
Canada	$1,468,000,000,000	$1,357,000,000,000
Indonesia	$505,000,000,000	$918,000,000,000
Switzerland	$454,000,000,000	$331,000,000,000
Israel	$209,000,000,000	$215,000,000,000
Singapore	$209,000,000,000	$204,000,000,000
Kenya	$35,000,000,000	$67,000,000,000

Source: *Economist, The world in 2009*

It may also be useful to relate a country's total GDP to the number of inhabitants—to get a more realistic view of how much wealth there is for each person living there. Imagine a small country like Sri Lanka or Costa Rica winning as many medals in the Summer Olympics as China or the United States. Each country's total economic output, therefore, needs to be divided by the number of people living in the country—to get a better idea of who is better off. It doesn't mean much to say that India is richer than Canada just because its nominal GDP is bigger. We need to look at its per capita GDP.

• •

INFORMATIONAL TOOL:

What is **per capita** income?

Think of capita as the Latin word for head. Per capita figures, dividing an economic statistic by the number of people in the population, allow us to better understand the effect of the statistic on the country's inhabitants. Per capita income tells us how much the economy's total production of goods and services—or the total gross domestic product—would be if divided among the economy's total population, putting a "human" dimension to an otherwise unfathomable economic statistic.

• •

In addition, when economic growth is compared on a per-person basis, it changes the picture markedly. Countries with growing populations, such as the United States, Brazil, and India, are seen to have decidedly smaller increases in economic output when their growing populations are factored in. In contrast, Russia and Japan, with stagnating or declining populations in the 21st century, show decidedly larger economic growth when measured on a per capita basis.

No measure of economic growth and economic power, however, is able to capture the complete economic picture. Quality of life, for example, isn't included in traditional mea-

Country	GDP (IN U.S. DOLLARS ADJUSTED FOR PPP)	GDP PER CAPITA (IN U.S. DOLLARS ADJUSTED FOR PPP)
United States	$14,839,000,000,000	$48,400
Singapore	$204,000,000,000	$44,200
Switzerland	$331,000,000,000	$42,940
Canada	$1,357,000,000,000	$40,540
United Kingdom	$2,277,000,000,000	$36,820
Germany	$2,989,000,000,000	$36,100
Japan	$4,546,000,000,000	$35,780
France	$2,226,000,000,000	$35,750
Spain	$1,470,000,000,000	$32,120
Israel	$215,000,000,000	$28,940
Russia	$2,310,000,000,000	$16,330
Mexico	$1,624,000,000,000	$14,610
Brazil	$2,114,000,000,000	$10,880
China	$9,128,000,000,000	$6,830
Indonesia	$918,000,000,000	$3,870
India	$3,728,000,000,000	$3,270
Kenya	$67,000,000,000	$1,700

Source: Economist, The world in 2009

sures of GDP. Which means that the small monetary outlay of a French family taking a five-week summer vacation in the family's country house in Provence or the Atlantic coast doesn't, in the end, contribute much to a traditional measure of GDP.

Japanese and American families, on the other hand, taking much shorter summer vacations in order to earn more salary—and paying a lot of money to send the children to summer camp or pay for expensive day care—would have a significantly greater effect on the country's calculation of GDP. This extra economic activity is seen by some economists as contributing to the economic well-being of the nation—albeit with minimal benefit to the family's overall quality of life, sometimes referred to as *gross national happiness*.

CHAPTER 3

CENTRAL BANKS AND GLOBAL CRISES—WHO REALLY CONTROLS THE GLOBAL ECONOMY?

THE WORLDWIDE CREDIT crisis that began with the collapse of the housing market in the United States was just one of many crises that central banks and other financial authorities have had to deal with during the first part of the 21st century.

But the enormity of the financial collapse required government and central bank intervention never before seen in the global economy. After Lehman Brothers, one of America's biggest investment banks, was allowed to go bankrupt, the Federal Reserve was required to bail out AIG, the world's largest insurance company. The $85 billion bailout was, until then, the biggest bailout in American economic history.

When banks began failing across the globe—primarily because of bad investments in U.S. subprime securities, but also because of the freeze in interbank lending—it was clear that a full-blown worldwide crisis had arrived. Stock market declines of more than 50 percent in some countries presaged a global economic meltdown. The concerted action of the world's central banks, including the U.S. Federal Reserve, the Bank of England, the European Central Bank, and the Bank of Japan, helped calm things down for a while. But when countries began failing—

Iceland and the Ukraine were the first of many national economies that had to be bailed out—it was clear that the fallout of the 2008 crisis would last for years to come.

The key to finding the right solution to economic crises is to somehow solve the immediate problem without making things worse in the future. Some say that the reaction of the Fed to the meltdown of the dot-com sector at the end of the 20th century—increased liquidity and drastically lower interest rates—set the stage for the meltdown of financial markets several years later, with massive defaults of mortgage holders who probably shouldn't have been given home loans to start with, but were lured in by artificially low interest rates. The result was a recession that was much worse than that which the central bank was trying to avoid.

• •

INFORMATIONAL TOOL:

What is the difference between a recession and a depression?

Think of the difference between having a cold or a long-term illness. Officially, a recession is a decline in economic output over two consecutive quarters. A severe recession, one lasting a year or more, is referred to as a depression. Often, recessions aren't recognized as such until they're over— the economic statistics that define recessions and depressions are notoriously volatile and can be evaluated with certainty only after a few months or even years. Falling prices, called deflation, sometimes accompany a long-term depression. When prices rise, however, despite the decline in economic activity, the mixture of stagnation and inflation is referred to as stagflation. Other than stagflation's "perfect storm" of negative economic effects, most economic downturns provide a mixture of positive and negative implications for the average consumer. Reduced inflation, which usually accompanies an economic downturn, means that consumers pay less than they normally would during boom times, but is often offset by lower, or nonexistent, salary increases and—in the worst case—significant job losses. As U.S. president Harry Truman once said, "It's a recession when your neighbor loses his job; it's a depression when you lose yours."

• •

Just as the speed of an engine is regulated by its fuel supply, a country's economy is controlled by regulating its money supply—and each country's monetary policy is the responsibility of its central bank. In Britain, it's the Bank of England; in Switzerland, it's the Swiss National Bank; in the United States, it's the Federal Reserve; in the *euro zone* countries, it's the European Central Bank; and in Japan, it's the Bank of Japan. These quasi-public institutions are set up by governments, but are then given the independence needed to keep an economy under control without undue interference from dabbling politicians.

Despite the tendency of the media to concentrate on the latest major economic statistic, there is no one single indicator that tells us how fast an economy is growing—or if that growth will lead to inflation down the road. And, unfortunately, there is no way to know how quickly an economy will respond to changes in monetary policy. If a country's central bank allows the economy to expand too rapidly—by keeping too much money in circulation, for example—it may cause "bubbles" and inflation. If it slows down the economy too much, an economic recession can result, bringing financial turmoil and rampant unemployment.

Central bankers, therefore, need to be prescient—and extremely careful—keeping one eye on inflation, which is the product of an overheating economy, and one eye on unemployment, which is the product of a slowing economy. In the 21st-century economy, however, regulating money supply has become a much more difficult task. With the amount of capital flowing around the world dwarfing many countries' money supplies, it's almost impossible to know with certainty what the effect of any monetary decision will have on a local economy—let alone on the world.

• •

INFORMATIONAL TOOL:

What were the biggest *financial meltdowns* in modern history?

The Great Depression, caused by a severe stock market crash in 1929— and exacerbated by the U.S. decision to erect onerous barriers to world trade—is perhaps the most famous financial meltdown in modern economic history. But many others have occurred since the beginning of the global economy, dating back to the heyday of the British Empire. Everything from war to weather to political turmoil has brought financial markets to their knees. In addition, cyclical forces—overproduction, speculation, and market euphoria being followed by stock market crashes, massive layoffs, and closed factories—are most often the major cause of financial crises. Many meltdowns are caused and resolved by global forces, often outside the control of any one country. The falling prices following the U.S. Civil War, for example, rebounded only at the end of the 19th century, when increased gold production in southern Africa led to a worldwide revival of economic activity. The outbreak of the Second World War in Europe and Asia brought American industry back to life, ending the Great Depression well before the United States entered the war at the end of 1941. And the recession in most of the industrial world in the 1970s was a direct result of the decision by oil-producing nations to impose an embargo. Most of the recent financial meltdowns, from the stock market crash of 1987 to the bursting of the dot-com bubble in the late 1990s to the severe market collapse following the terrorist attacks of September 11, 2001, have been quickly turned around by rapid central-bank intervention—mainly through massive injections of funds into the financial system. The catastrophic financial meltdown that ravaged the world economy in 2008, however, was another matter. What began as a U.S.-based housing crisis soon took on global proportions and no central bank was able to unilaterally stop the downward economic spiral.

Major Financial Crises Since the Late 20th Century:

1971: U.S. Dollar Crisis. Collapse of the Bretton Woods Agreement to fix currency prices.

1973: First Oil Shock. Oil-producing nations raise price of petroleum sharply, leading to economic downturn in most of the industrialized world.

1979: Second Oil Shock. Rampant stagflation—persistent inflation along with stagnating economic growth.

1982: Sovereign Debt Crisis. Many Third World countries default on loans.

1984: Failure of Continental Illinois Bank. Followed by collapse of forty-three more banks in the United States.

1986: Savings and Loan Crisis. Speculation on home loans leads to several spectacular failures in the United States.

1987: Stock Market Crash in United States. Leads to stock market crashes around the globe.

1989: Japanese "Lost Decade." Bursting of Japanese real estate and stock market bubble leads to long period of economic stagnation.

1992–93: Currency Crisis in Europe. British pound and Italian lira drop out of European Monetary System.

1997–98: Asian Economic Crisis. Currency crises and stock markets crash across south Asia, primarily in Thailand, Indonesia, South Korea, and the Philippines.

1998: Russian Economic Crisis. Leads to default on sovereign debt and years of economic decline.

1998–99: Brazilian Economic Crisis. Rampant inflation and currency free fall lead to default on international debt.

1998: Long-term Credit Bank Failure. Leads to instability of U.S. financial markets.

2000: "Dot-com" Bubble Bursts. Internet stocks plummet, leading U.S. Federal Reserve to lower interest rates drastically.

2001: Argentine Economic Crisis. Currency uncoupled from dollar link and massive default on international debt.

2007–08: Global Financial Crisis. Subprime mortgage meltdown in the United States leads to credit crisis and worldwide market meltdown. After bankruptcy of Lehman Brothers, a major U.S. investment bank, the Federal Reserve steps in to bail out U.S. banks and insurance companies. Governments and central banks around the world inject trillions to prevent complete economic collapse.

• •

Inflation and unemployment have become the yin and the yang of the 21st-century economy. When one rises, the other tends to fall. Although neither is perceived as good, in recent years, inflation has become the dominant preoccupation of economic decision makers. It used to be that reports of a surging economy brought euphoria to the markets. If factories and businesses were producing at full capacity and everyone had a job, the markets would greet the news with approval, confident that in a booming economy, everyone would be better off. However, after the severe inflation scares of the past decades, with prices rising out of control in many countries, leaders realized that an economy growing too quickly can be too much of a good thing. Reduced unemployment means that companies are forced to pay higher wages for scarce workers, and prices of goods and services need to be raised to pay for the increased cost.

• •

INFORMATIONAL TOOL:

What is the relationship between *inflation* and *unemployment*?

Think of a playground seesaw: When one side goes up the other goes down. It's not always the case, but unemployment usually goes down when an economy is growing and prices are rising. Declining unemployment makes it harder for businesses to hire new employees, so they tend to pay higher salaries to attract qualified personnel. This has the effect of raising the cost of doing business, which eventually leads to higher prices. Central bankers try to balance their decisions to allow for a reduction in unemployment while keeping inflation in check.

• •

In a booming economy, inflation can grow quickly as consumers and businesses begin to compete for increasingly scarce goods and services—and scarcity leads to higher prices. The result is usually a vicious circle of wage and price increases that end up hurting almost everyone, especially those on fixed incomes, who see their buying power decline when prices rise.

The international markets watch each country's inflation rate carefully—always on the lookout for signs that an economy is stalling or overheating. International investors, including gigantic pension funds, hedge funds, and international banks, move billions and sometimes trillions of dollars, pounds, euros, and yen around the world on any given day, looking for the best return on their investment. When a country's economy looks like it is growing too strongly, and inflation is about to rear its ugly head, international investors can move their money out of an economy at a moment's notice, preferring to invest their funds in countries with more stable economic growth and low inflation.

Just as a prudent driver keeps an eye on the road ahead, a country's central bank tries to keep the economy on a steady course. Central bankers need to look at all the economic data, such as factory orders, housing starts, consumer credit, retail sales, manufacturing, construction, and employment figures—some of which are leading and some of which are lagging indicators—in an ongoing effort to keep the economy from overheating or sliding into recession.

• •

INFORMATIONAL TOOL:

What is the difference between **leading economic indicators** and **lagging economic indicators**?

Think of being on the front of a train looking forward and on the caboose looking back. Leading economic indicators tell you where the economy is heading. Economists and political leaders look to them to tell how quickly the economy will be growing in the months—and years—ahead. Typical leading economic indicators are spending on new plants and machinery, retail sales, and housing starts. Lagging economic indicators tell us where the economy has been. Unemployment and previous GDP growth don't tell us much about what will happen in the future, but are useful for plotting the course of past economic activity.

• •

Normally, by increasing or decreasing the supply of money, the central banks have been able to control economic growth to a large degree. But in the 21st century, it is becoming increasingly difficult for central banks to know how quickly the economy is growing. In most modern economies, printed notes and coins constitute only a small percentage—less than 10 percent in most cases—of the total money supply. Nonetheless, the total money supply is still carefully controlled by the central banks. In the case of printed money, central banks print only enough to satisfy the everyday needs of businesses and consumers. And with electronic payments becoming increasingly popular, the use of printed money is declining rapidly. The amount of cash in circulation is now significantly less than the amount previously needed—to cover wage payments and bank deposits, for example. Some economists predict an end to the use of cash within a few decades.

The growth of other financial instruments, such as derivatives and securitized loans like mortgage-backed securities, has made it almost impossible for central banks to effectively control the supply of money and credit in modern economies. The Bank for International Settlements has estimated that the total value of outstanding derivative positions on the over-the-counter markets exceeded $400 trillion during the first years of the 21st century—when the entire U.S. economy, the world's largest, was estimated to be worth less than $15 trillion. The problem for central banks is that these new financial instruments give investors enormous amounts of nominal assets with a minimal outlay of cash. When the prices of these new financial instruments rise, investors can borrow against them—just as a homeowner can get a second mortgage on a house that has risen in value.

The globalization of the world money supply has also contributed to the creation of an entirely new paradigm for central bankers. It used to be that the world's rich economies that make up the Organisation for Economic Co-operation and Development pretty much controlled the world's money supply. But with the rapid economic growth in the developing world at the beginning of the 21st century, more than half of the world's broad money-supply growth was occurring in the emerging economies—mainly Brazil, Russia, India, and China—with considerable growth coming from smaller trading nations such as Taiwan, South Korea, and Vietnam that were building up considerable surpluses of foreign currency as well.

• •

INFORMATIONAL TOOL:

What is the **OECD**?

Think of a country club for rich countries. The Organisation for Economic Co-operation and Development, based in Paris, France, groups together the world's rich-country economies. In addition to providing statistics and documenting all aspects of the member countries' economies, the OECD serves as a forum for discussion and coordination of economic policy. It includes the United States, Canada, Mexico, Japan, South Korea, Australia, New Zealand, and most of the European Union members, such as France, Germany, and Spain.

• •

How is inflation determined around the world? Mainly, by using a basket of goods and services that represent the average citizen's daily needs. In some countries in the developing world, for example, more than 60 percent of the basket is made up of foodstuffs. In China it's 30 percent. And in the United States, only 10 percent, reflecting the fact that the average American consumer spends only about that much on food, and the rest on other goods and services. This means that increasing food prices have a much bigger effect on inflation in the developing world than in rich countries.

Since the basket of goods used to determine each country's inflation rate is defined by the country's government or government-controlled agency, there is the possibility for a certain amount of manipulation. For example, during inflationary times at the beginning of the 21st century, the Argentine government consistently understated the true inflation rate significantly by choosing goods and services that weren't rising as quickly as others. Other baskets of goods and services—for example, those used to compare currency values around the world, referred to as purchasing power parity—are determined by international organizations, banks, or even media outlets such as Web sites, magazines, or newspapers.

• •

INFORMATIONAL TOOL:

What is the **consumer price index**?

Think of a basket or a shopping cart full of goods and services like orange juice and DVDs. The consumer price index (CPI), referred to as the retail price index in Britain, tracks the prices of a wide range of goods and services, including computers, milk, rent, and haircuts, in an attempt to get an idea of how much prices are increasing in the economy as a whole. This index is often used to readjust fixed incomes, such as pensions and social security payments. The CPI basket of goods and services is determined by each country and is usually not the same as the one used to determine purchasing power parity, which allows economists to compare currency values between countries.

• •

Once a central bank confirms that inflation has gotten out of control—evidenced by a sharp rise in the country's consumer price index, for example—it can step in to control the economy in a number of ways. The most common tool, reducing the money supply, takes place in several stages. Since most easily accessed money is in the form of bank deposits, the most efficient way for a central bank to regulate the money supply is by regulating bank lending and bank deposits. Essentially, when banks have more money to lend to customers, the economy grows. And when banks reduce their lending, the economy slows.

The reason this works so well is because of the *multiplier effect*. Money deposited in a bank doesn't just sit there. The bank usually lends the money to someone else. A hundred dollars deposited in a bank in Seattle, for example, may end up being loaned to a business in Key West. After setting aside a small portion of each deposit as a *reserve*, banks are free to lend out the remainder. The effect is to increase the money supply without any extra currency being printed.

Basically, a bank's supply of money available for lending is limited only by the amount of its deposits and by its *reserve requirements*, which are determined by the central bank: Most banks are required to put a certain percentage of their funds— 10 percent of deposits, for example—on reserve, and are prohibited from lending these funds back to customers. When a central bank increases the reserve requirement, therefore, it effectively reduces the money supply, since banks have less to lend to businesses and consumers. On the other hand, by reducing the reserve requirements—as several central banks did during the credit crunch of 2008—they allow the banks to lend more, stimulating the economy by releasing more money for lending.

Reducing interest rates is the most visible tool central banks have to control economic growth. When a central bank decides that an economy is growing too slowly, for example, it can simply reduce the interest rate it charges on loans to banks. When banks get this "cheaper" money, they are able to make cheaper loans to businesses and consumers, providing an important stimulus to economic growth. Likewise, by raising interest rates, a central bank slows down the economy by making it more "expensive" for businesses and consumers to borrow money—and their purchases of homes, cars, computers, and factories will decline.

Like a locomotive pulling a long train, central-bank interest rates tend to affect rates throughout the economy at large. When a central bank changes its *discount rate*, the interest rate it charges for loans to other banks, interest rates across the economy almost always follow suit. For example, the interest rate on loans made between banks—called *interbank rates* in Europe and *Fed funds rates* in the United States—will rise whenever banks have to pay more to borrow from the central bank and will fall when they have to pay less. The higher cost of money is almost always passed on to consumers and businesses in the form of higher interest rates on every other form of loan in the economy.

• •

INFORMATIONAL TOOL:

What is the difference between the **discount rate** and the **Fed funds rate**?

Think of the strange fact that the discount rate is set by the Federal Reserve and the Fed funds rate isn't. The discount rate is the interest rate that the U.S. Federal Reserve, America's central bank, charges on loans to member banks. This rate is set periodically by the Fed in an attempt to influence interest rates throughout the economy, thus allowing the Fed to control economic growth. The Fed funds rate is interest that banks charge on overnight loans to other banks. It's called the Fed funds rate because the money being loaned between banks is usually kept at the Federal Reserve. Although heavily influenced by the Fed's policies, the Fed funds rate is actually set by the banks themselves.

• •

All interest rates are linked because money, like most commodities, is interchangeable. Banks and individuals will go wherever rates are lowest—wherever money is cheaper. A change in interest rates by the Federal Reserve in Washington, for example, will not only affect consumer and business loan interest rates in Miami or Minnesota, but now affect interest rates around the world. And the actions of central banks around the world increasingly are affecting domestic rates in the United States. In the global village of international money markets, interest rates have become the heartbeat of economic activity—and the world's economies are increasingly interconnected.

Perhaps the most dramatic way for a central bank to increase or decrease the money supply is through *open-market operations*, where a central bank buys or sells large amounts of securities, such as government treasury bonds, in the open market. By buying a large block of these bonds from a bank or securities house, the central bank pumps money into the economy, freeing up funds that were not previously part of the economy's official money supply—making those funds available for the banks selling the bonds to lend out to consumers and businesses.

How does this work? Essentially, a central bank "creates" money every time it dips into its vaults to buy bonds from banks in the economy at large. Whether it pays by cash or by crediting the bank's account, the central bank injects new money into the economy every time it makes a purchase in the open market.

Conversely, when a central bank sells bonds in the open market, it reduces the economy's money supply. The payments from banks and securities houses that purchase the bonds enters the "black hole" of the central banks' vaults—where the money sits, completely removed from the economy at large.

. . . .

INFORMATIONAL TOOL:

What is the difference between fiscal policy and monetary policy?

Think of the U.S. Congress as a homemaker, deciding how much to spend in a given year, and the Federal Reserve as the breadwinner, deciding how much money to inject into the home "economy." Fiscal policy is related to budgets, and fiscal deficits and fiscal surpluses refer to imbalances in government spending. Monetary policy, however, is set by the U.S. Federal Reserve and other central banks throughout the world. By regulating the money supply and interest rates, monetary authorities can effectively control a country's economy—and, hopefully, the rate of inflation and unemployment in the economy at large.

. . . .

Monetary policy is a difficult guessing game, and sometimes central banks end up creating bigger problems than the ones they try to solve. The American housing "bubble" during the first years of the 21st century, for example, was due in many ways to decisions made by the U.S. central bank years before to stimulate the economy after a sharp drop in dot-com share prices. In 2001, the Fed lowered interest rates a half a percentage point to 6 percent, and continued lowering them over the next three years in an attempt to soften the blows of the September 2001 terrorist attacks and rapidly falling consumer confidence. These extremely low interest rates encouraged consumers to go on a house-buying binge—taking advantage of increasingly lax requirements for mortgages.

In addition, a "savings glut" had been building up in the developing countries of the world economy and in the oil-producing economies of the Middle East. By the beginning of the 21st century the emerging economies of the developing world had accumulated trillions of dollars in excess reserves that had to be invested somewhere—and since most of their reserves were in dollars, they decided to invest them in the United States—providing money for mortgages and consumer loans. Even after the Fed began raising interest rates in 2004, money was still pouring in from abroad, fueling a consumer spending boom without precedent.

When the credit bubble burst in 2007 and 2008, many blamed the complex new financial instruments that made the mortgage boom possible—in addition to the failure of risk-management models, or even the role of ratings agencies. But in the end, it was the central banks that had to take ultimate blame, mainly for allowing interest rates to be less than the inflation rate—sometimes referred to as *negative real interest rates*.

• •

INFORMATIONAL TOOL:

What are **real interest rates**?

Think of Alice in Wonderland's looking glass—where things are not what they appear to be. Real figures, such as real interest rates and real wages, tell us what the figures really are when adjusted for inflation. It means nothing to say you're earning 10 percent interest on your bank deposits when inflation is several points higher and, at the end of the day, you end up losing money in real terms. During periods of insignificant inflation there is no difference between nominal financial figures and real figures. But when inflation grows it's important to compare all figures to the rising cost of goods and services. It may be better to borrow rather than save during periods of low or negative real interest rates, for example. And real wage growth is much more relevant than nominal. If you get a 5 percent raise during a year when prices rise by 6 percent, you've actually taken a pay cut.

• •

Faced with global crises, central bankers often face a serious quandary. Just as they were tested by the collapse of Long-Term Capital Management, the Russian debt default, and the Asian crisis of the previous century, the central bankers in the 21st century have to carefully weigh their twin duties of safeguarding stability and fighting inflation. The question is: How far can you go in preserving financial stability—bailing out failed banks and investors, for example—before you run the risk of encouraging further abuses or the creation of more market bubbles?

It is a difficult task. Because the benefits of recession—purging the excesses of an overheated economy, for example—may outweigh the costs: unemployment, lower wages and profits, rampant bankruptcies. Joseph Schumpeter, a visionary economist of the early 20th century, saw a sort of "creative destruction" taking place during an economic downturn, where capital would be freed up—removed from dying enterprises to give life to new ones. Central bankers may therefore want to encourage some form of recession, but a full depression—such as that which occurred in the 1930s—is not in the best interest of anyone, because of the disastrous effects on the economy.

• •

INFORMATIONAL TOOL:

What is **money supply**?

Think of a Monopoly game: When more money is made available to players—by giving more money for passing Go, for example—there's more money to spend on buying property from other players. A country's money supply has several different components, ranging from coins and banknotes to deposits in savings and checking accounts. The money supply most often referred to in the news is M1, which consists of all currency in circulation as well as money in "easy-to-access" bank accounts. Other, wider measures of money supply—such as M2, M3, etc.—include funds that are not so readily available, such as time deposits and other long-term investments.

• •

In addition to steering a country's economy through treacherous waters, a central bank often serves as supervisor of the country's banking and financial system. In most countries, the central bank is given a considerable degree of independence to carry out these duties effectively and efficiently. In the United States, for example, the president appoints the head of the Federal Reserve, but from that moment on the government has no significant say in how the Fed regulates the money supply and oversees the financial stability of the country.

In some countries, the central bank also takes on additional responsibilities. The Bank of England, for example, is responsible for printing the money as well as supervising the banking system. The European Central Bank, based in Frankfurt, oversees the monetary policy for all countries in the euro zone, but is limited in how much it can intervene in any one country's economic affairs. In the United States, the U.S. Treasury borrows money for the government's use by issuing treasury notes and bonds, while the Federal Reserve Board charts monetary policy and oversees the printing of money at the Bureau of Engraving and Printing. The Bank of Japan issues the government's checks and holds its deposits of foreign currency. Some central banks, such as the Swiss National Bank, are partly owned by private shareholders, which means that monetary policy isn't necessarily influenced by what's best for the country at large, but by what's best for the central bank's shareholders.

During times of acute financial turbulence, central banks usually act as a "lender of last resort" in order to preserve the stability of the country's financial system. During a major international financial crisis, central banks can also turn to their own "central bank," the Bank for International Settlements (BIS), based in Basel, Switzerland. To help solve global financial problems, the BIS often provides temporary funds to shore up failing banking systems around the world—providing short-term financing called *bridge loans* to member banks, which are paid back as soon as longer-term financing can be arranged.

The BIS also serves as a platform for establishing new rules for regulating the world banking community. In 2007, for example, a new accord was put in place that regulated the amount of capital that banks around the world needed to hold in reserve. This accord, dubbed *Basel II*, required banks to carefully evaluate the different types of risk found in the many new types of securities available to investors in the global economy. The failure of Merrill Lynch, UBS, and many other banks to properly evaluate the risk of owning large amounts of mortgage-backed securities, for example, led to multibillion-dollar losses and financial ruin for many.

The BIS also serves as a forum, bringing together the worldwide community of central banks to discuss financial globalization and the role of central banks in the converging world economy. With the rise of powerful new members in the global economy—China and India, for example—the number of members in the BIS "club" of central bankers rose sharply during the first years of the 21st century, going from thirty-six to fifty-five in less than a decade.

The International Monetary Fund (IMF) also provides bridge financing to countries in crisis. This IMF-mandated *structural adjustment* process is often a crucial first step before troubled countries are able to receive funding from other, more long-term sources. Although the IMF is based in Washington, D.C., it receives its funding from a wide variety of member countries around the world. In addition to being able to tap into the hard currency promised by its rich-country members to help the world financial system in times of turmoil, it also has considerable reserves of gold—more than three thousand tons of it at the beginning of the 21st century—that allow it to serve as a counterbalance to the turbulent markets and financially unstable governments during global crises.

The economic medicine prescribed by the IMF for countries in crisis is often painful—and often criticized as being harmful to the poorest members of society. For instance, the IMF often requires debtor governments to reduce subsidies to state industries during times of crisis—sometimes provoking severe civil unrest as these measures often raise the cost of previously subsidized services such as bread, milk, gasoline, and mass transit. Since many of the developing-world poor are already living at subsistence levels, a small increase in the cost of essential goods can mean economic disaster. It is not so difficult to go without a new refrigerator—but it is very difficult to go without the food to put in it. Acceptance of an IMF-prescribed plan, however, is usually seen as a sign that a country in crisis is prepared to seriously address its economic ills, regardless of the cost, paving the way for more long-term funding from the World Bank and other sources. In the end, many austerity plans imposed by the IMF eventually improve life for the poor people in developing countries, even though the short-term burdens of the readjustment plans are extremely difficult to bear.

Many developing countries—particularly the so-called *middle-income countries (MICs)*, which have an average GDP per capita in the $1,000-to-$6,000 range—have decided to insure themselves mainly by amassing large reserves of their own, allowing them to forgo having to turn to the IMF during times of crisis. Some countries, such as Argentina, Brazil, and Indonesia, have even paid off their IMF loans early. As a response, the IMF announced plans to allow developing countries to have a greater say, including increased voting power, in deciding how the IMF is run and how funds are distributed.

The G7/G8 summits, the World Economic Forum, and the United Nations also play a useful role in helping defuse and overcome global economic crises. The G7 "Group of Seven"— becoming the G8 whenever Russia joins the meetings—is made up of the leaders of Canada, the United States, Japan, Germany, Italy, Britain, and France. Annual meetings were originally intended to provide an economic forum, giving the leaders a chance to discuss global economic issues in an intimate setting. Because of the increasing demands of the global fusion economy, the G7/G8 forum has expanded over the years to cover a wide range of international issues, such as global warming and workers' rights. A larger group, called the G20, includes representatives from the largest developing countries; and another, even larger group, called the G77, brings together leaders of most of the developing countries to discuss issues of particular importance to the emerging economies.

• •

INFORMATIONAL TOOL:

What is the **World Economic Forum?**

Think of a rich man's clubhouse perched on a mountainside in the Swiss Alps. The World Economic Forum, founded by Geneva-based entrepreneur Klaus Schwab, holds an economic summit every year in the Swiss ski resort of Davos. These meetings have become the ultimate economic and political "schmooze-fest." Business leaders and politicians from prime ministers to party chairmen—and interested celebrities such as Angelina Jolie, Bono, and Sharon Stone—gather every winter at the WEF's "informal" summit to try to solve the world's major social and economic problems. Antiglobalization demonstrators often try to crash the party but are held at bay by heavily armed military and police forces. In an effort to make the Davos summits more egalitarian, the WEF has begun inviting international aid organizations and NGOs such as Amnesty International, Oxfam, and Save the Children. An alternative summit, called the World Social Forum, which generally coincides with the WEF forum in Davos, usually holds an annual meeting as well, to discuss world issues in a less capitalist setting.

• •

The United Nations also provides an important forum for solving crises and encouraging economic cooperation around the world. It is estimated that the United Nations and its agencies spend more time on economics and economic development than any other issue on their agenda. To confront the crisis of global warming, for example, the United Nations Development Program (UNDP) instituted a program to finance energy efficiency and antipollution programs in developing countries. This *adaptation fund* provides money for a wide range of climate change projects.

Most world leaders have come to realize that the world's economic problems are, in fact, inseparable from political and military conflicts. The World Bank, for example, has estimated that the majority of civil wars that have taken place over the last half century were—at least in part—motivated by access to commodities like oil, diamonds, and drugs. In the future, it is increasingly possible that wars may be fought for the most basic of economic necessities such as food and water.

In the end, the resolution of most international issues, such as credit crises, global warming, trade imbalances, and access to the world's resources, will depend on countries working together—often through coordinated central bank intervention and working with international organizations such as the World Bank and the United Nations, bringing together all of the nations of the world to tackle the challenges posed by global economic crises.

CHAPTER 4

FREE TRADE OR ISOLATIONISM—
HOW CAN TRADE WARS BE AVOIDED
IN THE 21ST CENTURY?

W E WOULDN'T HAVE a very high standard of living if we had to produce all of the goods and services we consumed in any given year. Imagine having to make your own clothes, car, and house—along with producing your own television programs to watch in the evening.

Most participants in the 21st-century economy agree that it makes sense to spend scarce material and human resources producing only those goods and services they are relatively good at—and use their export earnings to import the rest. However, some countries will always have more resources than the others. The problem is regulating foreign trade without disadvantaging any single player.

The goal of free trade is to have a level playing field, permitting individuals and companies to have the opportunity to sell their goods and services in other lands. In theory, when every country in the world is allowed to do what it does best—letting the French excel in fashion, or the Japanese in consumer electronics, or the Americans in aircraft and movies, for example— the world economy prospers. In general, trade increases income, and companies and consumers have more of a choice of what to purchase with their increased income.

Unfortunately, there will always be inequities—deficits and surpluses in the monetary value of goods and services traded—which leads some people to see free trade as a zero-sum game, with clear winners and losers. Free trade also exposes local producers to foreign competition, which can be hard on inefficient or poorly managed companies in the home country. This can lead to layoffs and idle factories, a disaster for small towns or countries that rely on a local industry for jobs and tax revenue.

But nothing in the fast-changing global economy stays the same for long. Confronted with foreign competition, many local companies are forced to take the painful steps to become more efficient, thus enabling them to compete and prosper at home as well as abroad. And companies with access to world markets can use economies of scale to produce large amounts of goods at a lower cost and, hopefully, pass on the price advantages to consumers on both sides of the border.

Even though it may make perfect economic sense for countries to open up their borders to trade, it is hard to convince politicians to suffer the outcry from the companies and individuals that are hurt by free-trade agreements. This can lead to the imposition of protective trade barriers and, eventually, an all-out trade war.

Although a trade war may not be as destructive as a military war, in both cases many suffer—often the very people the war was meant to protect. By protecting a few jobs in a few inefficient industries, governments end up forcing consumers and other businesses to buy relatively expensive domestically produced goods and services. For example, during the first years of the 21st century the sugar industry in the United States was able to get the U.S. government to ensure high prices for American-produced sugar that was roughly double the world average. Through a complex system of tariffs and subsidies, foreign competition was severely restricted, forcing local companies that use a lot of sugar—candy manufacturers, for example—to close factories and move operations to foreign countries where sugar was less expensive.

The trade barriers put in place by the U.S. government ended up protecting a few rich sugar producers, but eliminated thousands of jobs in industries that depended on a fair market price. In addition, the farmers and producers in many countries in the developing world were not allowed into the lucrative U.S. market, making them much poorer than they would have been without trade restrictions. A further result of these trade barriers on sugar was to limit the imports of foreign biofuel—ethanol made from sugarcane, for example—that would have allowed the United States to reduce its consumption of foreign oil, and reduce global warming by using a more environmentally friendly fuel to power U.S. automobiles.

Meanwhile, on the other side of the Atlantic, the European Union had refused to lift tariffs on imported products, such as energy-saving lightbulbs from China. Despite the fact that the tariffs were endangering plans to tackle climate change by phasing out the use of common incandescent bulbs for domestic use—basically, local producers could supply only a fraction of the energy-saving bulbs needed—political pressures from local manufacturers kept the trade restrictions in place.

The most common barriers to trade are quotas, tariffs, and subsidies. By imposing a *quota*, a country limits the quantity of foreign products that can be imported. A *tariff* is a tax placed on goods as they enter the country. Both quotas and tariffs raise the price of foreign-made goods. Governments can also use taxpayers' money to provide a *subsidy* to local producers, making the price of local goods artificially lower than the price of equivalent imported goods.

INFORMATIONAL TOOL:

What is a **subsidy**?

Think of a child receiving an allowance from his or her parents. Subsidies are government payments to businesses, ostensibly to help them through economic hard times. Most subsidies are criticized as being a waste of the taxpayers' money, because they often end up rewarding inefficiency. In many economies, badly managed and inefficient industries would not survive if they didn't receive generous government subsidies. Examples include shipbuilding, steelmaking, and some areas of agribusiness, such as sugar and cotton producers.

INFORMATIONAL TOOL:

What is a **tariff**?

Think of putting a tax on imports. Tariffs are, essentially, a penalty that governments put on imported goods. Tariffs usually take the form of a fixed percentage that is added to the imports' value to make them more expensive—and therefore less of a competition to domestically produced products. Tariffs in the United States during the first years of the 21st century included taxes on imports of orange juice, steel, and ethanol.

INFORMATIONAL TOOL:

What is a **quota**?

Think of a gate that allows only a limited amount of goods to enter a specific area. Quotas are usually the most effective way of reducing imports. Normally, producers can lower the price of the good to make it competitive in countries that use tariffs and subsidies to limit trade. But with quotas, once the limit has been reached, no more goods—at any price—may be brought in. Agricultural imports are often the most common items to be limited by the use of quotas. Fortunately, quotas are usually the first trade barriers to go when countries sign free-trade agreements.

• •

Trade barriers, like fences between feuding neighbors, are often imposed unilaterally—by one country acting on its own to limit imports. These barriers are usually designed to temporarily protect local producers from foreign competition and, in theory, allow them to improve their productivity. The problem is that local producers, once given the comfort of a protected market, rarely make the sacrifices necessary to improve their products or lower their prices.

Unfortunately, when a country unilaterally erects trade barriers, many other countries often follow suit, erecting trade barriers of their own, which can escalate into full-scale trade wars. To resolve trade disputes, governments often "barter" free trade, agreeing to remove a barrier to a specific product only when other countries have removed import barriers of their own. This is, in fact, a bit of a paradox, because free trade is almost always a win-win situation. Many countries, however, insist on making the removal of trade barriers a tit-for-tat process, mainly for political reasons. By appearing to be tough on trade, governments reap strong support at the polls, even though, economically, removing trade barriers is almost always beneficial for the country at large.

Historically, the developing countries have been some of the strongest proponents of free trade, primarily because their only hope for sustainable growth is to have access to international markets in which to sell their commodities, goods, and services. The irony is that many anti-free-trade activists justify their stance by saying they are trying to protect workers in developing countries. But tariffs and subsidies often end up hurting those workers in the developing countries the most. U.S. cotton subsidies, for example, are said to have led to a 30 percent fall in the incomes of cotton farmers in West Africa during the first years of the 21st century—principally in Mali, Chad, Burkina Faso, and Benin, where approximately twenty million people rely on cotton for their livelihood.

Since most developing countries export mainly agricultural products, farmers in rich countries in the northern hemisphere—principally in Japan, the United States, and Europe—fear the effects of low-cost competition on their profits. Consequently, they often oppose, sometimes vehemently, any efforts to allow developing countries to have access to their protected markets. In the European Union, for example, a complex system of quotas and tariffs keeps foreign agricultural products out while heavy subsidies allow rich country farmers to overpower competitors on the world markets, destroying the possibility for poor countries to increase agricultural exports and earn important foreign currency.

It may seem counterintuitive, but allowing developing countries to export food actually increases their ability to avoid famine. Prohibitive tariffs and quotas, along with massive subsidies for rich country farmers, often reduce the chances for agricultural sectors in poor countries to grow. Farming is a cyclical business where years of bounty are often followed by years of poor harvests, so removing the possibility for farmers in the poor countries to grow and prosper during the good years limits their ability to survive the difficult ones. Exporting surplus crops is, by far, the best way to ensure prosperity for farmers in poor agricultural nations. In addition, many aid programs require that the food they provide come from domestic sources in the developed world, particularly programs in the United States and the European Union. These aid exports often end up flooding markets abroad and destroying local production.

A universal free-trade agreement would, of course, solve the problem of deciding which barriers to eliminate, but getting every country in the world economy to agree on anything is not an easy task. The Doha round of free-trade talks, for example, languished during the first years of the 21st century, primarily because of the reluctance of rich countries in the northern hemisphere to lower barriers to trade in agricultural goods. A mitigating factor was also the growing reluctance of developing world countries to open their markets to manufactured goods.

Meanwhile, many countries decided to start small, by signing bilateral free-trade agreements (FTAs), which are easier to sell because the benefits are more tangible and major reduction of entrenched subsidies is not required. Malaysia's first FTA, for example, was signed with Japan, which was allowed to export automobiles to the previously protected Malaysian market in exchange for reduced barriers to imports of Malaysian plywood, tropical fruit, and shrimp into Japan—with no major change to Japan's system of agricultural subsidies. The United States followed suit by signing bilateral free-trade agreements with South Korea, Vietnam, and several countries in Latin America.

Once free-trade agreements are in place, some sort of mechanism is usually needed to ensure that countries respect their promises. In addition to bilateral commissions set up to monitor trade, the closest thing the world has to a worldwide trade watchdog is the World Trade Organization (WTO), which resolves disputes in an organized forum based in Switzerland.

• •

INFORMATIONAL TOOL:

What is the WTO?

Think of a trade tribunal, where countries meet to solve their trade disputes. The World Trade Organization began in 1995 at the former headquarters of the General Agreement on Tariffs and Trade, located in Geneva, Switzerland. Basically, the WTO's mandate is simple: When two or more countries have a dispute, they ask the WTO to help them resolve it through specially mandated dispute-settlement tribunals. Once a judgment has been made, the WTO permits the winning country to erect punitive tariffs, which are meant to allow it to make up for the losses caused by the offending nation.

• •

Despite the fact that the WTO, like many international and supranational organizations, is blamed for a wide variety of ills in the 21st-century economy, it must be underlined that its role was never meant to be more than as a global round table around which disputing parties could meet to air their grievances. Basically, the WTO has no power to force any country to do anything against its own national interests. And its only form of punishment is to permit the country that has suffered from illegal trade barriers to erect trade barriers of its own—usually in the form of tariffs. For example, when it was determined that the American economy had suffered from the European Union's refusal to allow unrestricted banana imports, the U.S. was allowed to impose tariffs on a wide range of EU goods, including Roquefort cheese and Italian truffles.

Most countries find it is in their own best interest to trade within the WTO framework, even if they do not agree with all of its decisions. A flawed arbitration system is usually seen as being preferable to the chaos of no framework at all for regulating trade. In the worst case, a country can opt to drop out of the World Trade Organization at any time, but would consequently be cut off from the benefits of being a WTO member, such as having an organized system for resolving trade disputes.

The WTO often has been criticized by protesters from wealthy countries for not taking stronger stands to protect the environment or labor standards, especially in the poorer countries of the world. On the other hand, those in developing countries criticize the WTO for catering to rich-country demands for stricter environmental and labor standards, fearing they are nothing more than yet another way for developed countries to keep them from having full access to the world economy. The WTO, pointing out that it is essentially only a forum to resolve trade disputes, has called for other bodies, such as the United Nations or the International Labour Organization, to settle disputes related to the environment and labor standards.

Despite the obvious benefits of free trade, trade barriers have always existed, and probably always will. The key is to find a way to promote more free trade with the minimum of harm to established industries and firms and in a way that promotes development in the world's poorer regions. Dismantling the world trading system would simply exacerbate existing problems and stall economic growth—essential for workers as well as captains of industry. In order for countries to increase real wages, for example, governments need to expand access to markets abroad in order to allow export industries to grow.

Foreign competition also acts as a catalyst for companies to become more productive, increasing the financial well-being of the country as a whole. Of course, displaced workers should be helped out with training and extended unemployment insurance as much as possible. But to close the door to trade, which by some estimates has added over a trillion dollars to the U.S. economy in the 21st century, would mean irreparable harm to the economy as a whole, not just those directly affected.

An effective way to stimulate trade is to form free-trade zones, either regionally or globally. The basic idea of a free-trade zone is to remove all barriers to the movement of capital, goods, and services between countries within the zone. This usually means dismantling tariffs and quotas between the member countries.

The European Union led the way in 1957 with the formation of the European Economic Community, joining together the economies of France, West Germany, Italy, Belgium, the Netherlands, and Luxembourg in a free-trade zone that, fifty years later, covered the entire continent. The addition of ten new countries in the first years of the 21st century brought a total of twenty-five members—with future candidates including Turkey and several countries from the former Republic of Yugoslavia.

Although the European Union had its beginnings as a purely trade-oriented union, the treaty of Maastricht, signed at the end of the 20th century, made the *common market* a true economic and political union. After Maastricht, citizens of Portugal could live and work anywhere from London to Athens; goods could flow from Finland to Italy without any extra formalities; and money could be transferred from Madrid to Frankfurt without restrictions.

The introduction of the euro in 1999 meant truly barrier-free trade among the eleven EU countries that decided to adopt the common currency. Denmark, Sweden, and the U.K. decided to continue their own currencies, as did several of the new members, awaiting approval from the European Central Bank to join the euro zone. Despite the failure of the European Union constitution to be approved, the members agreed in 2007 to streamline EU procedures—including the removal of the requirement for unanimity in EU decision making, and a president of the European Council who will serve two-year terms instead of the previous six-month rotating presidency.

The only Western European holdouts to the EU—Switzerland, Liechtenstein, Iceland, and Norway—decided to take a "wait-and-see" policy, choosing to take advantage of access to the EU market through bilateral trade agreements without entering the union officially. These relatively wealthy nations had previously ensured barrier-free trade among themselves through the European Free Trade Association (EFTA).

Unlike the European Union, NAFTA (the North American Free Trade Organization), between Canada, the United States, and Mexico, has remained true to its original purpose of promoting free trade in goods and services only—with no plans for economic, monetary, or political union. In addition, no attempt was made to impose common tariffs or quotas on goods coming from outside the bloc. Stretching from the cold arctic tundra to balmy Caribbean shores, NAFTA's goal was mainly to allow each country to benefit from the others' advantages. Instead of trying to grow tobacco or bananas in the Yukon, for example, Canadians figured that they would be better off if they imported these goods from their neighbors to the south, providing other goods and services in return—such as timber and banking services.

Canda Example ex

• • • • • • • • • • • • • • • • • • • •

INFORMATIONAL TOOL:

What is **NAFTA**?

Think of a swap meet with only three participants. The idea of NAFTA was to open up the economies of North America's three biggest economies to trade in goods and services. It wasn't an easy sell. Opponents predicted a "sucking sound" of jobs being lost south of the border. But, in the end, workers in all three countries benefited (on the whole) when all three economies expanded, aided by the benefits of increased trade with their neighbors. Unlike other trade groups, such as the European Union, NAFTA doesn't allow barriers to be erected to countries outside the trading bloc— it simply removed barriers to trade among the three NAFTA members: Canada, Mexico, and the United States. members

• •

Farsighted government officials in the United States and Canada calculated that—despite increased competition from low-wage industries in Mexico—in the long term NAFTA would lead to a net increase in jobs as local industries expanded to take advantage of the opportunity for expanded trade. And, in many ways, they were right. By the beginning of the 21st century, expanded trade in goods and services had created many more jobs than those lost to increased competition. In addition to increasing jobs and economic growth in the United States and in Canada, NAFTA succeeded in creating new jobs and businesses in Mexico, helping the country to reduce poverty and lower pressure for its citizens to emigrate northward in search of jobs.

Inspired by the success of free-trade zones in Europe and North America, many regions of the world have moved to build free-trade "megazones" of their own. In South America, Mercosur (Mercado Común del Sur, or in Brazil, Mercado Comum do Sul) joined the countries of the southern cone in the new free-trade bloc. Brazil and Argentina, two of the biggest economies in the southern hemisphere, were joined by Paraguay and Uruguay—and later by Chile and Bolivia as associate members. Like the European Union, Mercosur reduced tariffs on trade between the member countries while instituting common tariffs of goods from outside the bloc. Everything from beer and automobiles to fruit and banking services flowed in increasing numbers.

Meanwhile, farther to the north, the Andean Pact was formed to remove barriers to trade between Venezuela, Colombia, Peru, Ecuador, and Bolivia. The economies of Central America and the Caribbean also moved to form two more free-trade zones: the Central America Free Trade Agreement (CAFTA), removing barriers to trade between the United States and Guatemala, Costa Rica, El Salvador, Honduras, Nicaragua, and the Dominican Republic; and the Caribbean Community (CARICOM) free-trade zone, including Jamaica, Trinidad and Tobago, and thirteen other Caribbean island countries.

Even though Western Hemisphere leaders moved to join together all of these disparate groups into one hemisphere-wide trade zone, called Free Trade Area of the Americas (FTAA), political and economic pressure from groups within each country prevented any final agreement from being reached.

In an attempt to provide a free-market zone in Asia, the ten countries that made up the Association of Southeast Asian Nations (ASEAN) moved to create a trade zone of their own by the year 2015. In the meantime, they began discussions with China and Japan to sign free-trade agreements in an effort to counter moves by other nations in Asia—particularly South Korea and Vietnam—that had already signed free-trade deals with the United States. But opposition from entrenched groups within Japan, particularly the farmers who benefit from tariffs on agricultural imports of up to 800 percent, have made any deal with food-exporting countries extremely difficult to achieve.

• •

INFORMATIONAL TOOL:

What are the **free-trade zones** of the 21st-century economy?

European Union (EU): *Begun as a simple customs union with limited scope—the original idea was simply to reduce or remove tariffs on a limited number of goods—the European Union now covers a wide variety of cultural, financial, and economic fields, with its own currency, the euro, and its own central bank, the European Central Bank (ECB), based in Frankfurt. With a total GDP of more than €12 trillion (approximately $18 trillion), the EU has become the world's biggest free-trade union. The EU used to be called the European Economic Community, and later just the European Community, or simply the Common Market. Members include: Austria, Belgium, Bulgaria, Cyprus, the Czech Republic, Denmark, Estonia, Finland, France, Germany, Greece, Hungary, Ireland, Italy, Latvia, Lithuania, Luxembourg, Malta, the Netherlands, Poland, Portugal, Romania, Slovakia, Slovenia, Spain, Sweden, and the United Kingdom.*

European Free Trade Association (EFTA): *Consisting of Western European nations that opted out of formal EU membership, EFTA has set up a loosely grouped free-trade association of its own, even though the four members have preferential access to the EU through separate agreements. Members include: Iceland, Norway, Switzerland, and Liechtenstein.*

Central European Free Trade Agreement (CEFTA): *CEFTA originally included many more Central and Eastern European members, but several have left to join the European Union. The remaining members are principally ex-Yugoslavian nations. Full members include: Albania, Bosnia and Herzegovina, Croatia, the Republic of Macedonia, Moldova, Montenegro, Serbia, and Kosovo.*

North American Free Trade Agreement (NAFTA): *Originally set up only to remove trade barriers between the member countries, NAFTA has been subsequently altered to include agreements to address environmen-*

tal and labor concerns with the addition of the North American Agreement on Environmental Protection (NAAEP) and the North American Agreement on Labor Cooperation (NAALC). Members include: Canada, Mexico, and the United States.

Caribbean Community (CARICOM): Originally set up only to promote economic cooperation and development in the Caribbean basin, CARICOM now consists of a common market with reduced tariffs among member countries. CARICOM also operates the Caribbean Court of Justice, which serves as a sort of supreme court, providing a final court of appeals for member countries. Members include: Antigua and Barbuda, Bahamas, Barbados, Belize, Dominica, Grenada, Guyana, Haiti, Jamaica, Montserrat, Saint Kitts and Nevis, Saint Lucia, Saint Vincent and the Grenadines, Suriname, and Trinidad and Tobago.

Mercosur/Mercosul: Mercado Común del Sur (Mercado Comum do Sul, or Mercosul, in Brazil) was set up to provide a Latin American alternative to trade unions in the Northern Hemisphere. In addition to reducing trade barriers between member nations, Mercosur has imposed barriers to imports from outside the bloc. Associate members include Bolivia, Chile, Colombia, Ecuador, and Peru, with Venezuela having applied for full membership in 2006. Full members are: Argentina, Brazil, Paraguay, and Uruguay.

Andean Community (CAN): Awaiting membership in a full-fledged South American trade union with the members of Mercosur, the four Andean nations have grouped together in a trade union of their own: the Comunidad Andina (CAN), referred to in English as the Andean Community. Members include: Bolivia, Colombia, Ecuador, and Peru.

Economic Community of West African States (ECOWAS): Referred to by the French-speaking members as the CEDEAO (Communauté Économique des États de l'Afrique de l'Ouest), ECOWAS was set up to create an economic and, eventually, a monetary union in West Africa. The name chosen for the common currency is the eco. Members include: Benin, Burkina Faso, Cabo Verde, Côte d'Ivoire, Gambia,

Ghana, Guinea, Guinea-Bissau, Liberia, Mali, Niger, Nigeria, Senegal, Sierra Leone, and Togo.

Economic and Monetary Community of Central Africa is called **CEMAC** in reference to the French name of the group, Communauté Économique et Monétaire de l'Afrique Centrale. It not only provides an economic and free-trade zone to the member states, but has also created a common currency, the CFA franc. Members include: Cameroon, the Central African Republic, Chad, the Republic of the Congo, Equatorial Guinea, and Gabon.

East African Community (EAC): Originally begun as a customs union, with reduced tariffs between member nations and common tariffs on imports from outside the bloc, EAC has a further purpose: to prepare for a political union, called the East Africa Federation, with its own currency, the East African shilling. Members include: Burundi, Kenya, Rwanda, Tanzania, and Uganda.

Southern African Customs Union (SACU): The oldest customs union in the world, SACU was originally established between the Union of South Africa and several neighboring nations. Current members include: Botswana, Lesotho, Namibia, South Africa, and Swaziland. Partners include: Angola, Botswana, the Democratic Republic of the Congo, Lesotho, Madagascar, Malawi, Mauritius, Mozambique, Namibia, the Seychelles, Tanzania, Zambia, and Zimbabwe.

Common Market for Eastern and Southern Africa (COMESA): Stretching from Eritrea in the north to Zimbabwe in the south, COMESA is one of the pillars of the African Economic Union, whose eventual goal is to create an Africa-wide common trade area with a common central bank and a common currency. Members include: Burundi, Comoros, the Democratic Republic of the Congo, Djibouti, Egypt, Eritrea, Ethiopia, Kenya, Libya, Madagascar, Malawi, Mauritius, Rwanda, the Seychelles, Sudan, Swaziland, Uganda, Zambia, and Zimbabwe.

Greater Arab Free Trade Area (GAFTA): Created by the League of Arab States, GAFTA's purpose is to create a free-trade union among the

Arab countries of northern Africa. The original members (of the precursor to GAFTA, called the Agadir Agreement) were: Egypt, Jordan, Morocco, and Tunisia. Additional members of GAFTA include: Bahrain, Iraq, Jordan, Kuwait, Lebanon, Libya, Oman, Palestine, Qatar, Saudi Arabia, Sudan, Syria, the United Arab Emirates, Lebanon, and Yemen.

Association of Southeast Asian Nations (ASEAN): In addition to promoting trade and economic growth, ASEAN also supports social progress and cultural development in Southeast Asia. Members include: Brunei, Cambodia, Indonesia, Laos, Malaysia, Myanmar, the Philippines, Singapore, Thailand, and Vietnam.

South Asian Association for Regional Cooperation (SAARC): Set up to promote economic and political cooperation in South Asia, SAARC has the largest population of any trade bloc—more than a billion citizens. Members include: Bangladesh, Bhutan, India, Maldives, Nepal, Pakistan, and Sri Lanka.

• •

The holy grail of world trade agreements would be to include China and India—assuming they could be convinced to remove their many barriers to trade. It would certainly be an important step to creating a worldwide free-trade zone. Together with the other developing countries of east and south Asia, China and India constitute the home to more than half of the world's population and boast an economic growth rate that is often several multiples of that in the "developed" world. Referred to as "the Great Modernization" by some economic observers, the region's boom has begun to resemble the Industrial Revolution in terms of economic impact. In the absence of a worldwide free-trade agreement, any nation looking to expand a regional or bilateral agreement would have to include the booming Asian economies on their list of possible candidates.

Even though trade barriers have limited economic value,

they do have considerable power to change the behavior of nations. Many illegal practices in the world economy—such as human rights abuses, child labor, slavery, torture, war, and terrorism—can be altered through the use of economic sanctions.

Essentially, there are two kinds of economic sanctions: consumer boycotts and trade embargoes. *Consumer boycotts* can take many forms, from individual consumers making the decision to stop buying products from offending producers to well-orchestrated campaigns involving millions of consumers and store owners.

Unfortunately, the loss of one sale is not going to make a company change its practices overnight, but the threat of a worldwide consumer boycott can be an effective tool—mainly because it involves the most powerful economic incentive around: profits. By refusing to buy tuna that comes from drift-net fishing, for example, consumer groups were able to end the practice that had been contributing to the death of thousands of dolphins per year.

Trade embargoes are usually organized by governments or governmental organizations such as the United Nations to force a country to change a harmful or illegal behavior. Although trade embargoes have little economic value—the exporting country usually finds other, less demanding markets in which to sell their goods or services—they are often effective in bringing about political or social change. The economic sanctions imposed on North Korea, for example, were cited by Pyongyang as one of the principal reasons for giving up its plan to manufacture nuclear weapons. By deleting the Democratic People's Republic of Korea from the list of terror-supporting nations and lifting economic sanctions, the United States and other nations were able to accomplish something that years of military threats had been unable to do.

The key to any economic sanction is to have a "critical mass" of support. If only one or two countries impose economic sanctions, the offending country is unlikely to change their behavior. When the United States imposed economic sanctions on Iran, for example, refusing to deal with Iranian banks or buy Iranian oil until Iran renounced its nuclear ambitions and ended support for terrorism, other countries simply stepped in and signed business agreements with the affected Iranian entities. Nevertheless, many states and universities in the United States moved to divest: sell shares in any company that conducted business or traded with Iran. But without similar efforts in other countries, the sold shares simply end up in the hands of another pension fund or investment vehicle, with little effect on the offending power.

Unilateral sanctions can also create the opposite effect—alienating allies and reducing the possibility of getting other countries to cooperate with other international efforts. When the United States imposed economic sanctions on Iran—including the decision to prohibit American banks from doing business there—other countries in the region were invited to move in. Often, poorly coordinated trade sanctions provoke the targeted country into erecting trade barriers of its own, ultimately hurting consumers and businesses on both sides and limiting the influence the country imposing the sanctions may want to apply at a later date.

When many nations band together to send a clear economic message, however, threats of retaliation often lose their punch. Trade sanctions agreed to at the United Nations, for example, are much more effective because they need to be approved by a majority of the countries. Although many of these resolutions are nonbinding, enforcement is often not necessary if broad global support is obtained beforehand.

In the end, global trade can mean life or death to millions of people. Global famine and economic stagnation are major concerns for many countries in the 21st-century economy. Rich-country citizens often think they are doing the right thing by opposing free trade, justifying their stance by saying they are protecting local companies and local workers. But workers and farmers in countries around the world also need jobs and financial support. For many workers in the poor regions of the world, the only hope for sustainable long-term growth is to have access to international markets in which to sell their goods and services.

CHAPTER 5

MONEY, MONEY, MONEY—HOW DO CURRENCIES WORK IN THE NEW GLOBAL ECONOMY?

FROM THE VIRTUAL currency Linden dollars in Second Life to credit chips on bank cards to actual cash and coins in our pockets, money—in whatever form it's taking in the 21st-century economy—does make the world go 'round.

It used to be that anyone could issue a currency. In the 19th-century United States economy, for example, there were more than seven hundred banks issuing their own currency—and as many as one-third of all notes in circulation were fake. Today, currencies are issued by central banks or monetary authorities. In the United States, for example, the currency is printed by the Department of the Treasury and "sold" to the Federal Reserve, which injects it into the economy at large.

Basically, money has three purposes. First, it serves as a *medium of exchange*, allowing you to sell your goods or services for a fixed amount of paper, metal, or credits at an online site such as PayPal. Second, it allows people and businesses to *store value* from one year to the next. And third, it serves as a *unit of account*, telling us how much things are worth by providing us with a point of reference that is universally understood.

• •

INFORMATIONAL TOOL:

What determines the price of a **currency?**

Think of someone selling a Super Bowl ticket the day before the game—or the day after. Basically, currency trading follows the law of supply and demand. The more a currency is sought after by importers, foreign travelers, and speculators, the more its value goes up. And when a country imports significantly more than it exports, its currency's value tends to go down as the foreign exchange markets get flooded with unwanted greenbacks, yen, or pesos. The currency market is just like any other market in the world economy—the only difference is that a currency's "price" must be given in terms of other countries' currencies. A euro is worth so many dollars, which are worth so many yen, which are worth so many pesos.

• •

Buying a currency for use abroad is a simple matter. A tourist on vacation can go to a *casa de cambio* or a *bureau de change* and make the same transaction the big players do, selling one currency to buy another. This transaction involves choosing one of two prices: If you're selling you receive the trader's *bid price*, which is always a bit lower than the price the trader will charge for selling the currency back to you, the *ask price*. By trading all day long, always paying a slightly lower price to buy than to sell, the trader makes money. Theoretically, if an indecisive traveler were to trade back and forth enough times, there would be almost nothing left at the end of the day.

On the world markets, currency trading goes on twenty-four hours a day, seven days a week—on trading floors scattered around the world, from Boston to Singapore to Paris. The *market price* of a currency often changes several times a second. And in the 21st-century economy, it's the market that determines the currency's value, weighing buyers against sellers in a constantly changing environment.

There are a whole range of reasons currency speculators and traders buy or sell. One is a perception that the currency will change in value in the future. Who wants to buy a house in a declining market? You'd rather wait until prices go down, and then jump in. In currency markets it's the same story. If the view of the market is that the dollar will rise over the next few years, speculators and investors will buy, driving the price up—in a sort of self-fulfilling prophecy.

It works the other way as well. When countries run into debt problems or other economic problems, speculators and traders can be brutal, selling the currency in massive amounts on markets around the world, driving down prices and sometimes bringing down governments as well. During the Asia crisis in the late 1990s, for example, speculators drove down the price of the Thai currency, the baht, by almost 40 percent—leading to a meltdown in local financial markets. In the early 1990s, during a time of weakness in the British economy, currency speculators, betting on a weakening of the pound, were able to put so much pressure on the beleaguered currency that the government withdrew from the European Monetary System. The speculators were said to have made billions on their successful read of the currency market.

Central bank intervention to support a floundering currency can sometimes be effective. The euro intervention in 2000 led to a steady climb of the euro, eventually outpacing all other currencies in the world economy. Coordinated action, with all the major central banks and monetary authorities working in unison, tends to be the most effective way to change a currency's downward—or upward—course. Sometimes even too successful:

Plaza Accord action to devalue the dollar in 1985 had to be reversed two years later with the Louvre Accord when the dollar had fallen too much on world markets.

The efforts of central banks to control currency exchange rates are sometimes hampered in the 21st century by the fact that money is being held by an increasingly large group of players in the world economy. Almost 80 percent of dollar reserves, for example, were being held not by G7 central banks—such as those in Europe, Canada, or Japan—but by emerging-market central banks such as those in Taiwan, China, and oil-rich Saudi Arabia that had reinvested their massive export earnings in dollar-denominated securities such as U.S. government bonds.

• •

INFORMATIONAL TOOL:

What have been the most successful central bank **currency interventions** *during past financial crises?*

1985 Plaza Accord, to devalue U.S. dollar.
1987 Louvre Accord, to support U.S. dollar.
1995 First Yen Intervention, to halt dollar's slide against yen.
1998 Second Yen Intervention, to halt yen's slide.
2000 Euro Intervention, coordinated G7 action to support euro.

• •

The most common reason for a currency's rise or fall is usually based on fundamental market economics such as budget or trade surpluses and deficits. Trade between countries generates enormous transfers of funds, and the transfer of those funds can have a profound effect on the value of a country's currency. A California almond exporter, for example, earns millions of yen from sales to Japan and will usually trade those yen for dollars. The bank in Sacramento that exchanged the farmer's yen then will go to a bigger bank and they will "sell" it to an individual or company that may want it to pay for an investment in Sony shares or to buy a container of Nintendo Wiis.

What makes a currency go down in value? Imagine a French-made video game monopolizing world markets—with no one wanting to buy yen to purchase Sony or Nintendo products, the value of the yen would go down. Basically, when a country imports more than it exports—referred to as a *current account deficit*—over the long run the country's currency will go down.

But how long is the long run? That's the million-dollar—or million-euro or million-yen—question. During the first years of the 21st century, the United States ran enormous deficits in its current account—which measures a country's trade in goods and services as well as international transfers such as payments from foreign investments—to the tune of several hundred billion dollars a year. These dollars, spent on imports that were not balanced by exports, had to end up somewhere.

• •

INFORMATIONAL TOOL:

What is a **current account**?

Think of an accountant sitting down at the port, writing down everything—including money—that comes in and goes out during the course of a year. A country's current account measures a country's international trade in goods and services over a given period. Current accounts measure visible trade, such as rice and television sets, as well as invisible trade, such as banking services and movies. The current account also includes financial transfers, such as money sent home by citizens working abroad and interest paid on foreign debt. The current account is balanced by the country's capital account, *which includes all transfers of money related to the sale of goods and services abroad.*

• •

Fortunately, many countries with trade surpluses, such as China and Taiwan, have been willing to use their excess dollars to buy dollar-denominated securities. The result was that these countries ended up with trillions of dollars in U.S. investments that could, in theory, be sold at a moment's notice. The result of a precipitous sale would have catastrophic effects on the dollar—and the value of the U.S. government's debt. It was, therefore, in the interest of these countries to keep the U.S. dollar from falling too much.

It was also in their interest to keep the dollar strong, because their economic plan was to grow through exports. This *mercantilist* economic model had been successfully implemented by Japan in the 20th century, bringing untold wealth to the exporters and, later, to consumers.

• •

INFORMATIONAL TOOL:

What is **mercantilism?**

The idea of mercantilism is to encourage exports while restricting imports. This usually leads to an increase in foreign reserves. In the 21st-century economy, mercantilist economies can be encouraged to increase their currency's value by less violent means. Political pressure, for example. Or the threat of exclusion from trading groups such as the WTO.

• •

During the first years of a mercantilist expansion, a country tries to earn as much as it can by exporting as much as possible and importing as little as possible—and then investing the money abroad. The idea is to use the money to pay for a better life for its citizens at some point in the future. But what happens if the money earned from exports is invested in foreign securities that lose their value when the foreign currency falls—and the mercantilist country's investments abroad decline?

Some mercantilist countries—such as Japan in the 1980s and China at the beginning of the 21st century—have been forced, by a combination of economic and political pressure, to increase the value of their currency on the world markets, making imports less expensive and exports more difficult to sell on world markets. How is this done? Mainly by changing the currency's *pegged value*.

• •

INFORMATIONAL TOOL:

What is a **pegged currency**?

By intervening periodically in the currency markets, countries are able to keep their home currency trading roughly in line with the value of another currency—or basket of currencies. Most countries peg their currencies to the euro or the U.S. dollar. In recent years, Hong Kong, Shanghai, and Saudi Arabia have kept their currency pegged to the dollar, and countries in Eastern Europe have pegged their currencies to the euro. At the beginning of the 21st century, more than a hundred countries in the world economy had their currency exchange rates fixed in some way—mostly through pegs to other currencies. Pegged currency regimes are sometimes referred to as a dirty float to distinguish them from the freely floating currency regimes of the advanced industrial economies such as Britain, the euro zone, or the United States.

• •

Unfortunately, it's not always possible to keep a currency from rising or falling precipitously on world markets. Currency crashes around the world, from Britain to Argentina to Southeast Asia in past years, attest to the power of speculators to bring down a currency by selling enormous amounts of that currency on the world's foreign exchange markets. The speculators often succeed because governments with weak currencies are limited in what they can do. If they don't have enough foreign reserves, they can't support the currency by buying it on the foreign exchange markets. And if they raise interest rates to attract investment in the country and the currency, it can bring the country's economy to a screeching halt.

Countries with currencies that are too strong don't have the same problem. Even if they didn't want to spend foreign exchange reserves to support the currency on the world markets, all a country like China would have to do to keep speculators from driving its currency's price up would be to lower interest rates. This may bring on unwanted inflation, but even that would serve to foil the speculators' attempts to make a currency rise in value against the wishes of the home country's government and central bank authorities.

Instead of going to the markets to devalue the Chinese yuan, for example, the United States and other trading partners used political pressure to convince the Chinese government to "voluntarily" lower the value of its currency—an idea that was met with considerable reluctance from the Chinese authorities, who built their economy during the first years of the 21st century on ever-expanding exports. The idea played well to the home crowd, however—and Washington politicians were applauded for looking after America's best interest and forcing China to raise the dollar value of its currency, presumably leading to the eradication of the American trade deficit with China.

The effort to raise the Chinese currency's value, however, was eventually forced to confront economic reality—in this case, by ruthless foreign exchange markets. By calling for a rise in the value of the yuan, the U.S. authorities were, by definition, calling for a decline in the value of the dollar. And this, in effect, is exactly what occurred during the U.S. dollar meltdown of 2007, when it lost more than 20 percent in value against the euro and many other currencies around the world—including the Canadian dollar and the Brazilian real. It was only during the financial turmoil of the 2008 credit crisis that panicked investors pulled their money out of foreign markets and put it in "safe haven" currencies such as the dollar, yen, and Swiss franc, raising their value sharply.

Since the world has gotten used to using the dollar as the primary reserve currency, any action on the part of the U.S. authorities to manipulate the value of the dollar can have far-reaching consequences. How can creditor nations continue to pay for the U.S. trade deficit by investing in dollar-denominated treasury bonds if they thought the United States was going to let the dollar fall on the world markets?

When exactly is the right time to buy or sell a currency? Whenever there's a change in the home country's interest rate? When the economy of the home country is showing signs of strength or weakness? When there's a change in trade, evidenced by growing surpluses or deficits? Or should you buy or sell because you think that *other* traders in the market are going to buy or sell and you don't want to be caught going against an unstoppable market movement? It's hard to know for sure.

Interest rates are often a major factor in determining a currency's relative value. High interest rates generally occur when economic growth is strong—which implies increased demand for a currency, which will tend to drive up the currency's price.

The dollar's rapid fall against the euro in 2007, for example, was mainly attributed to the increasing differential between European and American interest rates. The relatively strong euro zone economies kept euro interest rates higher than those in the United States, leading many investors to sell dollars and buy the relatively stronger euro.

What can a central bank do to support a weak currency? The main tool is usually to raise interest rates, just as a bond issuer might raise interest rates to attract new buyers. But the higher rates may have a disastrous effect on the home country's economy, stifling growth and sending the economy into a tailspin—which may cause the currency to decline even more.

Another option would be for the central bank to let the currency fall so that imports—made more expensive because of the local currency's declining purchasing power on the world markets—decline drastically and the trade deficit is reduced. Unfortunately, this also leads to unwanted consequences, primarily an increase in inflation. Think of trying to buy Brazilian ethanol to power your car with dollars that have declined dramatically against the real.

Usually, when you're forced to buy more-expensive locally made alternatives, the cost of living goes up. And inflation, as soon as it rears its ugly head, is often perceived by the market as yet another reason to sell a currency. Who wants to hold a currency that's declining in value? It's often a vicious circle—difficult to stop once it starts.

An alternative reason to buy or sell a currency is arbitrage. The age-old trick of "buying low, selling high" is still alive and well in the international currency markets. Think of those bigwigs who have the wherewithal to borrow large amounts of currencies in one country, where rates are low, and switch into currencies that provide higher interest rates—or currencies where the return on investments is high.

Japan, for example, during most of the first years of the 21st century, had interest rates that hovered around 0 percent. If you could borrow a lot of yen, it would pay to convert them into investments in dollars or euros that paid a higher interest rate. This *carry trade* goes on whenever interest rates are so divergent that it's worth running the risk of fluctuations in the currency's price to make a quick buck.

• •

INFORMATIONAL TOOL:

What is the difference between speculation and arbitrage?

Think of the difference between someone betting on a horse race and someone earning money by buying and selling things at a swap meet. A speculator has an opinion of where the prices are heading and buys or sells accordingly, hoping, in the end, to make a profit. An arbitrageur spots discrepancies in world markets, and then acts quickly to buy where a product is sold cheaply and immediately sell it in another market where prices are higher. The difference between the two is risk. A speculator takes a risk that the price will go in the direction they predicted. An arbitrageur tries to avoid risk, spotting discrepancies in the prices of anything from stocks and bonds to commodities and currencies and buying and selling once the risk has been eliminated.

• •

Another reason to buy or sell a currency is to find a safe haven in periods of economic turmoil. The Swiss franc, for example, is often cited as a haven in troubled economic times. When it looks like the world is coming to an end—financially, at least—investors try to put their money into something that will hold its value. Even gold or other precious metals take on this "flight to safety" role during troubled times.

In the ever-expanding global economy, you don't have to

be a bank or a billionaire to invest in foreign currencies and profit from currency fluctuations abroad. The simplest but least remunerative way would be to buy a pile of foreign currency and keep it under your mattress—or in a bank safety-deposit vault. This wouldn't give you anything in terms of yield, but would still allow you to profit when the currency you bought goes up in value against your home currency.

A better way would to be to invest in a fund that invests in foreign stocks—or buy American Depositary Receipts (ADRs), which are repackaged shares from foreign stock markets that are sold in the United States as dollar-denominated securities. The advantage with ADRs is that everything is accounted for in dollars, even dividends, and the ADRs' value fluctuates with the foreign currency value of the underlying shares.

Another option would be to buy certificates of deposit (CDs) denominated in foreign currencies. International investors can buy CDs in a wide range of currencies ranging from New Zealand dollars, British pounds, Swiss francs, Norwegian kroner, and Mexican pesos. These foreign-currency CDs usually require a minimum investment of $10,000 and usually have a life span, referred to as a *maturity*, of six months or less.

There are also many currency-related funds in the global economy that allow investors to participate in pure currency plays—with no risk from movement in underlying securities like stocks and bonds. Several major U.S.-based mutual funds offer currency funds—often called *hard currency funds*—that allow investors to speculate on the rise or fall of anything from the Swedish krona to the South African rand. There are also funds that allow investors to invest in a blend of international currencies—reducing the risk from an individual currency going in the wrong direction.

Currency speculation can also have tax advantages. In the United States, for example, the tax treatment of many foreign currency investments is quite beneficial to the average investor because even though interest and dividends are taxed at the normal rate applying to ordinary income, any gain from the foreign currency is taxed as a capital gain, usually subject to a much lower rate.

Another interesting way for investors to benefit from currency fluctuations is to buy shares in companies that benefit from currency moves abroad. For example, a U.S. investor who thinks the euro will go up and the yen will go down against the dollar could buy shares in car exporters Toyota or Honda—and sell shares of BMW or Mercedes. A weak dollar also means increased exports for U.S. companies. After the dollar fell sharply in 2007, for example, containers in the Long Beach harbor were filled to capacity with U.S.-made computers and auto and aircraft parts, whose prices had suddenly become more competitive on world markets. On the other hand, because the strong yen and euro were making Japanese and European exports less interesting to U.S. consumers, car exporters such as Toyota and the Mercedes Car Group announced plans to move more production to the United States.

However, a strong currency can also cause problems at home. One example is the so-called *Dutch disease* that occurs when a local currency becomes overvalued because of temporary economic windfalls, such as the discovery of natural gas in Holland in the late 20th century that eventually led to a sharp decline in the competitiveness of Dutch exporters. The strong currency caused a steep drop in sales abroad and, consequently, job losses and layoffs at home.

Despite all the problems resulting from currency fluctuations, however, most modern economies have found that the advantages of not having the currency pegged or fixed far outweigh the disadvantages. It used to be that every currency's value was fixed by the government or was linked to some item of value. Even in the United States, until 1973, dollars could be converted into gold. This "gold standard" was meant to guarantee that currencies would always have a certain value, determined by the amount of gold held in each country's vaults.

• •

INFORMATIONAL TOOL:

What is the **gold standard**?

Think of a currency being backed by a piece of gold stored in Fort Knox. It used to be that a currency's value was linked to an item of value—such as silver or gold. This gold standard was used extensively in the 19th century in Britain, where gold coins in circulation could be melted down freely and gold coins and bullion could be exported and imported without restriction. The system broke down during World War I, but by the 1920s it had returned in most countries, only to collapse again during the Great Depression of the 1930s. After World War II, most countries pegged their currencies to the U.S. dollar or to gold. In the 1950s, in most European countries, for example, you could still convert local currencies into a fixed amount of gold. But when the Smithsonian Agreement of fixed exchange rates collapsed in 1973—mainly because of the catastrophic inflation and subsequent devaluation of the dollar following the 1972 oil shock—currencies were allowed to "float" on the international markets. From then on, it would mainly be the markets that would decide what the world's currencies were worth.

• •

At the beginning of the 21st century, the value of the world's freely floating currencies is determined mostly by economic and political factors—and sometimes by the speculation of individual traders. Foreign exchange traders, for example, may decide to bet that a currency will increase or decline in value just as a commodities trader bets that wheat or pork bellies will go up or down in value at some point in the future.

No one, however, knows for sure what direction currency markets are going to take. Since economic information is now immediately available to everyone in the global markets, exchange-rate forecasts are largely speculation. At any given point in time, about half the traders and investors in the foreign exchange, or *forex*, markets think that a particular currency will go up—and the other half think it will go down. If it were any different, the side "in the know" would keep buying a currency until it reached a new equilibrium. In the end, no one really knows where the currency markets are headed—if they did, they'd already have made their move and would now be sitting on a beach in the Caribbean, sipping a banana daiquiri and enjoying their newfound wealth.

CHAPTER 6

RAGE AGAINST THE MACHINE—WHY THE BIG FUSS OVER GLOBALIZATION?

AS THE FILM star Joan Crawford once remarked, "The only thing worse than being talked about is not being talked about." In the converging global economy, it's not all that different: In many ways, the only thing worse than opening your borders is *not* opening your borders. Sure, there are disadvantages to the free exchange of goods, services, and money. But the advantages are huge. And those countries that close their borders are going to remain in the back of the pack even during times of economic crisis.

"So what?" some may ask. "Who needs the trouble and disruption and pollution and all the other side effects of a burgeoning economy?" Well, the poor, for one. Obviously, the rich have benefited a lot from the exploding global economy—and rich countries more than poor ones—but other than a swath of languishing countries in sub-Saharan Africa, almost every developing country in the world is better off today than it was a few years ago, when more than half the world's population was forced to live on less than $2 a day. What about them? Would a return to the protected, insular ways of the past help or hurt the poor people of the world?

Let's look at the Great Depression. We've all heard about the rich tycoons who lost their shirts when the stock market crashed in 1929. But it was the farmers and the workers who suffered most. And when the United States closed its borders to trade with the Smoot-Hawley Tariff Act in 1930, it not only exported its recession to the rest of the world, it led other countries to close their borders in retaliation. Soon, an American recession became a global depression. The result? Most of those fat cats who lost money in the stock market suffered, of course, but many still had some in reserve—or were able to find new jobs. It was the poor, however, who were devastated by the depression. Some Americans actually starved to death.

All through history, those countries that opened their doors and traded were those that prospered the most: Greece, Rome, the Venetian Empire, Holland in the Golden Age, Imperial England, Japan, and the United States over most of the 20th century—and now a whole raft of emerging-market economies in the China, for example, before it opened its doors to the world economy, was a poor, struggling, backward economy. Now it's on track to become the largest economy in the world. And several hundred million people have been brought out of poverty in the process.

"But what's in it for me?" many people in rich countries ask themselves. It is true that even rich countries have workers who need to be protected from the hardships brought about by economic transition. The American middle class, for example, even during the "boom years" of the 1980s, saw real wages stagnate. Since then, the median income of America's workers has risen by only 17 percent. During that time, the income of the richest 0.1 percent of the population has quadrupled.

Worldwide it's even worse. By the beginning of the 21st century, the world's richest sixty-five million people were earning over five hundred times more than the world's poorest sixty-five million. Visitors to almost any city in the developing world are confronted with gigantic slums filled to capacity with people trying to eke out a living, sometimes under the most unsanitary conditions.

So what's the answer? Stop economic growth by putting an end to globalization? How will the poor in developing-country slums fare then? And what about the middle-class workers who saw their incomes stagnate even during the boom years? Will things get any better for them during an economic downturn? Most probably not. The modern global economy has to keep growing. Only then will it be able to create enough jobs to provide opportunities for growing populations.

Unfortunately, some people are against globalization mainly for cultural reasons. The French antiglobalist José Bové, for example, once used his tractor to destroy a McDonald's restaurant near his sheep farm, denouncing the evils of global domination by Anglo-Saxon multinationals and the proliferation of bad American food. But why was the restaurant being built there in the first place? Presumably, because a certain segment of the population had found it useful, indeed desirable, to eat at McDonald's.

Globalization, by definition, opens up doors. It gives us new opportunities—to buy, sell, and travel abroad. If it means that some may lose their job, it also means that many more will get jobs. Statistically, trade and exchange mean economic growth. Sure, the rich tend to benefit the most when profits increase. But a growing company also means increased demand for labor—either in the form of direct employment or by increasing the demand for a whole range of goods and services from outside the company—which creates jobs.

That doesn't mean we have to blindly accept the inequities that globalization exacerbates, but instead of blaming globalization for the unequally distributed wealth, why not blame the governments that allow the new wealth to be distributed unequally? There is something that governments use, and have used for centuries, to redistribute wealth—taxes. And the way they work is simple: You take more money from the rich than you do from the poor. Then you provide programs that help everyone. But, in the end, the poor get more. And everyone is better off.

Instead of killing the goose that laid the golden egg, why not try to distribute the eggs more equitably? In Sweden, for example, the government follows a policy of "protecting the worker, not the job." This *Scandinavian compromise* allows a government to accept the failure of certain industries—shipbuilding, for example, which in high-wage Sweden makes little economic sense—and concentrate on helping the newly unemployed workers, providing generous social services and subsidies to help them through the difficult period after losing their jobs. The United States has a similar program called Trade Adjustment Assistance (TAA) that helps workers who have lost their jobs to global competition. Approximately $1 billion a year is spent on retraining and unemployment benefits. Compared to the estimated hundreds of billions of dollars that are gained every year from free trade, it may not be much, but it's a start.

The annual added value of free trade is estimated to be more than a trillion dollars in the United States alone. How is this possible? The way trade works is simple. You usually buy from other countries only if it's cheaper than it would be at home. The idea is to allow each country to sell what it produces most efficiently—and then allow it to import the rest. Allowing countries to export what they have a comparative advantage in producing enables them to earn valuable foreign exchange, which allows them to import those goods and services that other countries are better at making.

• •

INFORMATIONAL TOOL:

What is the law of comparative advantage?

Think of the dictum "You scratch my back and I'll scratch yours." The law of comparative advantage was developed by the classical economist David Ricardo at the beginning of the 19th century. It deals with the synergies that occur when two or more countries are allowed to produce and export those goods and services they produce most efficiently—taking advantage of economies of scale to produce a lot of something at a reduced cost. In the end, the theory says that when each country is allowed to do what it does best, everyone is better off. Sometimes one plus one can actually equal three.

• •

The concept of *comparative advantage* is based on the idea that *every* country can compete on the world stage, even those countries that are not very efficient at producing much of anything. By allowing the value of the home currency to fall, at one point, certain goods and services will eventually be competitive in the world markets. And by keeping the door open to trade, countries—even those that are relatively poor—will benefit from having access to efficiently produced goods and services from abroad.

Let's take an example. Steel that is needed to make a wheelchair can be bought on the open market. It's irrelevant who made the steel. If it costs twice as much at home as it does abroad to make the steel, it makes sense to buy from another country—the money saved can be used to reduce the price of the wheelchair. The country exporting the steel can then use its earnings to buy other things, possibly even importing wheelchairs from our company. By choosing a cheaper steel input, the wheelchair maker has saved money—which can then be passed on to the consumer, distributed to shareholders, or used to make the price of exported wheelchairs more competitive in world markets.

The advantage to trade in this case is clear: Wealth has been created and wheelchair sales increase at home and abroad, creating more income for the wheelchair producer, which can be passed on to others in many ways: through increased dividends to shareholders, a rise in value of the company's shares, or increased investment—in a new factory, for example. Or even through the decision to hire a new employee or two—possibly the newly unemployed steelworker who was laid off when foreign imports stifled sales of the domestic steelmaking company.

• •

INFORMATIONAL TOOL:

What is economy of scale?

Think of buying in bulk. Economy of scale is based on the principle that goods and services can be produced more efficiently, and more cheaply, by increasing production. Instead of baking just one cookie, or teaching a class with just one student, it's more efficient to produce a lot of something and distribute the cost over a large number of goods or services. One of the first to put the theory into practice was Henry Ford, who found he could make Model T cars much more cheaply by using an assembly line.

• •

What about workers who lose their jobs because of foreign competition? Obviously, it would be wonderful if no jobs were ever lost in any economy—no matter what. But the fact is, in a free-market capitalist system, things are in constant flux.

Jobs are constantly being created and destroyed. What is essential is to find a way to make sure that the jobs created are more valuable than those lost.

No one, of course, wants to lose his or her job. But unless we live in a Disneyland-like economy, where governments pay people to do jobs for show—think of the blacksmith or the buggy-driver—it makes no sense to keep jobs that have no economic raison d'être. Unfortunately, many opponents of globalization see the status quo as something to be preserved at all costs. And somehow, globalization is seen as a recent phenomenon that's upsetting the perfectly ordered applecart.

Globalization, however, has been going on ever since the first man left Africa and settled abroad—approximately sixty thousand years ago. Ever since, man has been trading and exploring and fighting and preaching in other lands. Instead of using donkeys or small sailing vessels, today's global traders travel in comfort. Today, trade moves by rail, container ships, or specially fitted jumbo jets, but the idea is the same: Opening borders opens opportunities.

We tend to think that the world is moving inexorably toward a more integrated economy, but during the years leading up to the First World War, globalization was in some ways even more powerful and more effective than it is today. The European imperial powers—France, Belgium, Germany, and Britain—had succeeded in creating a de facto common market between their far-flung colonies and the mother countries. In many ways, trade and people flowed more freely then than they do today.

Globalization, whether new or old, isn't always benevolent. Just as illnesses during the Middle Ages were transported by rats hitching rides on trading ships, the 21st century's interconnected global economy has the potential for some negative impact. Outsourcing implies jobs lost to markets abroad; immigration implies ethnological and demographic change at home. In general, globalization implies change, and change can be abrupt, uncomfortable—even brutal.

The resistance to globalization has been growing in many countries. So many G7 summits have been disrupted by anti-globalization activists that tear gas and broken shop windows are almost thought of as inevitable by-products of these annual meetings. The rage, however, may have reached its apex the day two hijacked commercial airliners were flown into the twin towers of the World Trade Center. Although much has been written about the religious and political motives of the terrorists, in the end they chose to destroy the world's foremost monument to globalization to make their point—whatever it may have been.

Where will all this anger lead us? What do we want for our future, for the future of our children? A world where every country hides behind walls and tries to go it alone? Think of the butcher, the baker, and the candlestick maker trying to do their own jobs plus all the others—because of some misguided belief that it's better to do everything ourselves. All prosperous societies—even in biblical times—were built on the concept of *division of labor*. And in the 21st century, if some countries are better at making airplanes or answering phone calls or making blockbuster movies more cheaply, then they should be allowed to do it. The world will be better off.

Basically, with a minimum of trade barriers, consumers are given the opportunity to buy the best products the world has to offer—at the best prices. By opening up markets, a government allows its citizens to export those things that they are best at producing, and to import the rest, choosing from the best the world has to offer. And by importing cheaper goods from poor countries, the industrialized countries not only provide their own citizens with a wider range of products to choose from, they stimulate the growth of jobs in countries where people are desperate to earn enough just to live.

Obviously, working conditions in the developing world need to be carefully monitored, to make sure that no worker is abused—especially children. But having access to export-oriented jobs, with salaries that usually surpass the prevailing wage available in other industries, is often the best hope for families in developing countries to pay for their children's food and education—and build a better future.

By giving the developing countries an economic jump start, rich countries are also able to expand their own economies, in addition to contributing to the creation of jobs in poorer regions of the world economy. And as developing countries grow and their citizens have more disposable income, they often buy goods and services from the industrialized countries, such as automobiles, refrigerators, computers, and movies. In the end, the increased trade leads to more growth, which creates even more wealth—for both sides.

The key is finding the best way to distribute this new wealth. It's important to first distinguish between poverty and inequality. If globalization does make almost everyone better off, maybe we should be spending our energies on distributing the new wealth, not destroying the machine that created it.

John Kennedy's view that "a rising tide lifts all boats" may be even more appropriate in the 21st century than when he first pronounced it in the 1960s. We now have the tools to create—and distribute—enormous new wealth. Instead of fearing this new power, let's use it—and try to make the world a better place.

CHAPTER 7

WHAT IS THE VIRTUAL ECONOMY?

BELIEVE IT OR not, at the beginning of the 20th century there were still places in the world where you could pay your bills with shells and beads. At the beginning of the 21st century, in contrast, money is rapidly becoming obsolete. Electronic cash and the Internet have revolutionized the world economy, providing a "friction-free" marketplace where businesses and consumers can interact virtually—in ways that would have been unimaginable a few years ago.

With more than a billion people using the Internet, the possibilities for developing virtual business and virtual payments are enormous. But an even bigger market has emerged: economic transactions via other electronic media such as "smart" cards and cell phones. Suddenly, by waving a smart card or a cell phone over an electronic reader, consumers around the world can make payments, transfer money, pay the entrance fee to a movie, or buy soda or beer at the local sports stadium.

Business transacted electronically, sometimes referred to as *e-commerce*, has grown exponentially since the beginning of the 21st century. And when governments around the world allowed contracts signed on the Internet to have the same legal status as a contract signed on paper, any kind of transaction became possible in cyberspace.

Business-to-consumer (B2C) commerce began taking off

when online retailers such as Amazon.com and Schwab.com created billion-dollar industries by providing consumers with products and services that were cheaper and easier to get online than by going to a neighborhood shopping mall. The low-cost structure of the Web has also allowed businesses to access many hard-to-reach segments of the public, sometimes referred to as *long-tail consumers*, who are interested in rare products that were previously not even offered because of the high cost of traditional sales structures.

• •

INFORMATIONAL TOOL:

What is the long-tail theory of online commerce?

The long-tail theory of commerce describes the ability of online businesses to use low distribution and inventory costs to make a profit out of selling small volumes of hard-to-find items to a few scattered customers. The long tail refers to the graph that shows the line well beyond the belly on the normal bell curve, representing the long line of consumers that are interested in the hard-to-find, low-volume items that most businesses, especially before the arrival of online businesses like Amazon.com and eBay, didn't offer for sale because interest in them was minimal. The term was first used by Chris Anderson in a Wired magazine article in 2004.

• •

The Internet also allowed businesses to offer tailor-made products, providing consumers with the possibility to use the Web to order a watch or an automobile that exactly fit their needs and specifications. Henry Ford once said that customers could buy his Model T in any color they wanted—as long as it was black. Now, Ford can provide online customers with a complete survey of every car it produces, allowing them to choose from as many colors and models as they like.

In the 21st-century economy, most e-commerce takes place between businesses. The business-to-business, or B2B, marketplace initially was made up of companies creating online exchanges to buy materials and other goods and services from one another. These e-hubs or e-marketplaces provided a much wider range of suppliers and trading partners, leading to lower prices and increased productivity for the businesses that used them. In the late 1990s, for example, the major U.S. carmakers joined forces to create a B2B site that would allow them to buy billions of dollars of parts from thousands of suppliers scattered across the globe. This quickly led to lower costs—and not just because it became easier to find cheaper suppliers. B2B exchanges also allow companies better control over supply and inventories, so they can save on inventory overhead and administrative costs as well.

It used to be that the majority of electronic and online transactions were concentrated in a few wealthy countries. By the beginning of the 21st century, however, the virtual economy had spread across the globe. Within just a few years, France, Germany, and Japan have all overtaken the United States in terms of rapid Internet connections. And the connections are much more powerful. On average, French broadband connections are more than three times as fast as those in the United States. In Japan, they are more than ten times as fast. South Korea now has almost universal Internet access—at velocities that can only be dreamed of in many North American markets. And China's billion-plus consumer market for Internet-based economic transactions has only begun to be tapped.

One activity that benefits greatly from expanded access to markets and bandwidth is the rapidly expanding virtual-world sites such as Second Life, where people can create virtual personas called *avatars* and participate in an ever-expanding array of activities such as shopping, investing, banking, and gambling.

The booming population in many of these virtual-economy sites has attracted the attention of real-world companies such as Coca-Cola and IBM, which have set up shop in these virtual worlds, paying astronomic sums for prime virtual real estate to market their products. Consumers pay with a virtual currency—called Linden dollars in Second Life—that can actually be exchanged into real-world currencies, at fixed or semifixed exchange rates.

Economic activity in the virtual-world sites is starting to resemble the real-world economy in strange ways. During the credit crisis of 2007, for example, Ginko Financial, a bank in Second Life, actually experienced a run on assets. And a virtual land boom, with real-world investors using real-world money to buy virtual real estate, forced Linden Lab, the owners of Second Life, to add new servers to meet the growing demand. By the year 2007, the amount of digital land that had been purchased online expanded to more than seven hundred square kilometers—approximately eight times the size of Manhattan.

Meanwhile, online banking in the 21st century has made great inroads into the bricks-and-mortar worlds of finance and economics. This "virtual" banking is just one example of how consumers and banks can benefit from the reduced cost that electronic transactions can provide. Traditional bank transfers, for example, cost the bank more than a dollar per transaction if done by a teller, about 25 cents if done by a cash machine, and less than a cent if done over the Internet.

But it's not just services—bank loans are another area that is expanding electronically. Web sites around the world, such as Zopa.com in Britain or Prosper.com in the United States, provide online businesses that connect borrowers and lenders, without going through the traditional channel of a bank. Instead of giving money to a bank and collecting a low rate of interest on the deposit, someone with money to lend can be put in touch with borrowers directly, using the Web-based software provided by the online enterprises. Taking advantage of the drastically reduced need for personnel and no need for expensive real estate for superfluous branches, these online financial institutions are able to provide their services for a fraction of the cost of a traditional bank.

Similar to traditional credit unions, which pool lenders and borrowers from the same company, church, neighborhood, or profession, these online banks are able to bring together borrowers and lenders from the far corners of the globe. Users enter the site as lenders or borrowers and are put in touch with their counterparty using the same due-diligence procedures as a normal bank. Most online banks and their affiliates are subject to the same regulations as normal financial institutions. Zopa.com, for example, is regulated by the British Financial Services Authority, and Prosper.com is regulated by the U.S. Federal Reserve Board and subject to the banking laws of the various states in which it operates—ensuring that the default rate and reliability is as high as, if not higher than, traditional banks.

• •

INFORMATIONAL TOOL:

What is an affiliate?

In traditional business terminology, an affiliate is a company that is related to, but not specifically owned by, another. In the world of e-commerce, the word affiliate is used to describe a broad range of relationships between entities—such as companies that arrange their Web sites to link to another in an effort to generate more business, or bloggers who group together as affiliates to gain critical mass and more online readership.

• •

Increased Internet connectivity has also allowed users to participate in many forms of economic activity that were previously the domain of service providers. For example, when Google Earth began allowing users to create their own 3-D universes online, mixing real geography with virtual reality, a whole new form of economic interaction was born. When Housing Maps.com created a "mash-up" with Craigslist and Google Maps in San Francisco, users could use the Internet to locate and purchase housing online without ever leaving the geo-Web space they were logged into.

Social networking sites such as MySpace, Facebook, and LinkedIn have also provided new opportunities for economic activity in cyberspace—allowing users to exchange everything from job-hunting tips and online résumés to information on successful job searches. By relying on a new twist in online interaction called *crowdsourcing*, many sites and online businesses have enlisted online users to help build sites by contributing images and content in ever-expanding ways—creating a rich virtual world where everyone can participate and contribute.

• •

INFORMATIONAL TOOL:

What is **crowdsourcing**?

Think of getting the audience to help you answer the big question on Who Wants to Be a Millionaire? The idea of handing over tasks to a group of people, or the public at large, has been around for a long time— think of the use of referenda to make decisions in many democracies. But the idea of outsourcing business tasks to a wide audience surfaced only at the beginning of the 21st century, when large masses of people could be tapped to provide problem-solving skills on a global basis. The term crowdsourcing *was coined by Jeff Howe in a* Wired *magazine article in*

2006. As opposed to open-source solutions, where the activity is initiated and undertaken by volunteers, crowdsourcing is usually initiated by an individual or a business that turns to the public at large for help in finding a solution.

•••••••••••••••••••••••••••••••

A classic example of the use of crowdsourcing was the creation of the online encyclopedia Wikipedia, which was built from user-supported input and then expanded into geospace by permitting users to link articles to Google Earth sites through the use of *geotags*—allowing virtual citizens to use information in entirely new ways. In Britain a Web-based company called MyFootballClub.com bought an existing soccer team, Ebbsfleet United FC, and uses a fifty-thousand-member fan base to choose the starting lineup and decide which players to buy or transfer. In Canada, a gold-mining group, Goldcorp, has used crowdsourcing to find gold—allowing anyone on the Internet to have access to geological survey data for its Red Lake, Ontario, goldfields. The company reported that the contest yielded 110 targets, of which 80 percent were productive, yielding more than eight million ounces of gold.

The Internet has allowed commerce to evolve in new and exciting ways. When the rock band Radiohead decided to allow consumers to download their new album and decide themselves how much to pay, for example, they were able to still retain a sizable portion of their profits—having successfully removed the record companies and other middlemen from the economic equation. Although at first many online consumers downloaded the album for free, acting "rationally," according to traditional economic theory, many others actually paid more than they normally would have if they had bought the CD in a record store. Some paid the extra money as a form of protest against the domination of mainstream record labels, but some did it simply for the thrill of participating in the creation of a new form of economic activity—and creating a new economy in the process.

Other online purveyors of electronic media have been forced to take radical steps to compete in this new electronic market. One innovation is the increasing sales of unrestricted media—such as MP3 music in DRM-free format—that can be downloaded and transferred an unlimited number of times. This has become so prevalent that even large online purveyors of music, such as Amazon.com, decided to reevaluate their business model and began selling unrestricted media.

Online advertising has become another important component of the emerging virtual economy. Mainly thanks to its revenue from online advertising, Google, for example, has become one of the biggest companies in the world, in terms of market capitalization. The purchase of many online sites, such as MySpace, has been driven primarily by the opportunities for advertising revenues from the burgeoning "populations" on many social networking sites.

• •

INFORMATIONAL TOOL:

What is *market capitalization*?

Think of measuring a vineyard's total production by weighing a single grape and then multiplying. Market capitalization (commonly referred to as market cap) refers to the practice of determining the size of a company by multiplying the number of shares outstanding by the share price. This gives a figure that allows us to compare company sizes across borders and across market segments. Since the share price represents the public consensus of what the share is worth, the market capitalization represents the public consensus of the company's size and worth. The *market capitalization of all publicly traded companies in the 21st-century economy has been estimated to be more than $50 trillion—five times more than the United States' entire economy.*

• •

During the first years of the 21st century, the revenue from Internet advertising accounted for only about 5 percent of total advertising expenditures, but began rising rapidly. Advertising revenues have become a major revenue source in the virtual economy—from newspaper and media sites to blogs and online map providers. Since many consumers balk at paying fees to access most sites, the only way for most companies to make money has been to sell advertising. Now virtually all news sources—from CNN to the *Economist*—have free-access Web sites.

Pay-per-click advertising, one of the biggest revenue sources on the Web, allows companies to pay a small fee to insert ads in browsers and other Web sites based on keywords that the consumer is entering. A person entering the words *vacation* and *scuba diving*, for example, is immediately shown ads for vacations in dive sites around the world. The potential for such user-specific advertising in cyberspace is limitless—especially with computers being linked together in *clouds* to provide an ever-growing universe for companies and individuals to do business in. Because information from users can be easily accessed, analyzed, and processed, advertisers are finally getting close to the holy grail of marketing: being put in direct contact with the customers who are really interested in buying the product being advertised.

Web citizens can also make money from online advertising. Blinkx, an Internet video search company, began allowing bloggers to make money from the videos and other material they show on their blogs. Ads are inserted alongside the videos, and every time an ad is clicked by someone in cyberspace, the provider of the video receives a payment. A few cents only, but income—and incentive—nonetheless.

• •

INFORMATIONAL TOOL:

What is **cloud computing**?

Think of using electricity from a regional network instead of getting power from your own generator. The idea of cloud computing—originally developed by Google engineers at the University of Washington with IBM support—is to link together hundreds, if not thousands of small computers to achieve the computing power needed to process and analyze enormous amounts of data—to be used in a variety of applications, from Web-based word processing to simulation of global-warming scenarios. The idea is that no single computer or server can provide the power to use the almost limitless amount of data available in today's digital economy. What sets cloud computing apart from other linked-computer systems is that the users have no need to have any expertise or control over the computers they are using—basically, the cloud does all the work.

• •

In some ways, the virtual economy has become a victim of its own success. Because so much economic activity is taking place online, hackers and even mischievous governments have discovered the power of bringing the system to a screeching halt. When Estonia moved to remove a Soviet-era statue from a major square in 2007, for example, its economy was brought to a virtual standstill when attacks from the East swamped the Web sites of banks, government ministries, and many local companies that had built a complex network of economic interaction on the Web. Even telephone exchanges were targeted. Another form of cyberwarfare is the use of packet cyberbombs that can be sent in waves from *botnets*, groups of hijacked computers that are used to swamp targeted sites.

• •

INFORMATIONAL TOOL:

What is a **botnet?**

Think of a network of robot computers ready to do the evil deeds of a malevolent hacker. One of the most nefarious forms of cyberwarfare is the use of networks of hijacked "zombie" computers that are joined together in robot networks, or botnets, to send cyberbombs, swamping targeted sites with waves of unwanted mail and, in the process, bringing the target's online business to a standstill.

• •

In recent years, hackers have been able to penetrate highly sensitive sites in all areas of the world economy, from credit data processors to military command headquarters. Some companies also use various forms of cyberattacks to gain access to data and sensitive information in a form of industrial espionage that is just beginning to surface. As the use of botnets has evolved from relatively harmless vandalism to highly dangerous and economically disastrous industrial warfare, the world's authorities have tried to find better ways to prevent cyberattacks. But when hackers and other *bot-herders* are able to commandeer and hijack computers from all corners of the world economy—the attack on Estonia, for example, used hijacked computers from as far away as Kuala Lumpur and Brazil—the world's police are often powerless to act.

Despite the trouble caused by these rogue hackers, access to the Internet has allowed many small businesses to thrive in the new global economy. Farmers, for example, who used to rely on the newspaper or radio for weather information, can now use the Internet to check current crop prices and get up-to-the-minute information on the latest weather forecasts. They can also use the Web to get agronomic advice and risk-management tools that were previously reserved for the elite. Web-based exchanges also allow farmers to buy pesticides and fertilizers at lower prices and buy or sell farm-related futures, such as wheat or pork-belly futures, online—which translates into lower costs, increased production, and, eventually, lower prices for the end user, consumers around the globe.

In emerging markets many small entrepreneurs have discovered that they can use Web-based business to circumvent big multinational trading groups and access world markets directly. An automobile parts firm in Vietnam or South Africa can now sell directly to a factory in Detroit, and a dressmaker in Guatemala or Bangladesh can now sell to a dress shop in Copenhagen or Chicago—or directly to consumers who have provided a body scan over the Web. Instead of waiting decades for new ideas to filter down to them, businesses and consumers in developing countries now have instant access to new technologies and markets, making them more competitive and, consequently, more profitable.

As the high-tech revolution sweeps the globe, an essential step for all countries that hope to fully participate in the new virtual economy is to increase training in schools and provide retraining for adults who have lost their jobs to technology-driven restructuring—ensuring that Internet-related growth provides a fair chance to all. Digital literacy—along with economic literacy—will be essential for all levels of the population if they are to benefit from access to the new Web-based economy.

CHAPTER 8

GETTING OUR SHARE—HOW DO WE INVEST IN THE NEW GLOBAL ECONOMY?

THE 21ST-CENTURY economy has opened up a whole universe of possibilities for international investment. And, basically, we are all investors—even if we don't directly own a foreign stock or bond. The money that college endowments, insurance companies, and pension funds earn from their international investments ends up paying for our homes, health care, dorm rooms, or wheelchairs when we get old. As individuals, we can also invest directly, taking advantage of a whole series of new products that make investing internationally as easy as putting money in the bank around the corner.

Anyone who invests in the global marketplace does so for one of three reasons: speculation, hedging, or arbitrage. Most investors in the international markets are speculators in that they believe that the market is going to move in a specific direction—basically, up or down—and they buy or sell based on that belief. A California pension fund, for example, may invest money in a Chinese real estate company hoping to profit from an increase in land values in Shanghai or Beijing. Or the Scottish Widows Fund buys bonds issued by the World Bank, knowing that the implicit guarantee of the U.S. and U.K. governments will ensure that the bond will be reimbursed on time—with interest.

Unfortunately, there is no way of knowing for sure what will happen to any given investment. Which means that all speculators take a risk. If the market moves in the right direction, they make a profit. If it moves in the wrong direction, they suffer a loss. Anyone buying dot-com shares before the market collapsed in 2000 would have lost a bundle, but that same person would have earned a bundle buying Google shares when they were first issued—for a fraction of their value a few years later.

• •

INFORMATIONAL TOOL:

What is the difference between a bear market and a bull market?

Think of a bear, growling and pessimistic, as representative of a market with declining prices. A bull, charging optimistically ahead, symbolizes a rising market. It is generally accepted that a full-blown bear market is one that experiences a 20 percent decline in prices over at least two months. A bull market can occur over a shorter period of time, but is defined as one with rapidly rising prices. A bull market can also be referred to as a bull run.

• •

The activities of speculators are balanced by the two other "players" in the global economy: hedgers and arbitrageurs. Unlike speculators, hedgers have no idea where prices are heading—they simply want to protect themselves from unfavorable changes in the markets. An elderly New York retiree, for example, could buy a house as a hedge against inflation, assuming that the house's value will go up as prices in general rise. Exporters also act as hedgers when they buy currency options or futures that allow them to know for sure how much their foreign currency earnings will be worth—locking in the value of a foreign currency—guaranteeing them a profit in their home currency well before the goods have been paid for.

Hedging has existed since the beginning of time. Farmers hedge by planting more than one type of crop and companies hedge by selling a wide variety of products. Imagine being an automobile producer selling only SUVs when oil prices start to skyrocket. Essentially, the role of a hedge in the financial markets is to remove risk by making carefully selected investments that will balance potential losses. When one investment goes down, the other—it is hoped—goes up.

Arbitrageurs, on the other hand, take advantage of perceived discrepancies in the world markets. Essentially, an arbitrageur buys in a market where prices are relatively cheap and sells in another where prices are higher. A German tourist who buys inexpensive CDs in Hong Kong or San Francisco and sells them for a profit to friends at home is as much an arbitrageur as a trader sitting on a bank trading floor in New York or Tokyo. A true arbitrageur tries to eliminate risk by buying and selling simultaneously.

Markets are often made more efficient by the different activities of speculators, hedgers, and arbitrageurs. And they need one another to work efficiently. If the market consisted only of people trying to sell, prices would drop precipitously. Speculators and arbitrageurs keep the market from becoming a one-way street by stepping in to buy or sell whenever prices move too far in one direction or are out of line with prices in other markets around the world.

The most common form of speculative investment for individuals is to buy a share of a company. Essentially, a share of stock is a title to partial ownership. Anyone who owns a share of a company owns a part of the company, referred to as *equity*. If the company makes a profit, the shareholder benefits, usually in the form of a *dividend* that is paid to all the company's "owners."

• •

INFORMATIONAL TOOL:

What is a dividend?

Think of a company handing you a check to thank you for your investment. Companies issue dividends as a way of sharing the profit they have earned over the course of the year. If they don't pay this money out to stockholders in the form of dividends, they keep it in the company's till, for use at a later date. But even "retained earnings" are like dividends in the sense that they tend to increase the value of the company's shares.

• •

In the 21st century, most stock is issued and traded electronically, but the concept is the same as it was previously: The owner of a stock has a share of the company—and its profits—until that stock is sold to someone else. This means that every time a company makes a profit, the owner of the company's shares profits in some way. Either the company pays the profit to the shareholders by paying a dividend or the money is retained within the company, thereby enhancing the value of the company and often leading to a rise in the company's share price.

An equity investment is generally considered to be riskier than a bond. If the company incurs a loss, or future losses loom, the company's share price can decline considerably. In contrast, a bond's return is usually known in advance—most bonds have fixed interest payments and a fixed date on which the bond's original purchase price, its nominal value, is repaid.

INFORMATIONAL TOOL:

What is the difference between a **stock** and a **bond**?

Think of the difference between owning part of a company and loaning the company some of your money. A stock investment implies ownership. If the company makes money, part of that money belongs to each stockholder, sometimes referred to as a shareholder. A bond is a form of loan. The issuer of the bond—a company, government, or other organization—simply agrees to pay back the money loaned, with interest. Stocks are intrinsically riskier than bonds. If a company goes bankrupt, the shareholders have to wait until the bondholders are paid off. However, the big advantage of stock ownership is that the rewards are unlimited—if the company does well.

To reward investors for the extra risk of equity investment, stocks generally need to provide a higher return than bonds. Barring a major market meltdown like those that occurred in 1929 and 2008, over time, stocks provide approximately a 10 percent average annual return on investment—much higher than the average return on bonds and other fixed-income securities. Someone investing a thousand dollars into the stocks that make up the Standard & Poor's 500 Index at the end of World War II, for example, would have seen their original money rise many hundredfold during the ensuing years—mainly because of the effect of exponential growth where profit is earned on earlier profits.

For this reason, many financial advisers will recommend that long-term investments be placed into the stock markets, where the potential for long-term yield is greater. It is generally recommended that short-term investments be placed in more conservative vehicles, such as bonds, that tend to be less volatile. Most investors would prefer that money they invested over the short term retain its value and be readily accessible.

• •

INFORMATIONAL TOOL:

What is the connection between bond prices and interest rates?

Think of a playground seesaw—when one side goes up, the other must go down. A higher price means a lower yield; a lower price means a higher yield. Since a normal bond has a fixed interest rate, its yield will change— depending on how much you pay for it. A hundred-dollar bond paying 10 percent interest will end up yielding 5 percent interest if you have to pay two hundred dollars for the bond. As interest rates change in the economy at large, bond prices have to adjust as well—to keep them competitive with other investment opportunities.

• •

Stocks, bonds, and most other securities are traded on exchanges, found in almost every major city in the world economy. The largest exchanges, such as the New York Stock Exchange and the London Stock Exchange, haven't significantly changed the old *open outcry* trading system in use since exchanges were first invented centuries ago. Others, such as NASDAQ and upstart BATS, use computers to do their trading, allowing for more volume at a much lower cost.

The consolidation of stock markets from all corners of the globe is also transforming the world of equity trading. In 2007, the merger of the New York Stock Exchange with Euronext— comprising the previously merged exchanges of Amsterdam, Brussels, Lisbon, and Paris—created a global juggernaut to provide more liquidity and better compete with other exchanges. Even though the average investor will still go through a broker to buy or sell shares, the final purchase or sale almost always ends up going through one of the big international stock exchanges.

The value of shares traded worldwide has exploded in the 21st century, with close to $100 trillion of stocks and other securities trading in almost any given year. This is due in part to the dramatic increase in volume and value of emerging markets such as China, Brazil, and India. The boom in stock market trading has led to a steep increase in the value of the exchanges themselves. Originally broker-owned *mutual utilities*, most of the world's exchanges have evolved to become sleek for-profit entities—which are themselves traded on stock exchanges around the world. When the São Paulo BOVESPA stock exchange was floated in 2007, its shares almost doubled in value on the first day of trading.

In order to attract new clients, and keep the ones they have, major exchanges have moved to streamline trading and develop new technologies and techniques to trade the world's securities. Some Wall Street firms have even moved to set up exchanges of their own, such as the Atlanta-based IntercontinentalExchange (ICE), to trade many of the same stocks found on the New York Stock Exchange and NASDAQ. The Kansas City–based BATS Trading—the name stands for "Better Alternative Trading System"—has grown to become the third-largest stock exchange in the United States, after the NYSE and NASDAQ. The advantage of these "upstart" exchanges is their lower cost, in part due to their location—where salaries are often much lower than in the major financial centers such as Chicago, London, or New York.

Another option for big investors is to circumvent stock exchanges altogether, using *internalization*, a system whereby banks and big brokers deal directly with one another— eschewing the liquidity and transparency of large exchanges in an effort to cut costs and streamline the process. Some trading systems use computer software to search through brokers' order books, and when they locate counterparties both sides are alerted and trades are executed anonymously, without going through a major exchange. Access to advanced technology has been able to turn bank trading desks into "virtual" stock exchanges, with volumes starting to rival those found in some of the world's major markets.

One advantage that major stock exchanges have is their supplementary services, such as selling data on the companies traded on the exchange or the establishment of an index. An exchange index, such as the NYSE Composite or India's Bombay Stock Exchange Sensitive Index, are based on shares traded on the exchange and track their movements over time—usually "indexing" the results by weighing the movement of larger companies more than the smaller ones.

• •

INFORMATIONAL TOOL:

What is a **stock index**?

Think of a farmer who goes out to check on the progress of the crops every once in a while—instead of checking every plant in the field, it's usually easier to take a few representative samples to get a good idea of how the crop as a whole is doing. Stock indexes use the same principle, calculating the average of a group of representative stocks to give investors an idea how the market as a whole is doing. Stock indexes are usually calculated by a major bank or a news agency, such as Nikkei—the acronym of one of Japan's leading financial newspapers, the Nihon Keizai Shimbun. *In London, the* Financial Times *provides the most widely watched stock index, the FTSE, commonly referred to as the* footsie. *The word* index *refers to the weighting given to the movement of shares of larger companies. Microsoft's share price movement, for example, changes the S&P 500 Index more than the same percentage movement of a smaller company like Avon or Mattel.*

• •

Every stock market around the world has at least one index that tracks the movements of a group of representative stocks. The Dow Jones Industrial Average, for example, tracks the prices of thirty of the most prestigious *blue-chip stocks*, mainly from the New York Stock Exchange but now including stocks from the technology-laden NASDAQ exchange as well. Sometimes, it is more useful to look at a "broad" index that takes the weighted average of hundreds of shares, such as the Standard & Poor's 500 Index, which measures the movement of five hundred major stocks from several different exchanges.

Cross-border stock indexes are difficult to calculate because they often contain stocks denominated in different currencies. The EURO STOXX index overcomes this by looking only at stocks traded in euro-area countries. A wider European index, the STOXX, includes stocks from several noneuro countries, such as Switzerland, Denmark, and England, so its movement must reflect currency changes as well as changes in the price of the stocks it tracks. Basically, whatever the market, someone is compiling an index to keep investors informed of what's happening.

• •

INFORMATIONAL TOOL:

What are the **major stock indexes** of the 21st-century economy?

Argentina, Buenos Aires: Merval Index (Mercado de Valores)

Australia, Sydney: S&P/All Ordinaries Index

Austria, Vienna: ATX (Austrian Traded Index)

Belgium, Brussels: Bel 20 (Belgian 20 Index)

Brazil, São Paulo: BOVESPA (Bolsa de Valores de São Paulo Index)

Canada, Toronto: S&P/TSX (Standard & Poor's and Toronto Stock Exchange)

China, Shanghai: Composite Index

Czech Republic, Prague: PX (Prague Stock Exchange Index)

Denmark, Copenhagen: OMXC20 (OMX is derived from the fusion of two previously existing exchanges: Aktiebolaget Optionsmäklarna and Helsinki Stock Exchange)

Europe: DJ STOXX 50 (Don Jones Stoxx 50 Index)

Euro Zone: DJ Euro Stoxx 50 (only euro countries)

Finland, Helsinki: OMX Index (OMX is derived from the fusion of two previously existing exchanges: Aktiebolaget Optionsmäklarna and Helsinki Stock Exchange)

France, Paris: CAC 40 (Cotation Assistée en Continu—Continuous Assisted Quote)

Germany, Frankfurt: DAX (Deutsche Aktienindex)

Hong Kong: Hang Seng Index (compiled by Hang Seng Bank)

Hungary, Budapest: BUX (Budapest Stock Exchange Index)

India, Mumbai: S&P CNX 50 (Standard & Poor's and CNX Index— Credit Rating Information Services of India Ltd. and National Stock Exchange of India)

Indonesia, Jakarta: Jakarta Composite Index

Ireland, Dublin: ISEQ Overall Index (Ireland Stock Exchange)

Italy, Milan: S&P MIB Index (Standard & Poor's and Milan Stock Exchange—Borsa di Milano Index)

Israel, Tel Aviv: Tel Aviv 100 Index

Japan, Tokyo: Nikkei 225 Index (compiled by Nikkei—Nihon Keizai Shimbun newspaper)

Malaysia, Kuala Lumpur: Composite Index

Mexico, Mexico City: IPC Index (Índice de Precios y Cotizaciones)

Morgan Stanley Capital International World Index (MCSI—compiled by U.S. bank Morgan Stanley—denominated in U.S. dollars)

Netherlands, Amsterdam: AEX Index (Amsterdam Exchange Index)

New Zealand, Wellington: NZSX40 Index (New Zealand Stock Exchange)

Norway, Oslo: Oslo All Share Index

Philippines, Manila: Composite Index

Poland, Warsaw: WIG Index (Warszawski Indeks Gieldowy—Warsaw
   Stock Exchange Index)
Portugal, Lisbon: PSI General Index (Portuguese Stock Index)
Russia, Moscow: RTS Index (Russian Trading System Index)
Singapore: Straits Times Index (created by Straits Times newspaper)
Slovenia, Ljubljana: SBI 20 (Slovenski Borzni Indeks—Slovenian Stock
   Exchange Index)
South Africa, Johannesburg: FTSI/JSE All Share Index (Financial Times and
   Johannesburg Stock Exchange)
South Korea, Seoul: KOSPI Index (Korea Composite Stock Price Index)
Spain, Madrid: IBEX35 (Iberian Index)
Sweden, Stockholm: OMX Stockholm 30 Index (OMX is derived from
   the fusion of two previously existing exchanges: Aktiebolaget
   Optionsmäklarna and Helsinki Stock Exchange)
Switzerland, Zurich: SMI (Swiss Market Index)
Taiwan, Taipei: TAIEX (Taiwan Stock Exchange Index)
Thailand, Bangkok: SET (Stock Exchange of Thailand Index)
Turkey, Istanbul: IMKB National Index (International Markets for Key Bourses)
United Kingdom, London: FTSE 100 (joint venture between Financial
   Times and London Stock Exchange)
United States, New York: Dow Jones Industrial Average
United States, New York: Russell 3000 Index (founded by Russell
   Investment Group)
United States, New York: S&P 500 (Standard & Poor's name derived from
   merger of Standard Statistics and Poor's Publishing)

• •

As foreign markets have expanded their role in the world economy, investors have begun to expand their portfolios as well. Investors can now go online and buy shares in foreign markets with little more effort than it takes to buy shares in the home market. Web-based brokers, for example, allow Indian investors to buy Swedish or Argentine stocks online and pay for the investments in rupees, not kroner or pesos. However, unless you believe in the *random walk* theory of stock selection—under which any stock you pick is as good as any other, because the market is so efficient it has already factored the relative risk and reward into the price—it is usually a good idea to consult with a professional and study all the market fundamentals before making any decision on which stocks to buy.

For this reason, many investors still buy international securities through a broker who puts in an order to buy or sell shares that is executed on a foreign market and then booked in the client's brokerage account. Using this system, an investor in San Diego can buy Club Med shares in France or Toyota shares in Japan, for example, and have those purchases appear on the home brokerage account alongside Apple or Sara Lee shares from the United States. In most cases, however, foreign shares purchased in this manner are still quoted in the foreign currency, and the dividends and other payments, if there are any, will not be in the investor's home currency either.

To avoid these inconveniences, many companies have their shares listed as *stock certificates* on various exchanges around the world and accounted for in the local currency. In North America, for example, you can buy American Depositary Receipts (ADRs), stock certificates that are created by banks that buy shares of a foreign company and place them on deposit in the United States. These ADRs give the holder the right to the *underlying share*—just as if they owned it outright. When the foreign share changes its value, the stock certificate changes its value in tandem.

The advantage is obvious—the certificate translates the foreign values into the local currency. The buyer of an ADR for Toyota, therefore, doesn't have to worry about translating the value of the share from yen to dollars; it is done automatically—the ADR price is quoted in U.S. dollars and the dividends are credited, in dollars, to the owner's normal brokerage account.

One disadvantage of ADRs and other foreign stock certificates, of course, is the foreign currency risk, intrinsic to any investment abroad, which adds a second layer of risk—and possible reward—to any foreign investment. The value of the foreign share may go up in foreign currency terms, but if the currency itself declines against the investor's home currency, the gains abroad may turn into losses at home. But currency risk works both ways, which means that investors who choose mediocre investments in a country with a rapidly rising currency may see stellar returns when everything gets translated into the home currency. American investors buying Irish shares at the beginning of the 21st century, for example, would not only have benefited from rising share prices but would have had the investment increased even further by the rise in the value of the euro.

Some foreign-company shares are listed directly on various exchanges around the world. On the New York Stock Exchange, for example, the shares of several hundred foreign companies are traded daily. This provides investors with liquid, easy-to-trade stocks that have been approved by the Securities and Exchange Commission, as well as having their financial figures accounted for according to U.S. norms. This gives investors the comfort that the company's books are in order and that the risks are acceptable.

Besides traditional *registered* shares, some countries, such as Switzerland, offer investors the choice of *bearer shares*, which do not require the registration of the owners' names at the company's headquarters. Other investment vehicles, available in various countries around the world, include *preferred stocks* and reduced-rights *participation certificates*, which provide dividends like normal shares but do not allow the investor to vote at stockholders' meetings.

• •

INFORMATIONAL TOOL:

What is a **preferred stock**?

Think of Mommy's favorite child, getting the first piece of the pie. Preferred stock usually pays a fixed dividend to stockholders and is considered to be "senior" to common stock, which means that in the event of a bankruptcy, holders of the preferred stock are paid before those holding common stock. If the money runs out, the common-stock holders are left in the lurch. In some ways, a preferred stock is like a bond in that its fixed dividend resembles an interest payment. Like bond owners, owners of many preferred stocks have no voting rights. You can't have your cake and eat it too.

• •

Despite the ease of trading provided by all the new investment tools of the 21st century, cross-border investing is still not seamless. National accounting laws require companies to adhere to local accounting rules—which may not be compatible with those in other countries, nor legible to the untrained investor. To get around this problem, many global companies prepare different sets of books for various markets around the world.

Examining financial documents from diverse international companies is a daunting task for any investor, no matter how knowledgeable. Most investors, therefore, have come to rely on ratings agencies to help them judge the risk of countries abroad—as well as the companies that do business in them. The first question you should probably ask, when buying bonds or other fixed-rate securities, is, What are the chances of getting my money back? A bond investor needs to know not only whether the interest will be paid on time, but whether the principal, or the amount of money originally invested, will be paid back as well. Those investing in Argentine bonds before the country's financial meltdown at the beginning of the 21st century would have seen their investment crumble as the government defaulted—paying back only a fraction of the bonds' value.

• •

INFORMATIONAL TOOL:

What is **principal**?

For any loan, the part that needs to be paid back is referred to as principal. Only when the principal is paid off can the borrower stop paying the loan's interest. Since interest is always calculated on the remaining principal, anyone taking out a home loan needs to figure out how much of the principal to pay back each month, in order to reduce the outstanding debt. A bond's principal is also referred to as its face value.

• •

When investing abroad, it's always important to look at the country's sovereign rating. Usually, a sovereign government is almost always a better credit risk than a company in that country. This is because the government, in theory, will always be the last entity to go bankrupt. Essentially, if things get really bad in an economy, a company's assets could always be seized by the government—or the company's value could be eroded by increased taxes or diminished by increased inflation from the government's decision to print new money to pay off its debts. Although global companies with a lot of assets abroad—Nestlé, for example, has many more assets abroad than in its home country, Switzerland—could be better credit risks than the country they are domiciled in.

The easiest way to judge a company's risk is to look at its official rating. The world's largest ratings agencies use the term *triple A* to define the companies and countries with the highest rating—implying the lowest risk. Loans to AAA borrowers such as Switzerland and the United States, for example, are considered to offer the best chance of being paid back on time—with interest, of course. Duff & Phelps and Fitch Ratings also use the AAA system, while A.M. Best, which provides ratings primarily for the insurance industry, uses elementary school–style letters like A++ to denote the best borrowers.

• •

INFORMATIONAL TOOL:

How is **risk rated** in the world economy?

	Moody's	S&P	Duff & Phelps	Fitch	A.M. Best
Investment	Aaa	AAA	AAA	AAA	A++
Grade	Aa	AA	AA	AA	A+
	A	A	A	A	A, A–
	Baa	BBB	BBB	BBB	B++, B+, B, B–
Speculative	Ba	BB	BB	BB	C, C–
	B	B	B	B	D
Very Risky	Caa, Ca, C	CCC, CC	CCC, CC, C	CCC, CC, C	E, F

• •

Many of the world's ratings agencies have come under fire for not giving investors adequate warning of the risks associated with many new securities, such as mortgage-backed securities. Faced with the task of rating increasingly complex structured finance products—bearing such obtuse names as

CDOs (collateralized debt obligations) and CPDOs (constant proportion debt obligations)—the world's major bond rating agencies began relying on complex computer programs to help them determine the various securities' ratings. As it turned out, the computers provided AAA ratings for many securities that ended up being classified as nothing more than "junk" when markets began to plummet. Many banks that invested in these products, thinking they were getting a high return for low risk, faced financial ruin when their reserves weren't enough to cover the hundreds of billions of dollars of losses that these "toxic" securities produced. The ratings agencies defended their actions, saying that their recommendations are based on providing an idea of the "probability" of default and that individual investors are still the ones who have to decide what securities to invest in.

Unfortunately, ratings agencies are traditionally paid by the companies whose bonds they rate—a bit like a Hollywood studio paying critics to write about their movies. The other alternative, having investors pay the ratings agencies, has failed to gain much ground because investors have balked at being the ones to pay the ratings agencies' high fees. Some have called for more government oversight, such as requiring the SEC or another government entity to rate stocks and bonds and other securities.

• •

INFORMATIONAL TOOL:

What is **equity**?

Think of a homeowner subtracting the value of the mortgage from the house's value. Whatever is left over is referred to as the owner's equity. In economics it's the same story. On a company's balance sheet, equity *refers to the part of a company's assets that belongs to the shareholders—after all the liabilities have been subtracted, of course. A company's* net worth *is also referred to as* stockholders' equity.

• •

Since many of the big investors in the world economy—pension funds and other managed funds, for example—are allowed to hold only *investment-grade* securities, a country's sovereign rating is extremely important. When a country is upgraded, its leaders and company managers rejoice. Not only does a higher rating mean a lower *cost of capital*, in that governments and companies can issue bonds with lower interest rates, but companies have easier access to international bank funding as well. A biotech start-up in India, for example, becomes much more profitable—and more competitive—when it is able to borrow money at rates similar to those in more developed countries such as Britain, Japan, or the United States.

There is an increasingly wide variety of investment vehicles in the expanding 21st-century economy. Bonds, for example, are no longer limited to the plain-vanilla fixed-income or floating-rate versions that have been made available to investors in previous decades. Bonds have begun taking on all kinds of new roles and functions. With the advent of global warming, for example, bonds that allow insurance companies to hedge against catastrophic loss from events such as hurricanes and floods are becoming increasingly popular.

These *cat bonds* usually pay a much higher interest rate—to recompense the buyer for taking the risk that a catastrophic event may occur and significantly reduce the bond's value. Before Hurricane Katrina, insurance companies were awash with capital, but with the rise in the number of catastrophic hurricanes—especially in the Caribbean—property- and casualty-insurance companies need to spread the risk with bond investors willing to trade some risk for much higher interest rates. By the first years of the 21st century, more than $5 billion of such cat bonds had been placed with international investors—and some private investors who have taken advantage of the arrival of cat bond mutual funds on the international marketplace.

First-time investors in the global marketplace may want to make their first foray into a managed fund, benefiting from the expertise of market professionals. A mutual fund, for example, would allow you to diversify your investment across a wide range of stocks or bonds or other securities—ensuring that a sharp loss in any one investment has little effect on the total return. Funds normally use professional managers to choose the right mix of securities—for which they are paid a management fee consisting of a percentage of the amount of money under management and an eventual bonus if the fund does well. The idea is that professional fund managers have a better understanding of individual markets and securities and are therefore more successful than the average investor in choosing what to put in the fund. The downside is that the management fees sometimes eat into the total return, sometimes leaving only a small portion to the investor.

• •

INFORMATIONAL TOOL:

What is a **mutual fund**?

A mutual fund gives investors the benefit of diversifying risk over a wide range of securities within a single investment vehicle. Most mutual funds contain a variety of stocks or other securities that are carefully selected by professional fund managers. Investors can sleep soundly knowing that if any one investment in their fund goes bad, the overall impact to them will be small. Mutual funds are especially appropriate for people wishing to invest in foreign markets where information on individual companies is not easily accessible.

• •

As markets have expanded in the 21st century, a plethora of different funds are now available to the international investor. *Growth stock funds* invest primarily in companies that retain their earnings and concentrate on growing the enterprise. A typical growth stock is expected to appreciate in value over time because of the constant reinvestment of income. Growth stocks usually provide a high *return on equity* (ROE), which means that net income is usually higher than 15 percent of the value of the underlying stock.

Income stock funds hold the majority of their shares in well-established companies that pay consistent dividends. This may be of interest for a pension fund or for retired people who need a constant income. Some investors, such as Warren Buffett, have pointed out that there is no fundamental difference between growth and value investing—what is important is to look at the stock's *intrinsic value*, which is based on the value of the cash flows the company provides over time, as opposed to the tangible net worth or *breakup value*, which is what you would get by breaking up the company and selling off the individual parts.

• •

INFORMATIONAL TOOL:

What is **tangible net worth**?

Think of holding a company's assets in your hands. What can be held can probably also be sold. Tangible assets include things such as cash and cars,

*bank accounts and outstanding loans, factories and computers.
What isn't considered tangible are things that have no quantifiable
value, such as goodwill and brand names. Tangible net worth—
tangible assets minus tangible liabilities—gives investors a real-world
idea of what the company is really worth. Many 21st-century
companies, such as dot-com start-ups or Web sites, have virtually
no tangible value—the only thing they have to sell are a few computers
and an idea. But the idea may one day be worth millions—if not
billions.*

• •

There are many other types of funds available for investors
in the world economy—each responding to a specific goal or
area of interest. Some funds may concentrate investments in
emerging markets, recovery shares, or blue chips—the top-rated
companies in any sector. Other funds may concentrate on investing in companies specializing in technology, the Web, or the
environment. *Country funds* and *regional funds* also provide
investors with the opportunity to concentrate their investments
in particular countries or regions of the world.

Basically, there are two types of structures for equity
funds. A *closed-end fund* (called an *investment trust* in
Britain) has a limited number of shares available. These shares
are traded on the open markets, where their price is determined
by supply and demand. The fund's underlying investments
could, in theory, go down in value, but the shares of the fund
itself could rise if there are not enough to meet market demand.
In an *open-end fund* (called a *unit trust* in Britain), new shares
can be issued at any time, which means that the price is determined not by supply and demand, but by the underlying value of
the fund's holdings, commonly referred to as *net asset value*
(NAV).

An exchange-traded fund provides an interesting way for investors to limit volatility and reduce the fees charged by traditional mutual funds. Because most exchange-traded funds are not managed per se, but are based on the shares that make up a particular index, such as the S&P 500, investors can avoid paying the high fees, or *loads*, that traditional fund managers charge. ETFs provide investors with a wide range of indexes and underlying exchanges—including many vehicles that invest in foreign stock markets and provide the same ease of trading and accounting as domestic exchange-traded funds.

• •

INFORMATIONAL TOOL:

What is **volatility**?

Think of a small sailboat being rocked by gusting winds. A security's volatility is determined by the frequency of movement of its price, as well as the magnitude. Most investors don't like surprises, so stocks (and other securities) with high volatility usually tend to cost less than those with similar fundamentals but more stable prices.

• •

There are also many new vehicles for investing in real estate in the 21st-century economy. *Real estate investment trusts* (REITs), for example, are funds that invest primarily in real estate projects such as shopping centers or residential or office complexes. They are similar to exchange-traded funds, in that they tend to have low turnover and consequently low management costs. In addition, their underlying investments are usually provided in a much more transparent manner than traditional stock or bond funds, which may take many months to reveal the securities they are invested in.

* *

INFORMATIONAL TOOL:

What is a **REIT**?

Think of a mutual fund that invests in bricks and mortar instead of pieces of paper. Real estate investment trusts (REITs) are funds that allow investors to invest in a whole basket of real estate projects instead of just one house, office complex, or shopping center. The primary advantage, in addition to the diversified portfolio that most REITs offer, is that someone else takes care of fixing the leak in the roof or the heating system. The other advantage of REITs is the way they are taxed. Since the underlying investments are not corporations, but property, most of the income can be transferred directly to investors without paying a corporate income tax in many of the countries where REITs exist.

* *

Politically or socially conscious investors, including college endowment funds and pension funds, can invest in funds that correspond to their view of how the world should grow and prosper. A socially conscious fund manager, for example, may insist on investing only in companies that guarantee nondiscrimination for race, sex, or sexual orientation. Others may insist that the companies they invest in do nothing to harm the environment—by planting a tree, for example, for every one that is harvested in the production process. One socially conscious investment fund based in the United Kingdom, the Children's Investment Fund Foundation, concentrates on funding health care and education programs for children in the developing world.

Keen to attract these new sources of funding, many corporations have instituted reforms to encourage more *corporate social responsibility* (CSI), showing that they have made a concerted effort to ensure workplace diversity, for example, or a commitment to human rights or protecting the environment. Despite criticism by some observers that CSI is diverting attention from government programs that should be providing the solution to society's problems, others have pointed out that company leaders have simply realized it is in their own self-interest to build the global economy in socially conscious ways—that, in some ways, they have the skills and funds to find solutions to the world's problems that many governments are unable to solve.

Although it is hard to find companies that are 100 percent in tune with investors' social or environmental goals, many funds insist on buying shares of companies that are the "best in their group," doing the least amount of damage to the environment, for example, or having the highest scores for respecting workers' rights. Islamic investors, required by *sharia* law to avoid usury, or interest, may insist on investing only in securities that don't pay interest. They may also insist on shunning all investments in companies that earn money from gambling, alcoholic drinks, and tobacco.

In addition, most banks in Islamic countries have restructured their operations to become sharia-compliant. To get around the issue of paying interest, many of these banks issue fee-based credit cards or structure mortgages whereby the bank purchases the property in question and then sells it back to the "borrower" at a markup to the original price with periodic installment payments replacing the payment of interest. The most innovative sharia-compliant financial instrument is the *sukuk*, or Islamic bond, which, instead of paying interest, bases payments on the value of present or future assets.

Investors in other parts of the world, where the payment of interest is not only allowed but encouraged, can choose from a wide variety of funds that invest in interest-bearing securities such as bonds, preferred stocks, certificates of deposit, and high-yield securities, often referred to as *junk bonds*. High-yield securities provide an increased return for an increased level of risk. Most high-yield bonds are rated below investment grade because the probability of the interest and/or principal being paid back on time is significantly lower than that of other securities in the market. Some may even be delinquent in paying back their accrued debts. The extra risk of high-yield securities is usually compensated by interest rates that are several percentage points higher than those provided by more secure investments in the international marketplace.

• •

INFORMATIONAL TOOL:

What is the difference between current and delinquent?

Think of a train that's on time and one that's late. Loan payments—such as mortgage payments or credit card payments—that are made on time are classified as current on the lender's balance sheet. Loan payments that arrive late or not at all are referred to as delinquent and have to be placed in a separate category on the lender's balance sheet.

• •

Distressed-debt or distressed-equity funds also allow investors to reap high returns in exchange for incurring a certain amount of extra risk. These so-called *vulture funds*, usually managed by savvy managers with large amounts of ready cash, wait for the right moment—a market crash, for example—to swoop down and buy assets for a fraction of their price. The idea is to benefit when the markets turn, or at least benefit when the bond is partially reimbursed. In most cases, cash-strapped bond issuers prefer to pay at least something on a distressed security in order to avoid the shame of a full-fledged default, which often involves being barred from entering the international debt markets again at any time in the near future.

Owners who are forced to sell large blocks of securities at distressed levels—a bank with delinquent mortgages, for example, or a highly leveraged fund needing cash to meet margin calls from brokers—are usually happy to get the ready cash, even if it means giving up assets that are significantly undervalued. Many international funds have set up distressed-debt funds to allow investors to profit from buying cheap assets, including bankrupt companies, with the possibility of selling the assets for a significant profit when the markets improve.

• •

INFORMATIONAL TOOL:

What is **bankruptcy**?

Think of a broken bench on the trading floors of medieval Venice. Traders who couldn't pay their debts got their benches broken, called banca rotta *in Italian, and were removed from the game. Companies or individuals who can't pay their debts are removed from the world of business by clearly established bankruptcy laws. In some countries, failing companies are given an opportunity to try to pay off their creditors—called Chapter Eleven in the United States. If the company can find no other solution to its problems, it goes into liquidation, or Chapter Seven, and its assets are sold to pay off as many debts as possible.*

• •

Just as it would be limiting to shop at only one store, it's increasingly obvious in the 21st century that investing only in your local currency and local markets is financially unwise. For most of us, investing in the expanding global economy will be our only hope of having the financial wherewithal to weather the economic turmoil of the years ahead. With the precarious financial situation of social security and other national pension schemes—21st-century demographics are putting an enormous burden on almost all of the world's retirement plans—it's going to be increasingly important in the years ahead that we, as investors, put our assets where they can provide the best returns. And those returns can often be found in stock and bond markets outside our home countries.

CHAPTER 9

WINNERS AND LOSERS—HOW DO WE COMPARE INVESTMENTS IN THE 21ST-CENTURY ECONOMY?

WHAT DID IT mean when PetroChina became the first company in the world to be valued at more than $1 trillion dollars? How could a company in a poor, albeit emerging economy be worth so much more than the world's next-biggest enterprise, America's ExxonMobil, valued at the time of PetroChina's exploit at a mere $488 billion?

Valuing and comparing companies and investments is always a difficult venture—especially when you have to add in different accounting systems, different currencies, and different economic systems. How can you compare an investment in Japanese stocks to the purchase of a vacation house in Mérida, Mexico? How can you compare the purchase of a Brazilian bond to the purchase of a U.S. Treasury security?

Just as fields of crops can be compared by their yield, international investments can be evaluated by first looking at their total return—also referred to as *yield*. In economic terms, yield is the total increase in value of an asset over time, including dividends and other payments such as interest. It helps to translate the yield of various international investments into a common currency. Most people prefer to use their home currency. Most investors, therefore, convert all values into one *currency of reference*. For example, the Yale University endowment fund, which invests billions abroad during any given year, begins by translating all those international investments into U.S.-dollar values to see how they stack up against one another. In this way, the yield on any one investment can be compared to all the others.

• •

INFORMATIONAL TOOL:

*What would $10,000 have **yielded** by the end of the decade if invested in the year 2000?*

	FINAL
GOLD	$28,507
BRAZIL EQUITIES	$20,325
RUSSIA EQUITIES	$19,830
MEXICO EQUITIES	$19,694
PLATINUM	$18,893
U.S. TREASURY BONDS (30-YEAR)	$18,407
U.S. HOUSING	$18,215
PICASSO PAINTING	$17,309
INDIA EQUITIES	$14,283
U.S. MONEY MARKET FUND	$13,410
U.S. INFLATION OVER PERIOD	$12,781
CHINA EQUITIES	$12,338
TWO-CARAT DIAMOND	$11,600
EMERGING MARKET EQUITIES	$11,369
SWITZERLAND EQUITIES	$10,539
MONEY KEPT UNDER A MATTRESS	$10,000
HONG KONG EQUITIES	$7,438
U.S. EQUITIES (S&P 500)	$6,243
U.S. EQUITIES (NASDAQ)	$3,865

Source: Bloomberg, Bank of America

• •

Yield is generally defined as the percentage increase in value over a given period of time. In a simple investment, such as a bond with a fixed interest rate, the yield is easily calculated. A bond paying 5 percent interest over ten years would have a yield of 5 percent. But what about a bond that has a floating interest rate? Or a stock that provides dividends in some years and nothing in others? Or one that loses half its value over the time held? Most investors simply add up all the gains and losses of a particular investment over time.

Savvy investors, or their accountants, simply plug in all the cash flows, or the gains and losses that can be found in the financial figures of companies and investments—consisting principally of the *balance sheet* and *profit and loss statement*. This allows them to determine the *internal rate of return*, which summarizes the total return that any given investment provides. The internal rate of return of an investment that was sold for double the purchase price, for example, would be 100 percent. One providing a periodic interest payment during that time would have an internal rate of return considerably higher.

• •

INFORMATIONAL TOOL:

What is the difference between a **balance sheet** and a **profit and loss statement**?

Think of the difference between a snapshot and a home movie. Like a snapshot, a company's balance sheet shows what a company is worth at a given point in time. The balance sheet has two sides: assets—what the company owns—on the left, and liabilities—what the company owes—on the right. Whatever's left after subtracting liabilities from assets is called shareholders' equity, the extra value of a company that, in theory, belongs to the company's owners. The story of what happens to a company over time is told by the company's profit and loss statement (P&L). Like a movie, a company's P&L shows the change in the company's finances, usually over the course of a year. A typical P&L starts with income, called revenue, then deducts all the cost and expenses of doing business to arrive at the bottom line: net income, *which is what's left after deducting taxes and other fees from the profit.*

• •

Analyzing investments also involves taking into account political risk. If the government of a foreign country collapses, or if new laws are passed restricting the transfer of funds abroad, investments in companies based there may be lost. Even countries that are not directly affected by global troubles sometimes see their currency and stock markets come under pressure as investors flee for safer harbors. During the financial meltdown following the credit crisis that swept the world in 2008, for example, some international investors sold positions in emerging markets to cover losses in their home markets, leading to stock market crashes in parts of the world that had nothing to do with the original crisis.

Nevertheless, many investors still see the value of investing abroad. During the first years of the 21st century, the total return of international investments significantly outpaced that of traditional markets like the United States, Switzerland, Germany, and Japan. When Latin America, India, China, and the other rapidly growing economies of southeast Asia embarked on market-oriented reforms, high private-equity inflows immediately followed—bringing the *price/earnings ratio* of the emerging economies more in line with the rest of the developed world.

The price/earnings ratio (P/E), sometimes referred to as *price-to-earnings ratio*, gives investors a thumbnail estimate of how the money they're paying for a given share relates to the income the company is generating. *Growth stocks*—those of companies that are expected to grow significantly over the coming years—tend to have a higher P/E because earnings are usually lower than for stocks of established companies. In other words, the stock price is higher than it normally would be given current earnings. Health care or high-tech companies, for example, are often referred to as *growth companies* because they are expected to grow faster than those in more traditional fields, such as banking or manufacturing, which are often referred to as *value companies*.

Stock market bubbles can sometimes be predicted by looking at price/earnings levels of companies in specific markets. As long as P/E ratios are within historical averages, say from 10 to 30, markets tend to remain stable. When P/E ratios go outside traditional boundaries, trouble may be imminent. When the dotcom bubble burst at the end of the 20th century, for example, the NASDAQ index stocks were trading at P/E levels well above 50.

• •

INFORMATIONAL TOOL:

What causes **price discrepancies** around the world?

Why should buying an apartment in London cost so much more than buying one in Berlin, Mumbai, or Toronto—or Liverpool, for that matter? An overvalued currency is often the cause. Essentially, currencies, like other commodities in the world economy, are worth only what someone is willing to pay for them. And if a currency is overvalued, everything in that country's economy seems expensive. Basically, scarcity makes prices rise. And in certain cities—London and New York, for example—there is a limited amount of real estate to go around and a lot of demand. If hundreds of thousands of Middle East sheikhs and highly paid investment bankers all want to live in the posh areas of London, their price—and the prices of the goods and services that one uses there—tends to rise accordingly.

COMPARISON OF APARTMENT PRICES AROUND THE WORLD (DOLLARS PER SQUARE METER):

1	London (prime location), United Kingdom	$24,250
2	Upper Manhattan, New York, United States	$15,933

3	Moscow, Russia	$15,531
4	Paris, France	$13,826
5	Hong Kong, China	$12,599
6	Tokyo, Japan	$11,870
7	Singapore	$11,800
8	Mumbai, India	$10,222
9	Barcelona, Spain	$9,871
10	Geneva, Switzerland	$7,534
11	Zurich, Switzerland	$7,376
12	Sydney, Australia	$7,085
13	Madrid, Spain	$7,021
14	Tel Aviv, Israel	$5,021
15	Toronto, Canada	$4,737
16	Auckland, New Zealand	$4,438
17	Warsaw, Poland	$4,383
18	Dubai, United Arab Emirates	$4,066
19	Montreal, Canada	$3,779
20	Munich, Germany	$3,613

Source: Global Property Guide, 2008

• •

In the end, international investors have to pay attention to an ever-increasing number of financial and market indicators, not just prices and earnings. Balance sheets, profit and loss statements, country risk rankings, credit ratings, currency risk, etc., all play a part, but no one criterion can tell us whether an investment is wise or foolish. As the Romans said over two thousand years ago, *caveat emptor*: "Let the buyer beware."

Fortunately, Web-based trading and a wide array of financial news sites have facilitated access to investing in the expanding world economy, removing the need to channel all investments through a broker or investment adviser—who may actually be less well informed than clients about the wide range of foreign investment opportunities available today. The opportunities are limitless.

CHAPTER 10

PRIVATE EQUITY AND PUBLIC GOOD—WHO REALLY CONTROLS THE COMPANIES OF THE WORLD?

IN THE BEGINNING there is the idea. And these days it is usually someone sitting in a garage somewhere coming up with the next Internet wonder or a "better mousetrap." Either way, there comes a time when a company must be set up to provide a structure for the new business. But how do you set up a new venture without risking everything?

The heart of capitalism is private ownership, and limited-liability companies provide the possibility for people to own an enterprise without risking their personal assets should the company go bankrupt. The idea of limited liability is reflected in the *Ltd.* that follows company names in most English-speaking countries—although in the United States, companies are commonly referred to as *Inc.*, or *incorporated*. The abbreviation *S.A.* in Spanish- and French-speaking countries refers to the words *Sociedad Anónima* or *Société Anonyme*, which imply the same concept as Ltd.—the owners are "anonymous" in that the creditors of a bankrupt company have no right to force them to pay the company's debts.

Many countries make a clear distinction between large and small—or public and private—companies. Generally, *public companies* are those that are large enough to have their shares traded on recognized stock exchanges. Smaller companies, usually those with their shares in the hands of a small group of investors, are usually referred to as *private* or *unlisted*. In Britain, for example, *public limited companies*, or PLCs, are usually quoted on major stock exchanges, while Ltd. companies are not. In the United States, *S corporations* give businesses the advantage of limited liability without incorporation and provide investors with the advantage of being taxed only once—profits of S corporations are not subject to tax when the company books them, only when they are paid to the company's owners. Private companies, however, are usually limited in the number of shareholders they can have.

• •

INFORMATIONAL TOOL:

What are the different **types of companies** *in the world economy?*

COUNTRIES	TYPE OF COMPANY	ABBREVIATION	DEFINITION
United States	Public	Inc.	Incorporated
	Private	S corporation	(defined by subchapter S, chapter 1, of the Internal Revenue Code)
Britain, Canada	Public	PLC	Public Limited Company
	Private	Ltd.	Limited
France, Belgium	Public	S.A.	Société Anonyme
	Private	Sarl	Société à Responsabilité Limitée
Spain, Mexico, etc.		S.A.	Sociedad Anónima
Brazil, Portugal		S.A.	Sociedade Anônima
Japan	Public	Ltd.	Limited
Germany	Public	A.G.	Aktiengesellschaft (Share Corporation)
	Private	GmbH	Gesellschaft mit Beschänkte Haftung (Corporation with Limited Liability)

Netherlands	Public	N.V.	Naamloze Vennootschap (Anonymous Company)
Italy	Public	SpA	Società per Azioni (Share Corporation)
	Private	Srl	Società a Responsabilità Limitata (Limited Liability Company)
China	Public	Ltd.	Limited

• •

The traditional route for most large start-up companies is to eventually "go public" and sell the company's shares on a recognized stock exchange. This is usually accomplished by having an *initial public offering*, or IPO. Almost every major Internet company, from Google to Yahoo!, has gone through this rite of passage—the major exception being Facebook, which chose to take a $240 million direct investment from Microsoft in 2007 and put off an IPO in order to establish itself as a strong revenue-generating enterprise before going public.

The main advantage of an IPO is that it provides a growing company with access to a large investor pool. It also transfers a lot of money to the company's founders—and the venture capitalists who invested money in the fledgling company for a share of its stock. A publicly traded company also has the advantage of increased credibility with banks and fund managers, who often bid up the share price on the opening day of trading.

• •

INFORMATIONAL TOOL:

What is **venture capital**?

Think of the expression "Nothing ventured, nothing gained." Venture capital is money that is invested early—usually in start-up companies that have not shown any profit, but have a large potential for growth. The idea is to get in early: When the company finally takes off and starts showing a profit, the venture capitalists and others who invested early can reap huge rewards. Venture capital can be invested in anything from a dot-com start-up to a gold-mining company.

• •

Being a public company also has its downsides. After an IPO, a company is required to publish accounting statements quarterly, forcing it to consider the opinions of demanding investors who often concentrate on quarterly earnings instead of on long-term growth. Going public also requires disclosure of all relevant financial information, including the compensation of company officers, so competitors get a free look at the inner workings of the company. The cost of going public is also not insubstantial: Investment banks often keep a hefty share of the IPO's proceeds to pay for their expenses and fees.

Usually, the first in line to get IPO shares are the insiders—called *friends and family* by the Securities and Exchange Commission, which oversees IPOs in the United States. The next in line are the big institutional investors and fund managers that form the backbone of the underwriters' client base. The remaining shares are distributed on a lottery basis to individual investors who subscribed for the IPO shares. Companies often prefer that an IPO sell out quickly, ensuring that later issues of shares, called *secondary offerings*, find a ready and willing investor pool.

Instead of taking a company public, private equity funds use their amassed money to take control of a publicly quoted company with the intention of taking it off the market and making it more profitable, sometimes breaking it up and selling off the pieces individually. Eventually, usually after a period of three to seven years, companies can be relisted, usually through an IPO, which, in theory, nets the private equity funds a fat return on their investment. Assets that private equity firms have acquired include Dunkin' Donuts, Water Pik, and even one of the remaining copies of the Magna Carta.

• •

INFORMATIONAL TOOL:

What is *private equity*?

Think of the difference between a public school and a private school. A publicly traded company is open to anyone who would like to buy its shares, usually on exchanges like NASDAQ or the New York Stock Exchange. The private equity game involves one or more big investors buying enough shares in a company to be able to remove it from the publicly traded exchange—and put it in the hands of a few private owners.

• •

Just like the junk-bond traders and leveraged-buyout titans of the 1980s, private equity traders use enormous amounts of borrowed money to buy companies and other assets. During the first years of the 21st century, the number of private equity deals has exploded, quadrupling in value, from the $100 billion level to more than $400 billion. Ownership of most private equity funds includes high-net-worth individuals, pension funds, and other mutual fund investors looking for a bigger return on their money than that which can normally be gotten in the stock markets.

One of the hallmarks of the 21st century has been how ownership of companies has shifted. It used to be that the vast majority of ownership and investment was via investment in publicly traded companies like Microsoft or Apple or British Petroleum. Individual equity investors didn't have many other opportunities, and the other major stock investors—pension funds, insurance companies, and mutual funds—liked the transparency of publicly traded companies.

During the first years of the 21st century, many governments moved to make publicly traded companies even more transparent, requiring financial statements that described, in detail, everything the company had done over the course of the year—including how much the companies' directors were paid. The ensuing public criticism of CEO salaries and other intrusions on the previously private information led many companies to consider a return to the days before going public, when founders and owners could run the companies in a much more private and possibly more profitable way.

Funding can also be a difficult issue for publicly traded companies. In addition to fickle shareholders and disgruntled investment funds, companies have little leeway to arrange other sources of financial support. One option—in some countries, at least—is bank lending. In Germany, for example, banks have long been "partners" to so-called *Mittelstand companies* that remained unquoted and out of the view of public scrutiny. The problem for many companies is that a bank, like an investor group, can change its mind. When large groups of disgruntled investors sell their shares, stock prices plummet, reducing a company's freedom to pursue long-term goals, which may lead to lower profits. Likewise, banks can decide to reduce funding at short notice, or pull out altogether, leaving a company high and dry. This uncertainty can be anathema to running a company profitably over the long term.

• •

INFORMATIONAL TOOL:

*What is the difference between an **investment bank** and a **commercial bank**?*

Investment banks have traditionally concentrated on underwriting new issues of securities, such as stocks and bonds, and then trading those securities for their clients. Commercial banks have concentrated on taking in money as deposits and loaning this money to clients. In the 21st-century economy, investment banks have become increasingly rare. During the credit crunch of 2008, all five major New York–based investment banks ceased to exist: Lehman Brothers went bankrupt, Bear Stearns and Merrill Lynch were absorbed by healthier entities, and Morgan Stanley and Goldman Sachs opted for commercial bank status to benefit from Federal Reserve oversight and protection during troubled economic times.

• •

The arrival of the 21st century has brought a wave of new funding opportunities to many companies and individuals. Just as a mortgage company is able to arrange a loan and then pass it on, repackaging it or securitizing it and selling it to buyers on the other side of the world, banks or finance companies can arrange loans for companies, then offer the repackaged loans to outside investors such as hedge funds or other deep-pocket investors. Bonds have also become much more liquid and investors less risk-averse—allowing for the emergence of huge amounts of high-yield securities to be issued for companies that would otherwise have been refused credit by the local bank.

The holy grail of company funding with few strings attached is private equity, because it allows companies the possibility of getting large amounts of cash to develop or expand, without all the restrictions of more traditional sources. Private equity can take the form of an early investment in a small start-up company—usually referred to as venture capital—or the purchase of a publicly traded company by an investor or investor group that supplements their own cash with large amounts of borrowed money. Because this form of private equity investment uses borrowed money to *leverage*, or extend the reach of the investors' own funds, it is referred to as a *leveraged buyout*.

• •

INFORMATIONAL TOOL:

What is a **leveraged buyout**?

Think of using a crowbar or another type of lever to lift up a heavy object. In a leveraged buyout, an investor, or investor group, uses large amounts of borrowed money to take over a company. Ample financing allows the buyer to use a relatively small amount of cash to acquire a company that would otherwise be out of the investor's reach. After taking over control of the company, the investors try to find ways to generate cash so they can pay off the loans that are a drain on cash flow—the interest rates for many junk bonds or high-yield securities are usually much higher than those on more traditional corporate or government bonds. The goal is to restructure the company, or sell off parts, as quickly as possible—to bring in the large amounts of cash needed to pay off the debt the investors incurred in acquiring the company.

• •

The theory behind leveraged buyouts and other forms of corporate takeovers is that the new owners will be much more efficient in getting a high return on the money they've invested. Traditional equity investors and asset managers who invest in publicly traded companies are, for the most part, passive— allowing the company's management and board of directors to make most of the decisions on how the company is run. Private equity investors tend to take a much more hands-on role in making the companies they've bought more profitable.

Most private equity investors hold on to their purchases for just a few years—hoping that their efforts to restructure and reform the acquired company attract the attention of another big investor—or eventually listing the company, selling shares on a stock exchange, where small investors can purchase the new-and-improved company or parts thereof—and, hopefully, pay more than the original private equity investors did initially.

• •

INFORMATIONAL TOOL:

What is a hostile takeover?

Think of a military coup, removing a country's government and replacing it with another. In the mergers-and-acquisitions game, companies can be taken over by an investor or investor group acquiring enough shares to control the company's decision-making process. In a hostile takeover, the acquired company's board usually tries to oppose the acquiring company or investor group and uses a wide variety of defenses, called poison pill defenses, *to keep the acquiring investor from taking control of the company. If they fail, the acquiring investor uses its voting power to take over control of the company and often removes the board members who opposed the takeover.*

• •

One of the reasons for the success of private equity funds in raising so much money is that pension funds, college endowments, and other funds—usually restricted from holding direct stakes in risky companies—are, however, allowed to invest in funds that invest in unquoted companies and other ventures. Unfortunately, private equity fund managers ask for extensive fees for their work. These fees can sometimes reach into the billions. Venture capitalists and buyout specialists use the *2-and-20 structure* to reward themselves for their work: taking a management fee of 2 percent of the total amount invested every year and another 20 percent of profits. Many companies also give private equity managers an added benefit by taxing their "income" performance fees as a capital gain, which is usually taxed at a much lower rate than normal income.

The high fees paid to manage private equity funds have also led many investors to question the advantages of giving them the enormous amounts of money they have to invest. During the first years of the 21st century, the gross return of private equity funds has achieved a significant *alpha*—providing much higher returns than those found in more traditional investments. Once the fees are deducted from the earnings generated by private equity managers, however, the return is often lower than a traditional stock investment.

• •

INFORMATIONAL TOOL:

What is *alpha*?

Think of alpha being the first letter in the Greek alphabet—the first in line, better than the others, perhaps. Alpha is the term used to describe the extra return that fund managers say they provide to investors who give their money to them to manage. Many private equity and hedge-fund managers justify their high fees by saying that their special skills help investors beat the normal market returns. When compared to standard market indexes such as the Dow Jones Industrial Average and the S&P 500, for example, many fund managers provide several percentage points more in return per year. In addition to the beta provided by the normal market, the fund managers call all extra returns alpha—for which they charge several percentage points in extra fees.

• •

The estimated return of a simple stock index investment in the S&P 500 between 1980 and 2005, for example, was approximately 12 percent, and that of an average mutual fund investor was approximately 7 percent. The difference for you, the average investor, is enormous when applied over many years: $10,000 invested in the above-mentioned index fund would have grown to $170,000 during those twenty-five years, whereas the same $10,000 invested in a typical mutual fund over that same period would have grown to just $48,000, less than a third of the index fund's return.

Some private equity investments take the form of investments in "funds of funds," groupings of various hedge and private equity funds into one *superfund*, which is said to ensure reduced volatility. The reduced volatility of a fund of funds often comes at a high cost. Because of the extra level of management fees, investors often end up paying up to 3 percent in those fees, plus a *success fee* of up to 30 percent, reducing the final return substantially.

Another criticism of private equity funds is that they are heartless, that in their rush to break up companies and sell off unprofitable divisions or subsidiaries, they put people out of work—even though in the long term many of the surviving parts prosper and end up adding new employees. Many private equity fund managers say that their actions provide high returns to the funds invested in them, including many college endowments and pension funds that need to generate money to provide student aid or retirement assistance.

In the 21st-century economy, private equity firms control an increasing amount of companies and employ large parts of the population in many countries where they operate. Up to 20 percent of workers in Britain, for example, work for companies owned by private equity firms. The expanding range of private equity funds has begun sounding alarm bells among citizens and governments around the world who are concerned about the long-term effects of private equity investment on the declining power of local and national governments to control and direct economic growth.

CHAPTER 11

CORPORATE GOVERNANCE AND CORPORATE GREED—HOW ARE BUSINESSES MANAGED IN THE 21ST-CENTURY ECONOMY?

THERE IS A strong correlation between corporate and personal well-being. Poverty rates tend to increase whenever corporate bankruptcies do. And increased corporate revenues usually translate into increased government revenues, used to provide everything from education and health care to services for the elderly and disabled. Which is why governments take such an interest in promoting corporate well-being along with economic and social well-being.

The spectacular bankruptcy of Enron and other corporate disasters at the beginning of the 21st century were partly responsible for the U.S. government's decision to pass the Sarbanes-Oxley Act, which overhauled the way American companies were governed and attempted to restore confidence in American business. The new rules—forcing companies to publish extensive amounts of additional information on how money was earned and spent—were described by President Bush, who signed them into law, as "the most far-reaching reforms of American business practices since the time of Franklin Delano Roosevelt."

The collapse of other companies around the world—the wave of bank and corporate collapses during the 2008 credit crunch, for example—led many governments to insist on a much higher level of corporate governance, the rules that govern the way corporations are managed and controlled. The idea was to avoid large financial failures that could lead, in addition to massive layoffs and investor losses, to further contagion in the economy as a whole.

One of the many new accounting principles for the 21st century is the requirement that companies use truly independent auditors to oversee their books. Previously, accounting firms often had lucrative contracts for consulting and other work for the companies they were supposed to be overseeing. The conflict of interest led to many abuses and a lack of independent oversight, such as at Enron and WorldCom, which used the same accounting firms working as consultants as well as auditors. In the United States a new regulator was created to oversee the accounting industry: the Public Company Accounting Oversight Board, which would make sure companies respected the new laws—including a ban on company loans to executives, and guarantees that whistleblowers, employees who disclosed fraud and other unlawful activities, would not lose their jobs.

• •

INFORMATIONAL TOOL:

What is **insider trading**?

Think of a bank robbery being planned by someone who works inside the bank. A company's insiders are those who have access to the company's financial statements or other company secrets that haven't yet been made public—and usually consist of the company's top managers or their friends. The activities of insiders are carefully watched by the markets and by financial oversight authorities. In some countries, insider trading—purchasing or selling securities based on inside information—is tolerated with the rationale that someone has to be the first to trade on new information, so why not let the insiders be the ones? This first-come-first-served mentality is losing sway: Insider trading is now illegal in almost every major country in the world economy.

• •

Of the three entities that control a company—management, the board of directors, and the shareholders—management traditionally has been able to do things pretty much its own way, counting on tacit approval from shareholders and directors. But at the beginning of the 21st century, things started to change. Increasingly assertive shareholders and increasingly active board members have forced management to adapt to new ways of doing business.

After numerous scandals involving inflated CEO pay packages and other abuses of power by corporate management, many small shareholders have begun taking a more active role in 21st-century corporate decision making. In the United States, for example, shareholders have ended up winning seats on the boards of major companies such as Heinz, Wendy's, and Home Depot. Government entities that bailed out banks and other companies during the global credit crunch have also insisted on more control of how these companies are managed—and how the managers are remunerated.

One of the first actions of newly empowered shareholders is to insist on *say on pay* resolutions, which require shareholder approval of executive pay packages. The pay packages of CEOs have come under increasing criticism—particularly since company-oversight groups such as the Securities and Exchange Commission have moved to force publicly traded companies to reveal all compensation paid to executives. The biggest surprise—when companies started complying with the rules—was how much the executives of the world's companies were earning in addition to their salaries. Perks, such as use of the company jet, often add up to hundreds of thousands, if not millions of dollars. In addition many executives are given *deferred pay*, allowing them to avoid paying taxes on money that is "loaned" back to the firm.

Stock options are another form of executive remuneration that has also come under increasing scrutiny from shareholder groups. Since stock options are usually not taxed and not accounted for on the company's books until they are exercised, the amount of hidden value can be enormous. During the first years of the 21st century, the average total compensation of S&P 500 company heads in the United States exceeded $10 million, once stock options and other benefits were included. In addition, the average corporate executive's pay package in the United States was estimated to be approximately four hundred times the average wage for a production worker.

• •

INFORMATIONAL TOOL:

What is a **stock option**?

Think of a theater ticket giving the option, but not the obligation, to see the show. A stock option gives you the right, but not the obligation, to buy a particular share at a particular price. If the market price of the share goes up, the option's value goes up as well. But if a stock option is out of the money, *which means that the price of the share has gone below the striking price, or purchase price, option holders let the option expire, unused. The reasoning behind providing stock options to management is that they provide a powerful incentive to increase the value of the company's shares.*

• •

A further target of activist shareholder scrutiny is the issuance of *golden parachutes* to departing executives. These payments, sometimes amounting to hundreds of millions of dollars, are often promised to executives in the event they are forced from power. However, the question of many shareholder groups is, Why should an executive be rewarded if they are forced to leave because of poor performance?

Many shareholder groups have also insisted on having greater say on poison-pill defenses, strategies used by management to restructure a company to defend it against unwanted takeover groups. Poison-pill defenses protect the managers by allowing them to stay in power, but often hurt the shareholders by making the company's shares less valuable than they would have been if the takeover artists had been allowed to purchase the company.

With the advent of private equity, many publicly traded companies have become the targets of investors who hope to take them private. It used to be that management made the decisions to sell or not, but shareholders—institutional investors, especially—are also insisting on having a greater say in any decision to sell the company, and at what price. They are also insisting on the option of retaining shares in the company once it has gone private. In many cases, their insistence has paid off. A Web site that tracks takeovers and poison-pill defenses, Shark Repellent.net, has reported that shareholder campaigns against capricious decisions on accepting takeover offers has had positive results—leading to better offers more than 25 percent of the time.

Investor groups are also becoming increasingly vigilant of management taking their companies private in an operation referred to as a *management buyout*, or MBO, where the manager of the company, usually the *chief executive officer*, or CEO, sells the company to a private investor or investor group, often including the CEO instigating the deal. This, of course, can lead to a serious conflict of interest.

• •

INFORMATIONAL TOOL:

What is a white knight?

Think of King Arthur sending an ironclad warrior to save a damsel in distress. In the business world, a white knight is an investor who comes in to save a company from an unwanted takeover. The company's management, fearing the loss of their jobs among other major changes in the company's structure, often encourages a white knight investor to buy enough shares to block a hostile takeover and protect the status quo.

• •

In order to effectively monitor management's activities, most activist shareholders rely on the support of other shareholders, particularly the big institutional investors, which include pension funds, college endowments, mutual funds, and insurance companies. These shareholders, or *stakeholders*, as they are sometimes called, are fighting for a greater say in how the companies they "own" are run.

While ownership and voting rights tend to be relatively straightforward in the United States, in Europe ownership itself is often shrouded in a complex web of cross-holdings that allow some shareholders to increase the clout and voting power of the shares they own. These *control-enhancing mechanisms* can take many forms. In Germany and France, for example, these webs of cross-holdings have allowed banks and other investor groups to control a large swath of companies in various sectors of the economy—in some cases giving them monopoly control.

Another control-enhancing mechanism is the use of secret shareholders' agreements committing one group to always vote with another. In some countries this is illegal, but not in most of the advanced industrial economies—especially those that make up the European Union—which is why secret shareholder agreements are so prevalent in countries like Germany, Holland, and France.

• •

INFORMATIONAL TOOL:

What is a **monopoly**?

Think of the board game—when you own all the properties of a particular color, you can decide what to build on them. Complete control of one sector of service or production within an economy is called a monopoly. A sole producer of a good can pretty much decide what prices to charge. There are very few real monopolies—consumers generally find an alternative if prices get too high. For example, the OPEC oil producers thought they had a near monopoly in oil back in the 1970s, but when they raised prices too much, consumers found alternative sources of energy. When Microsoft was accused of monopolistic behavior at the beginning of the 21st century, Bill Gates countered that the company had been lowering most prices, not raising them—the European Union fined Microsoft anyway, to the tune of a half a billion euros.

• •

Pyramid structures are also a common mechanism for shareholders to obtain more control of the companies they own. Legal in most countries, a pyramid structure allows an individual or a company or even a family to use a company it already controls to buy a controlling share in another company. That company then buys a controlling share in another company, and before long the original owner is able to spread ownership and risk among a wide range of shareholders—but keep the control to themselves. Although these pyramid structures are most common in Italy, they occur in such diverse countries as Germany and Sweden, where some shares are allowed to have multiple voting rights at shareholder meetings, giving additional power to the shareholders who own them. The criticism of many of these structures is that too much power gets into the hands of a small minority of shareholders.

Another criticism is that too much power in the hands of shareholders runs the risk of limiting the power of management to make bold decisions and increase shareholder value over the long term. The fear of many managers is that companies in the 21st century will suffer from *management by referendum*, where every decision is subject to the often conflicting influence, and scrutiny, of a wide range of investor groups. Highly talented individuals may refuse to serve on boards to avoid the endless intervention and probing of investor groups. And some shareholders with special interests—political activists, for example—may force companies to make decisions that are against the interests of shareholders in general.

It could be that most shareholders will use their new power sensibly, however, realizing that they lack the intimate knowledge of management and the inner workings of a company necessary to micromanage the company on their own. Many will opt to use their influence to elect board members who are able, and willing, to force management to do the right thing—and in a way that ends up being in the best interest of the shareholders, the true owners of the company.

During the last decades of the 20th century, the *Washington Consensus* set out clear guidelines for economic growth—it was thought that if a country had the right level of inflation, the right level of budget restraint, and the right exchange rate, economic growth was pretty much ensured. But the collapse of several developing economies during the Asian crisis of 1997–98 and the market turmoil following the 2008 credit crunch changed many policymakers' way of thinking. *Rule of law* and sensible corporate governance were seen as major factors for economic growth.

It has been shown that countries with a significantly higher level of rule of law—along with strong public and corporate accountability—provide far more economic growth than those that have less respect for rule of law. This relationship between strong rule of law and higher standard-of-living levels—defined as GDP per capita—can be found in many country comparisons: Spain and South Africa, Portugal and Morocco, Ireland and Botswana. In these and many other cases, a higher respect for law in the first country has been shown to encourage more foreign investment and long-term economic growth than in the second— providing, in the end, more wealth for the country's citizens.

The World Bank in Washington, D.C., has begun compiling a *Worldwide Governance Indicators* project that compiles data from every country in the world—examining more than sixty indicators, such as the quality of each country's police and judiciary—and creates a quantifiable score, on a scale from 1 to 100. Some countries, such as those in Central and Eastern Europe, increased their scores significantly after the European Union forced them to revamp legal procedures and upgrade police and judicial forces in order to be considered for EU membership.

• •

INFORMATIONAL TOOL:

How are the world's major countries ranked according to **governance**?

The World Bank's Worldwide Governance Indicators (WGI) project ranks the governance in the countries of the world according to six *categories: voice and accountability, political stability and absence of violence, government effectiveness, regulatory quality, rule of law, and control of corruption. The category for rule of law, for example, covers the way contracts are enforced and the efficiency and fairness of the police and the courts. Under this category, the world's largest economies would be ranked as follows (WGI rule-of-law ranking—100: highest ranking, 0: lowest):*

Germany	94.3
United Kingdom	92.9
United States	91.9
Japan	90.0
France	89.5
Italy	61.4
India	56.2
Brazil	43.3
China	42.4
Russia	16.7

Source: The World Bank, 2007, info.worldbank.org/governance/wgi

• •

Proper corporate and national governance is becoming an increasingly important factor for economic success in the 21st-century economy. The United States, for example, began in 2004 to require all recipients of U.S. foreign aid to fulfill minimum rule-of-law standards. And more than half of all projects receiving World Bank financing now have a rule-of-law component, such as providing well-defined conflict-resolution programs in order to receive money for village development.

There are, of course, exceptions to this rule. Despite criticism of China's human rights policies, for example, its economic growth and foreign investment have been among the strongest in the 21st century. And despite Russia's rampant *crony capitalism*, where insiders and those with access to government leaders have reaped enormous economic benefits, the general economy grew quickly over the first years of the 21st century—attributed, by some, to the belief that a strong central government, albeit flawed, could still guarantee investors' rights. Statistics show, however, that only a sustainable commitment to rule of law and proper governance procedures can guarantee long-term economic growth and respect for citizens' economic rights.

CHAPTER 12

HEDGE FUNDS AND DERIVATIVE TRADERS—THE WILD CARDS OF THE NEW GLOBAL ECONOMY?

WHENEVER THERE'S A global economic catastrophe such as a stock market crash or a currency meltdown, the first culprits people turn to are hedge funds and derivative traders. During the global credit crunch, for example, pension funds and university endowments lost billions of dollars when the hedge funds they invested in collapsed or were forced to close. Market crashes, even the crash following the terrorist attacks of September 11, have been blamed on hedge funds and derivative traders swooping in and selling hundreds of millions of dollars' worth of stocks and other securities, causing markets to implode worldwide.

It used to be that only the big players in the world economy, with millions to invest, could have access to sophisticated investment vehicles like hedge funds. But now, high-net-worth individuals are increasingly being drawn to the stellar returns that some hedge funds have been able to deliver. Hedge funds are generally not subject to the same restrictions and reporting requirements applicable to normal investment vehicles—hedge-fund investors are considered to be more sophisticated and market-savvy than normal investors—and the universe of potential investors has grown considerably. Even banks have become big hedge-fund investors and traders in recent years, using the enormous wealth they manage, hundreds of billions of dollars in some cases, to invest in the world economy.

• •

INFORMATIONAL TOOL:

What is a **hedge**?

The original purpose of a financial hedge was to prevent losses by investing in something that would go up when the other things in your portfolio go down—investing in a house, for example, is a classic hedge against inflation: the house's value usually goes up during inflationary times. The irony is that hedge funds, large investment funds run by savvy managers for a highly sophisticated clientele, have become associated with risky bets—for example, by investing clients' money in speculative instruments such as highly volatile derivatives.

• •

With total funds under management reaching nearly $2 trillion during the first years of the 21st century, hedge funds are a rapidly expanding but still relatively small subset of the mutual-fund universe—which grew to more than $20 trillion worldwide during the same period. However, the money controlled by hedge-fund managers is used in ways that give them enormous power to influence the world economy.

How does it work? Typically, hedge-fund managers use computers and trading algorithms to analyze the market in ways that were impossible before the computer age, spotting discrepancies and opportunities that often go unseen by the ordinary investor. They then act on this information, and on their own intuition in many cases, to buy or sell securities in such volume that they generate enormous profits—or enormous losses—for their investors.

Hedge-fund investors are usually asked to share up to 20 percent of the fund's profits with the fund managers, in addition to a management fee. Why are they willing to pay so much? Because they think the higher returns more than compensate for the extra cost. Recent estimates of the amount of money invested into hedge funds worldwide range from $1 trillion to $2 trillion. Basically, a hedge fund uses fluctuations in the markets to make money, buying hundreds of millions if not billions of dollars' worth of securities and other assets when prices are cheap and selling when prices rise.

They may also choose to use derivatives—such as options or other sophisticated financial instruments—to sell when prices are high, only to buy everything back later when prices fall. In this way, hedge funds are able to make money in rising *and* falling markets, finding market anomalies and quickly acting on them, buying or selling in such large amounts that they make money on small or otherwise insignificant discrepancies.

Hedge funds invest in such large amounts that their actions often end up influencing the market they're investing in. Since most normal mutual funds are almost always fully invested, with less than 4 percent in cash during normal times, there's little for traditional stock fund managers to do during a market crisis but sell or sit back and watch their portfolios decline. And private equity funds, which use enormous amounts of borrowed money that can dry up in a flash during market crises, find it difficult to act aggressively during market downturns. But hedge funds use their money to buy a wide array of securities and derivatives—anything from commodity futures to currency options to credit default swaps—to swoop down and profit from market turmoil, wherever it may occur.

• •

INFORMATIONAL TOOL:

What is **program trading**?

Think of a market-savvy computer that's been programmed to track markets around the world, looking for slight discrepancies in prices. Program trading is kind of like buying large amounts of sale items in one supermarket and selling them to another where the prices are higher. In the global markets, program traders take advantage of small discrepancies in the markets, buying large amounts of stocks—or options, or bonds, or futures— in a market where prices are out of line with prices in other markets around the world. Program trading is often blamed for market crashes—such as the Black Monday crash of 1987, the Asia crisis of 1997, or the credit crunch beginning in 2008—the traders say they're just following the market fluctuations. Others say they're the tail wagging the dog.

• •

Hedge-fund managers are criticized for being ruthless, coldhearted traders, exacerbating market fluctuations—but dispassionate trading strategies often tend to be most profitable during tumultuous times, when prices rise and fall dramatically, opening up many new opportunities. Hedge funds can have a positive effect on the world economy, providing loans and credit to distressed companies that traditional banks won't lend to. Under a *loan-to-own* strategy, some hedge funds extend credit to companies under the condition that the loans can be converted to equity, giving the hedge fund an equity stake that allows it to benefit if the company is able to recover from its woes at some point in the future.

Hedge funds and other big investors are able to play a much bigger role in the world economy than they normally would, mainly by investing in *derivatives*. For a relatively small amount of money invested, derivatives allow investors to get a much bigger bang for their buck. Basically, a derivative is a security that "derives" its value from another item of value. Although the most traditional derivatives are stock options, futures, and swaps, the 21st-century economy has been flooded with a whole range of derivative securities. Collateralized debt obligations, or CDOs, for example, have become increasingly popular as investors look for more returns at a previously defined level of risk. The problem is that the risks for many CDOs are not properly understood by investors—or even by the banks that issue them—and losses can mount rapidly if the underlying collateralized assets go sour.

• •

INFORMATIONAL TOOL:

What is a **collateralized debt obligation?**

Think of an IOU with the deed to a house attached to it. Collateralized debt obligations (CDOs) are loans with an asset or a bundle of assets attached to them. The assets can be anything from a flow of money—from mortgage payments, for example—to a flow of goods such as a farmer's future crops or an orange juice factory's future production. The loan and the assets are usually grouped together and sold as a single instrument. A CDO can also be based on a wide variety of assets, such as a series of different mortgages with different levels of risk. In theory, this reduces the risk to the final investor, because the chance of a wide range of assets going bad is much smaller than that of any single asset going bad.

• •

Other, more traditional forms of derivatives are options, *futures*, *forwards*, and *swaps*. Just as options give the owner the right, but not the obligation, to buy something of value at a certain point in time, futures and forwards give investors the right—and sometimes the obligation—to purchase something of value at a later date. A corn farmer, for example, can sell next year's harvest by going to the futures or forwards markets to find a counterparty—someone who will agree to buy at a price that is set in advance. Futures are unlike forward contracts in that their terms are standardized. Because the time and date on future contracts correspond to other contracts, they can be traded on exchanges around the world. A swap is a prearranged financial operation that exchanges one asset for another. A bank could trade one series of income flows—from bonds, for example—for another that better matches the bank's funding and risk requirements.

The idea of derivatives is to reduce risk for one party while offering the other party the potential for a high return for being willing to take on that risk. Someone selling a derivative based on the Standard & Poor's 500 Index, for example, is expecting the index to move in a particular direction. If they think that the index will rise, they'll sell a future on the index, allowing the buyer to lock in a fixed return. In this case, the seller assumes the risk—for a price.

Basically, anyone buying a call or a future is willing to pay something in order to remove risk and know exactly what they'll be earning at a certain point in the future. A soybean exporter in Des Moines, for example, can use foreign currency derivatives such as options or futures to lock in the value of earnings coming in from sales abroad. Or a retired homeowner may use an investment in interest-rate derivatives to counterbalance the effect of inflation on the value of the house or apartment they own. Even insurance companies use derivatives, such as *credit default swaps*, which allow them to insure credit risk without the oversight of regulatory authorities. Basically, the person or institution selling the derivative takes on the risk that the underlying item of value—currencies or interest rates, for example—may move in the wrong direction.

• •

INFORMATIONAL TOOL:

What is a **credit default swap**?

Think of buying an insurance policy for a bond. The world's major insurance companies discovered at the beginning of the 21st century that most regulatory authorities would allow them to freely issue derivatives, securities based on the value of another item of value, that had basically the same function of guaranteeing credit risk. The advantage of these credit default swaps (CDSs) was that the insurance companies could issue them in almost limitless amounts, without worrying about setting aside reserves required by more traditional insurance vehicles. A credit default swap works basically like any other insurance policy. The seller agrees to indemnify the buyer if a specified bond defaults or if a specified financial institution goes bankrupt. Big investors, such as college pension funds, bought trillions of dollars' worth of credit default swaps, assuming that they were buying a guarantee that their investments wouldn't disappear in the event of a financial meltdown. Unfortunately, when markets crashed in 2008, major insurance companies that had issued CDSs, including the biggest insurer in the world, AIG, had to be bailed out or declare bankruptcy themselves.

• •

What makes a derivative especially risky is the way it can rise or fall sharply when the underlying item changes in value. When markets change direction quickly, with currencies and interest rates rising rapidly, for example, investors in derivatives can see their portfolios rise or fall precipitously. The 21st-century economy is full of examples of institutions or individuals who have lost fortunes investing in derivatives. Enron, for example, went bankrupt speculating on derivatives based on the price of energy, and banks and insurance companies around the world lost billions when their portfolios of collateralized debt instruments plummeted following the global housing market collapse of 2008.

The universe of underlying assets that derivatives can be based on has expanded greatly over recent years, and now includes such items as weather conditions, exchange rates, or the consumer price index. You can even go to the Web and buy options based on sports scores—in order to hedge a previous bet, for example. There are even *freight derivatives*, forward contracts that allow shipowners and manufacturing companies to lock in a fee for renting a ship—facilitating the transport of goods and commodities from one part of the world to another. In fact, freight derivatives trading has experienced a big surge as a result of the booming Chinese manufacturing sector, which relies heavily on cargo ships to send exports to foreign markets and bring in raw materials from abroad.

Most derivatives are traded on specialized exchanges such as Eurex, the CME Group—formed in 2007 by merging the Chicago Mercantile Exchange and the Chicago Board of Trade—and the Korea Exchange, which has become one of the biggest derivatives exchanges in the world, when ranked by number of transactions. The Bank for International Settlements (BIS) has estimated that the amount of derivative trading on recognized exchanges totaled more than $300 trillion per year—at a time when the total size of the United States' economy was slightly more than $10 trillion.

Many derivatives are also traded on *over-the-counter exchanges* (OTC), including trading floors in banks and other financial institutions scattered across the globe. The more exotic derivatives, such as swaps and forward rate agreements, are usually traded OTC because they are made-to-order, with unique dates and structures, limiting the feasibility of trading them on formal exchanges. The value of trading on these over-the-counter derivatives is hard to determine, but is estimated to amount to hundreds of trillions of dollars per year.

What is a derivative really worth? Because the value of most derivatives is so difficult to determine—how can you say how much a stock market will go up or down over a given period of time?—many investors refuse to trade in them. Berkshire Hathaway fund manager Warren Buffett, for example, has referred to derivatives as "financial weapons of mass destruction." And some governments have called for greater control of derivative trading and derivative traders, seeing the potential for unexpected derivative losses leading to an economic crisis as extremely likely in the interconnected global economy. The irony is that derivatives were originally meant to reduce risk, not increase it. If used properly, derivatives allow companies to spread risk and can have many positive benefits, facilitating trade and softening the impact of economic downturns.

Sovereign funds have also come under criticism for the way they have begun to control large parts of the 21st-century economy. It is estimated that several trillion dollars are being managed by governments as diverse as those of Norway, Kuwait, China, and the state of Alaska. Basically, a sovereign fund is an investment vehicle set up by a government or governmental entity to recycle excess foreign reserves or a windfall income. The Norwegian government, for example, used part of its earnings from natural-gas sales to set up a pension fund with more than $300 billion in reserve, more than the entire gross domestic product of most countries.

The Alaska Permanent Fund also uses the income from more than $40 billion it earned from oil sales to provide a yearly dividend to all residents. Abu Dhabi, Kuwait, Russia, and others have also used income from oil and natural-gas sales to set up sovereign funds, ranging from $100 billion to $600 billion, to provide a cushion for market downturns and provide a nest egg for future generations.

• •

INFORMATIONAL TOOL:

What is a **sovereign fund**?

Think of a government breaking open its piggy bank to invest in the global marketplace. A sovereign fund is an investment vehicle set up by a government to recycle excess foreign reserves or windfall profits. When a country makes a lot of money from foreign trade or from the sale of a commodity like oil or natural gas, it may want to invest this money for future generations. Instead of investing this money in bonds or overnight deposits, many governments have set up sovereign funds to make equity investments, buying companies or shares of companies from around the world.

LARGEST SOVEREIGN WEALTH FUNDS, WORLD RANKING

SOVEREIGN FUND	ASSETS IN BILLIONS IN U.S. DOLLARS
United Arab Emirates: Abu Dhabi Investment Authority	$875
Norway: Government Pension Fund—Global	$380
Singapore: GIC (General Investment Company)	$330
Saudi Arabia: various funds	$300
Kuwait: Reserve Fund for Future Generations	$240
China: China Investment Corporation	$200
Singapore: Temasek Holdings	$159
Libya: Oil Reserve Fund	$50
Qatar: Qatar Investment Authority	$50

Algeria: Fonds de Régulation des Recettes	$38
U.S.: Alaska Permanent Fund Corporation	$38
Brunei: Brunei Investment Authority	$30

Source: *Economist*, Morgan Stanley, 2008 figures

• •

Many mercantilist countries, such as China, Singapore, and others, have begun using their enormous foreign exchange reserves—earned from years of exporting more than they import—to invest abroad. China alone had amassed more than a trillion dollars by the first few years of the 21st century. Initially, the majority of these reserves were invested in dollar-denominated securities in the United States—U.S. Treasury bonds mostly. In 2007, however, the Chinese central bank decided to set up a sovereign fund and began investing the money in a more lucrative—and riskier—way. One of its first investments was a $3 billion stake in New York's Blackstone Group, which promptly lost more than $500 million. Despite the criticism that this money should have been more safely invested, the China Investment Corporation continued to diversify its holdings in equity investments around the world.

Critics have called for greater accountability and transparency in the way sovereign funds are invested. The fear is that when sovereign funds invest in or buy companies abroad, they gain an enormous amount of economic control. The proposed purchase of five port terminals in the United States, for example, was blocked because the purchaser, Dubai Ports World, was owned by the Dubai emirate. China's attempted purchase of Unocal, the U.S. energy group, was also blocked for security concerns.

For these reasons, Germany and other countries have moved to limit acquisitions by foreign state-run funds in any sector related to national security. The fear is that some state investors will not act like individuals, attempting solely to maximize returns and promote efficiencies. Sovereign funds may, indeed, invest in a company abroad to gain technology know-how or influence sensitive sectors of the world economy. Other possible solutions include requiring sovereign funds to publish internationally audited reports giving full details of their investment portfolios—or limiting ownership to 20 percent of any given company.

In the end, sovereign funds—like hedge funds, private equity, and derivative trading—need not be any more dangerous than traditional investment tools, as long as foreign ownership can be limited and the risks of the 21st century's many new investment vehicles can be properly evaluated and controlled.

CHAPTER 13

INCOME GAPS AND DEVELOPMENT— WHAT CAN BE DONE TO ELIMINATE POVERTY IN THE 21ST CENTURY?

LIVING ON LESS than a dollar a day, the generally accepted measure of poverty, may seem an impossible task for many of us. But the World Bank has reported that well into the 21st century, more than one billion people in the world do precisely that, every day, 365 days a year—and virtually all of them live in the developing world.

The United Nations Millennium Development Goals project, established by world leaders in 2000, was supposed to cut poverty in half by the year 2015. At the halfway point, on 07/07/07, the majority of the intermediate goals were not even close to being met. Despite a reduction in the number of people living on less than a dollar a day in every country except Bangladesh and Pakistan, many of the goals, such as reducing the rate at which mothers die during childbirth, improving access to clean water, reducing infant mortality, etc., were showing little signs of improvement, mainly because of the lack of resources and commitment from developing-country and developed-country governments.

The global income gap is much more than a difference in salaries. It reflects an immense gap in the quality of life between the rich and the poor. In India, for example, more than a third of all women have never been taught to read. And in Nigeria and Kenya, electricity shortages affect poor areas on a daily basis, depriving many hospitals of power during operations. More than a hundred million school-age children around the world have never seen the inside of a school, and at the dawn of the 21st century only 4 percent of Africans had access to the Internet.

The expanding global economy has generated enormous gains in prosperity, but this is mainly in the developed and developing economies in Europe, North America, and Asia. But what effect has this wealth had on the world's poorest countries? Despite the efforts of individuals, governments, and a wide range of global philanthropic organizations, the income gap between the world's richest and poorest countries is still growing wider rather than smaller.

The most commonly accepted method for measuring income equality is the *Gini coefficient*, which assigns a score of 0 to countries with perfect equality (utopia, for most observers) and a score of 1 to a country of complete inequality—where one household holds all the wealth. Denmark, with low income inequality, had a Gini coefficient of approximately 0.23 at the beginning of the 21st century. Namibia, the country with the world's highest income inequality, had 0.70. The United States, with a Gini coefficient of 0.45, has one of the most inequitable distributions of wealth among developed countries.

• •

INFORMATIONAL TOOL:

What is the *Gini coefficient*?

Think of high-diving scores, giving 0 for a perfect dive and 1 for a flop. The Gini coefficient, developed by the Italian statistician Corrado Gini, measures the inequality of income distribution, or wealth distribution, in countries around the world. Countries are rated from 0, for the least income inequality, to 1, for the most. To make the numbers easier to visualize, the Gini index was created, multiplying the Gini coefficient values by 100— the ranking remains the same; the numbers just get bigger.

GINI INDEX INEQUALITY RANKINGS FOR SELECTED COUNTRIES (LEAST INEQUALITY: 0, MOST INEQUALITY: 100):

Denmark	23.2
Sweden	25
Belgium	25
Slovakia	25.8
Hungary	26.9
Germany	28.3
Ukraine	29
Ghana	30
European Union average	32
India	32.5
Switzerland	33.1
Canada	33.1
Egypt	34.4
Indonesia	34.8
Australia	35.2
South Korea	35.8
Vietnam	36
United Kingdom	36.8
Japan	38.1
Russia	40.5
Ecuador	42
Singapore	42.5
China	44
United States	45
Venezuela	49.1
Hong Kong	52.3
Brazil	56.7
Chile	57.1

| South Africa | 59.3 |
| Namibia | 70.7 |

Source: 2007 CIA World Factbook

• •

At the beginning of the 21st century, the trend is for developing countries to have ever-increasing gaps between the incomes of the rich and the poor. In China, for example, the gap was increasing by more than 5 percent per year during the first years of the century. Even though the booming Chinese economy had succeeded in bringing more than a hundred million citizens out of poverty, hundreds of millions more were still earning less than a dollar a day.

As incredible as it may seem, the net worth of the ten wealthiest people in the world is more than the total yearly earnings of everyone living in the world's developing countries— essentially 90 percent of the world's population. Meanwhile, more than a million children die each year from lack of access to clean water. A visit to any big city in any developing country— Mumbai, Rio de Janeiro, or Mexico City, for example—shows the disparity with amazing clarity, with millions living in makeshift housing, with open sewers, rampant diseases, and no access to public services like education and health care.

And in the countryside, it isn't much better. In Africa, India, and China, for example, rural households are usually the poorest in the land—and, in many cases, getting poorer. Since productivity in agriculture has grown more slowly than productivity in other areas, the income of rural dwellers, most of whom rely on agriculture for the majority of their income, has declined relative to their urban compatriots. This, in part, explains the exodus of the rural poor to the rapidly expanding cities of most developing countries.

The shift to a market-based economy in many developing countries has increased the importance of proper education. Skilled workers earn much more in the expanding trade-oriented economies of China and India, for example, than their unskilled neighbors. Improving education, therefore, is a priority for reducing income gaps. But in many countries, teachers—and funds for elementary education—are often lacking.

Improving rural infrastructure—building new roads and train lines, for example—would also increase productivity in farming and increase job opportunities for the rural poor. But cash-strapped governments often lack the money to get things started. New techniques in agricultural production can provide valuable help. When new rice seeds were developed for African farmers, for example, it was estimated that yields would more than double, since they took less than half the time to grow compared to normal rice varieties. These *New Rices for Africa,* or *NERICAS*, were expected to revolutionize the farming sector in most sub-Saharan African countries. But since most farmers lacked the know-how and had no access to capital or credit, they were unable to pay for the seeds—or the fertilizer to make the seeds grow faster. At the beginning of the 21st century, after several years of promotion—mostly by well-meaning rich-country advisers—NERICA rice was being planted on only approximately 5 percent of the land where it could thrive. And without the infrastructure to get the crops to market, or fertilizer and seeds to the farmers, the project appeared doomed to failure.

One promising solution is the Millennium Villages project, which attempts to reduce world poverty by using ground-level support to empower the rural villages themselves to find the solutions to escape from the "poverty trap." Under a typical Millennium Villages project, villages get a jump start in development, with foreign donors providing basic investment in health, education, and basic infrastructure, including upgrading access to water, power, and Internet connectivity. The villages, many of which are located in Africa, are usually chosen because they are in *hunger hot spots*—areas marked by extreme poverty, high incidence of diseases, and chronic malnutrition. At the end of five years, the plan is for the community to be on the path to sustainable economic growth—ready to move on without foreign funds.

Debt reduction, such as that proposed by U2's Bono, has allowed many stagnating countries to get out from under the burden of paying a huge foreign debt—the original borrowed funds having often been squandered through mismanagement or corruption. Many developing governments, in Africa especially, spend more on interest payments than on health and education combined. Debt servicing, consisting primarily of principal and interest payments on the country's debt, is often the biggest drain on the meager financial resources of many developing countries. Canceling the debt, or rescheduling it—which means delaying repayment of loans until the economy is in better health—can help governments to devote precious resources to development instead of transferring money to rich-country lenders. But debt reduction is only one step in the process. What happens after the debt burden has been removed? How does the country access funds for further growth and development?

One of the most effective steps in encouraging economic development in the poor countries of the world is to provide opportunities for people to sell their goods and services. Even though many workers in developing countries work for low salaries by Western standards, farm work or a factory job is often an essential first stop on their way to economic independence. Trade barriers, therefore, need to be reduced in order to provide the opportunity for developing-country workers to sell their goods. And rich-country consumers should encourage imports from poor-country producers—as long as it can be verified that the workers' rights were respected in the production process. In the end, a job, even a relatively low-paying one by Western standards, is often the best hope for a worker to start building a better life.

Proper job training is a sine qua non for sustainable development. And without proper training for the children of the developing world, there can be no hope for a more equitable distribution of income. Educating girls—unfortunately, a low priority in many countries—has been shown to be one of the best development investments a country can make. In some developing countries, as incredible as it may seem, millions of girls are not sent to school. But statistics show that girls who have had some schooling, even just to the primary level, are able to increase family income significantly and are also more likely to have children who survive, who are healthy, and who will be given a proper education when they reach school age.

Direct investment by foreign entities also encourages development in the world's poorer countries by providing funds for factories, power plants, and other businesses. In India, for example, foreign investors contributed significantly to economic development by investing in infrastructure projects such as electricity-generating plants—allowing the Indian economy, already one of the biggest software developers in the world, to set up new high-tech plants and call centers in areas where people previously had no access to high-paying jobs. Many developing countries look to foreign direct investment in infrastructure to allow them to leap over the industrial stage of economic evolution, going directly from rural economies to service economies based on "clean" industries such as technology and media. In addition, foreign direct investment provides a stable source of funding that can't be pulled out of the economy at a moment's notice.

• •

INFORMATIONAL TOOL:

What is **foreign direct investment**?

Think of someone staking a claim during the gold rush. A foreign direct investment is defined as a controlling interest held by a foreign owner—if it weren't a controlling interest, it would be classified simply as investment. Essentially, when a foreign firm buys a domestic one, or even a controlling share of the company's stock, it needs to be accounted for as foreign direct investment under international accounting rules. FDI often provides needed capital to companies and countries that is longer-lasting than "hot-money" investments, which can come in and go out at a moment's notice.

• •

Private organizations and individuals have also begun to play a big role in reducing poverty in the 21st century. Bill Clinton's network of corporate and private donors, for example, has formed the Clinton Global Initiative (CGI), which has made a concerted push to fight HIV/AIDS, poverty, and climate change in the first years of the 21st century. It has been most effective in Africa, where the need for such philanthropy is probably the greatest. The CGI, like the Millennium Villages project, strives to create a businesslike approach to giving the money raised. Both have negotiated agreements with generic-drug makers—to cut the price of antiretroviral drugs in poor countries, for example, or arrange bulk-purchase agreements between governments of the developing world's biggest cities and makers of energy-saving products and infrastructure.

In many cases, major charities such as Save the Children, Oxfam, and Doctors Without Borders play a big role in reducing poverty and increasing the quality of life for millions of people in the world's poorest countries. Many of these organizations have evolved from simply providing food or medical care to trying to create an environment where famine and epidemics can be eradicated. As the Chinese proverb says, "Give a man a fish and you feed him for a day. Teach a man to fish and you feed him for a lifetime."

The Internet can provide an important boost to developing economies. Even if local populations don't have the same widespread access to computers and the Internet found in developed countries, entrepreneurs and businesses in many developing countries have discovered that even minimal access to consumers and businesses means profit, growth, and new jobs. A rug maker in Nepal, for example, can use the Web to sell to shops and designers as far away as Sydney or New York City. And software can be developed in India just as easily as it can in Silicon Valley.

Instead of waiting for new ideas to filter down to them, a process that used to take years, many enterprising people in the developing countries of the world are finally being given the opportunity to participate with the other players in the expanding global economy. Unfortunately, in many countries—in Africa especially—access to the Internet is limited, if not nonexistent. And those who do have access are forced to pay hundreds of dollars per month—more than their total monthly salary—for even the slowest bandwidths and Internet connections.

To help developing countries make the leap across the digital divide, the United Nations embarked on a drive for "digital solidarity" in 2005 that was meant to boost Internet connectivity. With support from the World Bank and the African Development Bank, many local governments were encouraged to slash red tape and encourage international investment in technology, including efforts to extend fiber-optic networks across the continent and to try to close the digital gap by providing millions of secondhand computers to first-time users. The ultimate goal was to get large sections of the economy, including governments, hospitals, and schools, on the Internet over the coming years.

Another way of helping people out of poverty is microlending—providing small loans for a fraction of the interest rate small borrowers would have to pay to a local moneylender. Nobel Prize winner Muhammad Yunus, noticing that poor entrepreneurs in his native Bangladesh were paying up to 10 percent a week to moneylenders to buy needed materials, set up Grameen Bank to provide small loans to the poor with no requirement for collateral. His first loans were to impoverished basket weavers who used the money to buy bamboo.

• •

INFORMATIONAL TOOL:

What is a **microcredit**?

Think of tiny loans allowing entrepreneurs in developing countries to set up small businesses. Microcredit refers to the practice of providing small amounts of credit, called microloans, to poor-country entrepreneurs who are not able to get money from traditional banks to set up a business. Because they lack collateral, steady employment, or a verifiable credit history, many people in developing countries cannot meet even the most minimal qualifications to gain access to traditional credit.

• •

When it became apparent that the repayment rate from microcredits was exceptionally high, even by commercial bank lending standards, many other banks and aid organizations set up microfinancing operations throughout the developing world. PlaNetFinance.org, Kiva.org, MicroPlace.com, and Village Banking.org are just a few of the successful operations that provide small loans to artisans, farmers, and small-business owners in developing countries. In Mexico, a microlending group called Compartamos began as a nonprofit organization, successfully lending to high-credit-risk entrepreneurs such as sock makers or shop owners. The secret to its success was creating groups of like-minded entrepreneurs—women, mostly—who agreed to guarantee the debts of the group's members. At the beginning of the 21st century, business had become so lucrative that Compartamos became a for-profit company and eventually opened a full-fledged bank in 2006 with a portfolio of a third of a billion dollars lent to more than 750,000 clients.

When venture capital firms, such as California-based Sequoia, began investing money in microfinance operations from India to Mexico, it was clear that microfinance had arrived on the world economic scene. And when JPMorgan launched a microfinance unit as part of its emerging-markets operation, the world had accepted microfinance as a viable, and profitable, business in its own right—in addition to providing new opportunities and promoting growth in the developing world.

The secret of microfinance operations is to use a labor-intensive approach to loan management, providing money only to borrowers known to the loan agent. To cover the defaults that occur, interest rates are somewhat higher than normal bank loans, but far below the rates charged by traditional moneylenders in most developing countries.

International development banks are another successful tool in fighting poverty. The World Bank, for example, loans billions of dollars every year to developing countries—mainly for long-term projects to fight poverty and encourage economic growth. The bank's aid arm, the International Development Association (IDA), provides most of the funds for schools, hospitals, and programs to fight AIDS and other diseases in the poorest countries of the world. Many loans to kick-start the private sector in many of the world's middle-income countries, such as Turkey and China, are funneled through the International Development Association.

• •

INFORMATIONAL TOOL:

*What is the difference between the **World Bank** and the **International Monetary Fund (IMF)**?*

Think of the IMF as the paramedic and the World Bank as the family doctor. The International Monetary Fund and the World Bank—both based in Washington, D.C.—serve very different functions. The IMF is responsible for helping countries in financial difficulty—providing short-term lending and helping them restructure their economies. The World Bank takes the long-term view, providing long-term loans and development assistance to developing countries. World Bank projects include construction of schools, hospitals, and financing programs to fight AIDS. Both the IMF and the World Bank get their money from rich-country contributions and by borrowing money on the international capital markets, taking advantage of guarantees provided by the world's highest-rated economies.

• •

Led by the government of Venezuela, several South American countries have moved to set up a development bank of their own, the Bank of the South—Banco do Sul in Brazil and Banco del Sur in the Spanish-speaking countries. The idea was to provide an alternative to the World Bank and the IMF in Latin

America, particularly in helping countries out of difficult economic situations during financial crises. Venezuelan president Hugo Chávez led the effort, citing the failure of the Washington Consensus—both the World Bank and the IMF are based in Washington, D.C.—to solve economic problems in a socially conscious manner. Many IMF restructuring plans, for example, were criticized for putting macroeconomic stability ahead of concerns for the poor. But IMF and World Bank leaders point out that strong macroeconomic health in developing countries benefits everyone, especially the poor.

Development assistance, however, doesn't always lead to a reduction in inequality. In many cases, it actually makes it worse. For example, the IMF has found that several of the main forces for development—new technology, financial globalization, and foreign direct investment—often increase inequality. New technology, for example, primarily benefits those who know how to use computers. Financial globalization benefits those who have the language skills and education to profit from increased access to global markets.

In some cases, foreign aid is diverted by corrupt government officials and often ends up in the hands of a small powerful elite. A study in Chad, for example, has shown that only 1 percent of the €20 million provided to support health clinics there actually reached its intended target. Much diverted money ends up deposited in bank accounts abroad, far away from those it was meant to help. To fight this problem, the World Bank and other development authorities have begun refusing new loans to countries that have a history of corruption—insisting that any new funds sent to developing countries be linked to guarantees that the money ends up helping the poor and not the wealthy.

Another reason for income inequality is that much foreign

direct investment is directed toward segments of the economy that already have high salaries, such as call centers or high-end manufacturing. In general, however, foreign trade tends to reduce inequality by providing consumers at all income levels with access to cheaper foreign goods—and allowing even those with low skills to find jobs in export-oriented industry. In Brazil, for example, the export-oriented economic boom of the first years of the 21st century brought more than 20 million poor people into the middle class, the so-called *class* C, with the means to finally purchase computers, cell phones, automobiles, and refrigerators—things people in many rich countries take for granted.

Even though income inequality among nations fell during the first years of the 21st century—mainly because of the "convergence" of countries like China, Brazil, and India, which become richer as they trade and grow—inequality within many developing countries has still been rising. When seen from a macroeconomic perspective, this is not inherently bad—as long as *everyone's* income is growing.

Unfortunately, the gap between rich and poor in many countries is causing support for trade and globalization to be undermined. And even though trade and globalization have been shown to help all sectors of society, on average, to profit and increase their standard of living, it is clear that those with high education and high skills are profiting the most. In Latin America, for example, the income of the richest fifth of the population is almost twenty times higher than the poorest fifth. In Africa, the continent with the highest income disparity in the world economy, the rich hold almost two-thirds of all wealth. It is clear that without a more equitable distribution of per capita income, it will be difficult for globalization to find ongoing support.

In the end, reducing poverty is not only a question of

increasing incomes. The human development index of United Nations Development Programme (UNDP), for example, measures poverty in terms of literacy, infant mortality, and life expectancy as well as purchasing power. Unfortunately, providing money to build schools and hospitals is only the first step. Efforts have to be made to make sure the schools and hospitals are properly staffed—and that children actually attend school. In Brazil, for example, life expectancy and literacy—two of the criteria for the UNDP's human development index—increased dramatically when families' benefit payments were linked to their children's attendance in school and visits to the doctor.

There is no magic bullet to solving world poverty, but concerted efforts from governments, aid organizations, and concerned individuals—when applied properly—can harness the forces of the world economy in ways that end up making the world a richer and, hopefully, more egalitarian place.

CHAPTER 14

DRUGS, SLAVERY, AND SHADY DEALS—THE ILLEGAL ECONOMY OF THE 21ST CENTURY

FOR MANY BUSINESSES and citizens around the world, corruption and other illegal activities are a way of life. From the subsistence coca farmer in Peru to a government official in Africa or the Middle East for whom bribes are the major source of income, illegal activities form a big, and growing, part of the world economy. Even purchases of counterfeit Viagra and fake Swiss watches or French handbags—on the street or on the Web—are part of the trillion-dollar economy that is made up of all the world's illegal and semilegal activities.

Drugs are by far the most commonly traded commodity on the world's black markets. Hundreds of billions of dollars of illegal drugs are sold every year—from the back streets of Kabul to dorm rooms in Ohio. With the amount of trade in illegal drugs surpassing the total economic output of most developing countries, it is impossible to ignore their importance to many global citizens' daily lives. Poor farmers in Afghanistan or Peru, for example, have a difficult time switching from coca or poppy production once they have gotten used to crops that generate more than ten times the income they would receive from planting traditional crops such as corn or wheat.

• •

INFORMATIONAL TOOL:

What is the difference between a black market and a gray market?

Think of the difference between being in jail and being in detention. The world's black markets provide a marketplace for clearly illegal goods and services. Sales of heroin and crack, contract killing, and trade in illegal body parts are just some of the activities that take place on the world's black markets. Gray-market trading involves those activities that are only semilegal, or legal economic activities attempting to avoid taxes. Anything from cigarette smuggling to prostitution—in some countries—to the offshore laundering of legally earned income is part of the world's burgeoning gray-market activity. The thing most people don't know is that the money flow— from the sale of anything from a pirated DVD on the streets of Hong Kong to a fake Louis Vuitton handbag or Rolex watch on the streets of New York— ends up in the hands of well-organized smugglers, some of whom even have connections to terrorist organizations such as Hezbollah.

• •

Eliminating the production of illegal drugs is a bit like squeezing a balloon. Restricting illegal activity in one place at a time—as authorities do sporadically in the world's drug-producing regions—often just pushes production somewhere else. Eradication efforts can also have unintended and undesired consequences. Efforts by Western governments to eradicate opium production in Afghanistan, for example, have been criticized by some as driving the local populace into the arms of the Taliban, which began promoting heroin production after the post-9/11 invasion as a way of undermining the United States' influence in the region.

Can anything be done to stop the drug trade? Some leaders point out that drugs, like alcohol, will always be a part of society and that it is a waste of resources to try to eliminate their production. Others say that instead of trying to suppress the supply, more efforts should be made to reduce the demand through more education or stricter enforcement of drug laws in the countries where they are consumed.

Demand-side solutions can also be applied to limit the trade in a wide variety of products found on the world's markets, from shark fins to elephant tusks. But the results can also be mitigated by unintended secondary effects. Making it illegal to sell ivory from elephant tusks on the international market, for example, helped to stop the slaughter of elephants in many African countries, but progress was mitigated by the fact that the price for ivory on the world's black markets rose dramatically—providing, for some, even more incentive for poachers to kill elephants in defiance of international bans. In response, some environmental groups decided to experiment with a controlled sale of ivory, allowing legally harvested ivory—from overpopulated elephant herds, for example—to be sold in carefully controlled conditions.

Poorly policed borders or poorly enforced legislation often lead to thriving black markets or semilegal gray-market economic activity. Many porous borders—such as the borders between Paraguay and Brazil and between Pakistan and Afghanistan, not to mention the U.S.-Mexican border—provide many opportunities for importing anything from heroin to counterfeit handbags—even animal parts such as sea-turtle eggs, which are poached in great numbers because of their supposed aphrodisiac qualities, and rhinoceros horns, which are ground up and sold as male potency medication. In some countries, legal drugs, such as those used to treat HIV/AIDS and tuberculosis, are also sold on black markets, as long as they can be obtained cheaply in one country and sold for a large profit in another.

As strange as it may seem, international black-market trading can involve human body parts. In Malaysia, for example, where the average wait for a new kidney is over a decade, patients often turn to the black market to buy new kidneys from neighboring countries—some coming from executed criminals. The process usually involves paying bribes to doctors or prison officials in the countries that are providing the body parts. The Transplantation Society, a leading international medical group based in Montréal, has banned the use of organs from executed criminals and other unwilling donors, calling the practice barbaric. But as long as there are patients around the world whose only alternative is a life tied to a dialysis machine or an early death, the illicit trade in body parts will probably continue.

Some black-market activity can lead to war—or help finance wars that have already begun. In several African countries, for example, rebels have used illegally mined diamonds to purchase guns and other war material. And some conflicts, such as that in Sierra Leone, have been shown to have their roots in access to local riches, including lucrative diamond mines. The UN Security Council has banned the sale of diamonds from war-torn countries, but the difficulty of differentiating "illegal" diamonds from legally mined diamonds has made enforcement difficult.

One black-market commodity can actually be used to fight wars: highly enriched uranium, which has become a subject of special concern in the post-9/11 world. The possibility of dangerous nuclear material falling into terrorists' hands has led some countries, principally the United States and its NATO allies, to work closely with officials from the former Soviet Union to make sure that weapons-usable uranium isn't sold on the world's black markets. Even though most terrorists lack the capability to build a nuclear bomb, fears that a "dirty bomb" could be easily constructed—by packing conventional explosives around nuclear waste or other radioactive materials, for example—have led world leaders to push for a world moratorium on the trade of hazardous radioactive materials, overseen by the United Nations's nuclear guardian, the International Atomic Energy Agency.

Human trafficking and slavery is another major problem in the modern global economy. According to the United Nations Office on Drugs and Crime, tens of billions of dollars were being earned from illegal human trafficking at the beginning of the 21st century. Basically, there are two kinds of modern-day slavery: *forced labor* and *debt enslavement*. Forced labor may involve anything from prison labor to traditional slavery—such as that practiced in southern Sudan, where slave traders literally kidnap young men and women, exactly as slave traders did centuries ago, and force them to work for their new masters, far from their families—sometimes for the rest of their lives.

Another practice is to entice young people to leave their families on the pretext of being given a job in another city—or another country. Once they get to their new home, however, they realize that they have been sold as virtual slaves, being forced to work off their transportation and other expenses incurred. Many end up in the sex industry, where they work for years—often being released only when they have gotten too old or when they contract an incurable sexual disease. By then, it is frequently too late: Many cannot go home because of the ostracism they would face for "dishonoring" their families.

• •

INFORMATIONAL TOOL:

What is the difference between migrant smuggling and migrant trafficking?

Think of the difference between paying to be taken across the Rio Grande or being forced or coerced. The International Office for Migration makes a clear distinction between smuggling and trafficking of migrants. Migrant

*smugglers are paid to help their customers get across borders illegally.
Migrant traffickers coerce their victims—often through fraud or
misrepresentation—to cross borders, often against their will. Most victims
of trafficking are young women who are lured to work in foreign
countries—being told they will be given jobs as waitresses or dancers.
Once they get to their destination, they are forced into prostitution and are
given their freedom only when their "debts" to the traffickers have been
paid off.*

• •

Another form of slavery, debt enslavement, exists in
almost every country of the world economy—including rich
countries such as the United States and Spain, where agricultural
workers are hired for a season and are encouraged to make purchases on credit at the company store. Often, these purchases
consist of nonessential goods such as cigarettes and liquor at
highly inflated prices. By the end of the season, these workers
often end up owing more to the company store than they have
earned in wages. These employees are often not allowed to
leave, under threat of physical force in some cases, until their
debts are paid off. In Kuwait, pearl divers sometimes work their
whole lives to pay off debts incurred by previous generations.

Although it is not exactly slavery, child labor is still
another form of exploitation that is all too common in the 21st-
century economy. The International Labour Organization,
based in Geneva, Switzerland, has estimated that more than two
hundred million children from ages five to fourteen are forced to
work in various countries around the world in any given year—
mostly in factories and in agriculture. Many of them are forced
to work up to fourteen hours a day in particularly dangerous
conditions. When police raided a brick-kiln operation in China's
Shanxi Province in 2007, for example, many of the workers who

were being held against their will and forced to work unusually long hours under brutal conditions were children.

What can consumers do to stop the practice of slavery and child labor in the world economy? Organizing consumer boycotts of products made by exploited labor can be quite effective. In India, for example, the use of child labor in the rug industry and in the making of soccer balls was drastically reduced after boycotts from consumers in other parts of the world. Now, many rugs coming from India and Nepal carry tags certifying that they have not been made by children or by forced labor. It is up to consumers in rich countries to insist on seeing a *fair trade* certificate—provided, for example, by the International Fair Trade Association—that guarantees the social and physical well-being of those making products sold on the world's markets—from bananas to roses to tennis shoes.

Like many problems in the world economy, the use of child labor is not easily dealt with. In many agricultural societies, children are often asked to help the family plant and harvest crops—in many cases involving no real harm to their health or education. In some ways, this is not so different from the practice of children holding summer jobs in many rich countries such as Canada, the United States, or in Western Europe. Many international children's aid organizations, therefore, try to make a distinction between *child labor* and *child work*, pointing out that some work, as long as it doesn't interfere with their schooling, can allow many children to earn a small income and develop skills and self-confidence. In the end, all workers should have access to jobs that do not compromise their health or well-being. But if a child or adult worker is forced to work under conditions indistinguishable from slavery, it is up to consumers, governments, and aid organizations around the world to help stop the offending practices.

• •

INFORMATIONAL TOOL:

How can product certification *help us know which things we buy may have been produced using slavery or child labor?*

Think of an international fair labor seal of approval. The Fairtrade Certification, provided by FLO-CERT, is just one of many certificates that are available to assure consumers that what they buy has been produced in accordance with international standards of fair trade and without abusing workers' rights. Originally limited to shops run by organizations like Oxfam or Traidcraft, fair trade certifications can now be found on products ranging from bananas to wine. Two pioneers of product certification, Max Havelaar and TransFair, joined forces to produce the International Fairtrade Certification Mark, which assures us that the products we are buying have been tracked back to the origin and have been produced in a way that not only doesn't exploit workers, but makes sure they receive some of the profits that the products generate.

• •

Corruption and bribery have also become major activities in many economies around the world. In areas where the average wage is often less than a hundred dollars a month, the opportunity to earn thousands or even millions is sometimes impossible to resist—even for those who are supposed to be enforcing the law. In many countries, poorly paid policemen and government officials receive bribes, as a "supplement" to their normal income, that are worth several times their normal salary. In Guinea-Bissau, for example, military officers are paid enormous bribes to secure landing strips for drug dealers to make deliveries. In Liberia, former president Charles Taylor was put on trial for having stashed away more than $3 billion in illegally acquired assets, including blood diamonds—a sum roughly equivalent to the entire Liberian GDP.

Many policemen and government officials who accept illegal payments point out that their salaries are extremely low because it is assumed their income will be supplemented by bribes—just as a waiter or waitress in New York will accept a lower nominal salary knowing that a large portion of the day's income will be in the form of tips. *Mordida* in Mexico City, *baksheesh* in Cairo, *dash* in Nairobi—many business deals around the world would be impossible without some sort of supplemental payment.

For many international businesspeople, it often seems impossible to compete abroad without getting dirty. Some countries have passed laws, however, that make corruption illegal—even in countries where it's accepted as a standard business practice. The United States, for example, prohibits all forms of international bribery through the Foreign Corrupt Practices Act. In practice, these laws have helped modify illegal behavior in the international marketplace—foreigners who know that certain businesspeople are prohibited from providing bribes by their home countries have learned not to ask for one.

Nonprofit organizations, such as Berlin-based Transparency International, fight against corruption by providing greater visibility for international business transactions. For example, Transparency International has teamed up with the Paris-based Organisation for Economic Co-operation and Development (OECD) to fight international corruption by formulating a convention among the OECD member states that specifically prohibits the practice of bribing foreign public officials while conducting business abroad.

The rise of the Internet in the world economy has opened a Pandora's box of illegal and semilegal activities. From the online downloading of protected music to espionage, the possibilities are endless. Identity thieves, for example, use the Internet to obtain credit card numbers and Social Security numbers, which are actually worth more than the credit card numbers—especially if they can be linked with other valuable data about the individual's life. This information can then be used to establish a new identity, online or off, and commit all kinds of fraud. Even *rogue traders* have used computers and the Internet to carry out billion-dollar scams on their employers.

• •

INFORMATIONAL TOOL:

What are **rogue traders**?

Think of pirates of the financial seas. Rogue traders speculate without their employers' knowledge, taking unauthorized positions to make money in rising markets. If the positions lose money, spectacular losses can sometimes ensue.

Most notorious rogue trading scandals:

1995: Rogue trading at Barings Bank destroys major British financial institution. The oldest merchant bank in England, called "the bank to the queen," lost so much money that it was forced to be sold for a symbolic one British pound.

2001–02: Enron is forced into bankruptcy by traders taking speculative positions in energy markets. The firm's accountants helped to hide the losses from investors by using separate companies called special-purpose entities. Massive losses during a downturn in the market led creditors to demand repayment of loans, and the company was forced to declare bankruptcy. Investors in the companies' shares lost virtually everything.

2008: Rogue trading at Société Générale, a major French bank, leads to spectacular losses when unauthorized trading causes losses of approximately €5 billion, more than $7 billion at the time. The rogue trader's intimate knowledge of the bank's computers and accounting system allowed him to hide unauthorized trades that were more than *the bank's total market capitalization. Not only was the rogue trader fired, the president of the bank was forced to resign as well.*

• •

In addition to personal espionage, industrial espionage has found a valuable ally in the Internet. Electronic eavesdropping, for example, which includes the use of spyware to track companies' e-mail and Web activity, can provide a wealth of information about a rival company's business—and business strategy. In 2003, the U.S. Air Force sued Boeing after finding out that Boeing had used industrial espionage to acquire thousands of confidential documents during intense contract negotiations. It was also alleged that the U.S. Pentagon's computer was hacked into by the Chinese military in 2007—a charge vigorously denied by China, even though it had admitted to pursuing other activities of cyberespionage, like many countries around the world. According to McAfee, the information technology security company, more than one hundred countries are believed to be using the Internet for espionage in the 21st century.

Malware is another form of industrial espionage, resembling classic blackmail scams in many cases. By initiating a well-orchestrated attack on a company's reputation in the world marketplace, attackers can have this information spread around the globe within hours, using online chat rooms and blogs. The attackers often request a large sum of money to stop the campaign, or to avoid future campaigns from occurring.

Online robbery, like phishing, also uses the virtual economy for malfeasance. In 2007, for example, a teenager was arrested by the police in the Netherlands after he had cheated other players of the online game Habbo Hotel. Even though the property he stole was virtual, it had a street value of several hundred euros. By stealing the property from other players, he had broken the laws not only of cyberspace, but of the real world as well.

• •

INFORMATIONAL TOOL:

*What is **phishing**?*

Think of fishing for any information you can drag out of the Web. Criminally fraudulent, phishing consists of sending out e-mails that appear to come from legitimate sources—from your bank or credit card company, for example. The idea is to ask for personal information in order to solve a problem concerning the recipient's credit card or account with an online business like eBay or PayPal. The fraudulent e-mail sometimes even includes a hyperlink connecting the victim's computer to a site that is supposed to belong to the sender, but in fact belongs to the gang of scam artists—often based in another country. Once the information has been collected, the scammers use the information to make purchases or conduct other online business under the victim's name. The word phishing has its origins in the word fishing, transformed for the virtual economy.

• •

Some Internet scams use the victims' greed to generate illegal payments. One common scam begins in Nigeria—or other African countries where the laws are perceived as being lax. The e-mail tells the reader that an auditor or other government official has discovered a huge fortune waiting to be transferred abroad—after the owner and the owner's kin all died in a plane crash or some other disaster. The e-mail recipient is told that they will get a sizable percentage of the money if they agree to give their name as the next of kin. After many exchanges of e-mails, the foreign partner is then asked to supply a few thousand dollars to "grease the wheels" of the local officials. Then a few more thousand are needed for further "fees," and the game continues until the victim figures out the scam and backs out.

Not everything is negative in cyberspace, however. The

Internet can also help in the fight against corruption—by providing more transparency to the world economy. And with business dealings online and in full view of everyone, there are fewer opportunities for corruption and shady deals. Transparency International provides a yearly survey of 180 countries and territories over the Web, ranking them from most corrupt to least corrupt—at the top of the list in 2007 were Somalia and Myanmar, and the least corrupt were Denmark, Finland, and New Zealand. Some individuals have set up individual sites to fight corruption. A site in India, for example, was created by the wife of a famous anticorruption whistle-blower who feared for his life. By making him famous, the wife explained, she was able to protect him from the corrupt officials who wanted to silence him.

With more and more business being done over the Web, and less with anonymous cash trading hands, it has become much easier to trace the flow of money. Bank transfers, which are almost entirely electronic in the 21st century, can provide important tools for tracing the movement of illegally earned money from one part of the world to another.

• •

INFORMATIONAL TOOL:

What is **money laundering**?

The purpose of money laundering is to take illegally earned money—from the sale of illegal drugs, bribery, extortion, etc.—and pass it through a legitimate business operation. It used to be a pizza parlor; now it's a secret bank account or an offshore company in a place with little financial oversight. In the end, the idea is to make the money look like it's been earned legally so it can then be spent without arousing suspicion.

• •

Money laundering almost always accompanies illegal behavior in the expanding 21st-century economy. Criminals usually need to cleanse their "dirty money" of its illicit past in order to use it in the economy at large. Since there's a limit to the number of Miami condominiums or luxury automobiles a drug dealer can pay cash for without creating suspicion, illegal money somehow has to get into the banking system without creating suspicion of how it was earned.

One popular money-laundering scheme is to make hundreds of small deposits into a bank account rather than one single large deposit, which could attract the attention of law enforcement authorities. In the United States, for example, transactions over $10,000 are usually reported to the government. Another option is to mix the money with legally earned money—using a restaurant's bank account, for example, or any other business that generates a lot of cash. The idea is to get the money into a respectable bank, such as one in Switzerland or another legitimate financial center, and then transfer the money to where it can be used—to buy a nice house or a sports car, for example.

Once illegally earned money has been deposited into a legitimate bank account, it can then be transferred around quite easily—most international transfers are simply electronic messages sent from one bank to another. A bank in Miami, for example, usually transfers money to London or Hong Kong by using a correspondent bank that credits the account of one bank and debits the account of another. The sheer size of these legitimate international transfers—more than a trillion dollars a day on some days—makes it difficult to control money laundering effectively. The illegal transfers simply disappear into the sea of legal ones.

Another way criminals get illegal money into the banking system is to start by putting the money in a bank that asks few questions about the money's origin and then transfer it to more reputable financial centers. Switzerland used to be a popular center for illicit-money transactions because of its strict policy of bank secrecy. But after the banking scandals of the 1990s, the Swiss banks have insisted on a "know your client" rule and begun requiring all customers to sign a form declaring the beneficial owner—the real person behind the trust or company setting up the account. This policy may have gotten rid of some nefarious clients, but it increased the attractiveness of Switzerland as a banking center for those with legally earned money.

• •

INFORMATIONAL TOOL:

How does a **Swiss bank account** work?

Think of a safe with only two people knowing the combination. Switzerland is one of the few countries that has bank secrecy enshrined in law— the Swiss bank secrecy laws were put in place in the 1930s, and are still in place today. Under Swiss law, ostensibly to protect Jewish account holders, it's a criminal offense for someone who works in a bank to divulge the name of account holders to anyone—especially foreign governments and tax authorities. The only way Swiss banks can be forced to divulge the name of a client is if it can be proved that the client has committed a crime—but it has to be considered a crime in Switzerland. Fortunately for many people trying to avoid reporting income in their home countries, tax evasion isn't a criminal offense in Switzerland—it's a civil offense, and therefore not subject to criminal penalty. Usually, there are only two people in a private Swiss bank who know the identity of a numbered account holder: the account manager and one of the bank's partners—that's all.

• •

Other banking centers, such as those in the Caribbean or other *offshore* tax havens, are often criticized as being easy on money launderers. Law enforcement officials point out that once an offshore bank sends money to an onshore bank—in Singapore or New York, for example—it is often too late to track the money's source. Money launderers traditionally use several different bank transfers to get the money into the bank where they actually use it, by which time no one has any idea of where it originated.

What can be done? Some countries in the European Union have threatened to ban all transactions with banks that are known to encourage or turn a blind eye to money laundering. Others have proposed making international loans and aid contingent on honest banking standards. Several international groups—such as the Financial Stability Forum (FSF) and the Financial Action Task Force (FATF)—have made efforts to investigate money laundering around the world, and have even gone so far as to list the countries that are seen as being lax or uncooperative in dealing with the problem. After the terrorist attacks of 2001, they added terrorist financing to the list of activities to be monitored.

• •

INFORMATIONAL TOOL:

What is a **tax haven**?

Think of a country that has no tax man. Almost any country that offers minimal tax rates to individuals or companies can be referred to as a tax haven. By reducing or eliminating taxes on profit or income, tax havens, such as many islands in the Caribbean or Pacific, are able to attract business and large amounts of private wealth. Some countries, such as Monaco, are considered to be tax havens even though their tax rates aren't as low as many of the offshore islands'—they're just a lot lower than neighboring countries'. Many high-net-worth individuals, such as tennis stars

or Formula One drivers, make their home in tax havens such as
Switzerland and Monaco, often making deals with local tax authorities to
pay a lump-sum tax, regardless of how much they earn in any given year.

• •

Several offshore tax havens, such as the Cayman Islands, have made concerted efforts to clean up their banking systems, preferring to concentrate on creating a respectable low-tax environment for companies from around the world to set up business. Many offshore financial centers have no income tax or capital-gains tax, so companies and hedge funds from around the world have flocked there to avoid paying taxes, at least on part of the income that can be justified as being offshore and, therefore, out of the reach of the tax authorities in their home countries.

The amount of illegal money in the world economy that remains undetected is enormous. Estimates of illegal activity in the world economy range from 10 to 20 percent of total economic activity. And global money laundering moves anywhere from half a trillion to 1.5 trillion dollars a year—more than the entire economic output of most countries.

CHAPTER 15

WHAT IS THE BEST ECONOMIC SYSTEM FOR THE 21ST CENTURY?

IN THE CONVERGING 21st-century economy, it is becoming increasingly important to find a system that allows us to deal with the problems of the future, and not just those of the past. Is capitalism, for example, really the best economic system to ensure sustainable economic growth in the years to come? During the 20th century, you could look at the failed economic model used in the former Soviet Union and then at the glaring wealth found in any major city of the capitalist world and be reassured that the free-market system would always provide more of everything to its citizens—allowing them, in the end, to lead healthy, wealthy, and productive lives. But what about the communist "miracle" of 21st-century China? Or the social welfare free-market model found in Scandinavia and some developing countries? Or the oligarchic capitalism found in modern Russia?

• •

INFORMATIONAL TOOL:

*What is the difference between **capitalism** and **communism**?*

Think of parents who let their children participate in the family's decision-making process and those who don't. Capitalism is an economic system that permits individuals to decide how much to produce and at what price. Under the communist system, decisions are made by a central authority. Instead of letting the markets make the major economic decisions, the communist system puts economic and financial decision making in the hands of the government, or a powerful leader, in the hopes of creating a more egalitarian "communal" society. The utopian movement of Marxist communism began in the 19th century as an alternative to the abuses of the capitalist Industrial Revolution, when child labor, unsanitary work conditions, and worker abuse were rampant.

• •

When we hear the word *capitalism*, many think only of its Western form, with its emphasis on pluralism, the rule of law, independent media, free markets, and democracy. But the success of the Chinese economy and other rising Asian stars such as India, South Korea, and Vietnam lead us to examine capitalism variations more closely. Some economic analysts have noted that countries tend to blend at least two varieties of capitalism. The United States economy, for example, is a mixture of big-firm capitalism—which was prevalent in the first half of the 20th century, when big firms, such as General Motors and U.S. Steel, dominated the economic landscape—and entrepreneurial capitalism, with a preponderance of small businesses and entrepreneurs leading the economy forward. The combination of these two types of capitalism—with Microsoft and Google existing alongside thousands and thousands of dot com start-ups, for example—has allowed the United States and similar economies to create unprecedented prosperity, mainly by generating significant increases in productivity, on which most economic well-being is based.

In contrast, China, although nominally communist, has succeeded in blending entrepreneurial capitalism with state-guided capitalism—where major economic decisions are made by the central government—putting it on track to become one of the largest economies in the world. And Russia has ensured astounding economic growth—albeit mostly based on exports of raw materials—by mixing *oligarchic capitalism*, where the bulk of the power is held by a small group of entrepreneurs, with state-guided capitalism not unlike that which existed under the czars.

Every system has its advantages and disadvantages. The oligarchic capitalism of Russia did bring order to a chaotic post-Soviet economy, but growth has been slower than in the other BRIC countries—China, India, and Brazil. And Japan, where the government and big companies form complex networks of interlocking relationships, achieved enormous growth in wealth and prosperity during the 20th century. However, during the first years of the 21st century, Japan's growth rate was one of the slowest of any major country in the world economy.

In the case of China, the "social harmony" that allowed it to become an economic superpower has depended largely on an authoritarian power that would be completely unacceptable in most democratic societies. But China's openness to the world—at least in the areas of trade and development—may be the main reason for its economic success. China joined the World Trade Organization in 2001, while Russia's membership plans were still being formulated.

Chinese foreign interaction, from hosting the Olympics to allowing hundreds of thousands of students to study abroad, has allowed the Chinese economy to grow exponentially. Meanwhile countries like Russia and North Korea have remained relatively aloof—fearful of the influences and foreign control that too much openness could bring. Moscow's universities, for example, are almost completely staffed by Russian professors, while some of China's top universities nearly always hire professors from abroad.

Unfortunately, the environmental destruction that has accompanied China's rapid rise to wealth and prosperity has brought doubts to the viability of the Chinese model. In its drive to modernize and grow, vast areas of the landscape have been devastated, water has become scarce in many areas, and people have been relocated and resettled without having much say in the process. According to the World Bank, ten out of the world's twenty most polluted cities are found in China.

What can be done to provide economic growth while preserving the environment and respecting human rights? Some look to environmentally friendly Sweden and the *Scandinavian model*, which attempts to combine the entrepreneurial spirit of capitalism with the social safety nets found under the communist, or socialist, system. With cradle-to-grave health care, free education for all segments of society, and extensive welfare and unemployment benefits, Sweden provides one of the most generous social support systems of any country in the world. Virtually all of Sweden's citizens have health insurance, while in some countries, such as the United States, up to 30 to 40 percent of the population have had to go without.

In order to pay for all this government largesse, the Swedish tax rates, extending well beyond 50 percent for top earners, need to be high. But high tax rates often discourage people from working and producing. There is also the fear that overly generous welfare and unemployment benefits end up encouraging people to remain unemployed much longer than necessary. Nevertheless, Sweden maintains one of the highest standards of living in the world. In the end, the socially conscious economic models of some Scandinavian countries—as well as those found in parts of Asia and Latin America—may provide a viable alternative to the "pure" capitalist model found elsewhere.

In France, the economic model also has been changing. With a bloated bureaucracy and the value of state-owned enterprises amounting to more than four times the GDP—more than ten times greater than the amount controlled by the state in neighboring Britain—France has seen the need to try something new. For example, upon taking office, President Nicolas Sarkozy called for a return to entrepreneurship and a reduction of state spending and state control of the economic machine.

Converting state firms into limited and listed companies without selling off the government's share did little to change the relative power of the government in France's economy, however. In typical *dirigiste* fashion, the French government continued to use a state-controlled entity, called the *Agence des Participations de l'Etat (APE)* to oversee its vast holdings in such companies as France Telecom, Air France, and the producer of Airbus. This meant that the true reins of power were still held by the government in Paris, instead of ending up in the hands of the newly empowered entrepreneurs. Further efforts to restructure the French tax and social security systems—as well as loosen stringent labor laws that had been keeping many French companies from hiring new employees—met with stiff opposition from trade unions and employees keen to protect their jobs and generous tax-supported benefits.

• •

INFORMATIONAL TOOL:

What is **privatization**?

Think of a government's going-out-of-business sale. Privatization involves the selling off of state-owned companies such as railroads or electricity companies. Countries burdened by the debt and losses of poorly run public companies often turn to privatization to improve efficiency and get more cash into public coffers. The opposite of privatization is nationalization.

• •

Alternative or *fringe* economic systems can take many forms. In Israel, for example, a communal economic system has been built around the kibbutz, an economic community based on a mixture of collective labor, love of the land, and no-frills egalitarianism. During the last decades of the 20th century, many kibbutzim were closed as their system of decision making by committee led to declining profits, mounting debt, and an exodus of young members to more lucrative careers in town. Many former kibbutz residents traded the promise of lifetime security for the opportunity to earn higher salaries and own their own homes outside the kibbutz. But at the beginning of the 21st century, a renaissance of sorts has taken place, based on a mixture of free market and communal economic ideas. Younger residents were lured back with the promise of being able to purchase homes and keep a greater share of the income they generated each month. Some kibbutzim began selling off plots of land to nonmembers, who were allowed to take advantage of some of the kibbutz services—such as child care, schools, and access to the organic food produced on the farms.

On the other side of the Atlantic, some countries have attempted to create a socialist utopian system with the central government controlling all major means of production. Venezuelan leader Hugo Chávez, for example, has called for a "Bolivarian revolution"—modeled on the ideas of the 19th-century economic and political revolutionary Simón Bolívar. However, many of the aspects of Venezuela's "revolution" were modeled on Cuba's Marxist-Leninist economic model—a dictatorship of the proletariat that would, in theory, pave the way to true socialism, where the pain and inequities of capitalism would be replaced by the communist system, in which life would be organized on the principle "from each according to his abilities, to each according to his needs."

Chávez was greatly aided in his "redistribution" efforts by skyrocketing prices of il, Venezuela's major export. He also imported, at times, thousands of Cuban doctors to help out. Fortunately, Cuba was not lacking in educated health care personnel. Unlike the situation in many developing economies following the capitalist model, Cuba's system of free education and emphasis on higher education for all has allowed it to boast nearly 100 percent literacy and a surplus of doctors and scientists.

In many ways, all successful economies use a mixture of various economic models, and what needs to be determined in each case is the right mix, preferably the one that creates the best conditions for improving the quality of life of the people who live there. Vast cultural differences ensure that not all countries will thrive under any one particular system or mix of systems. In the end, it's up to the people to decide—if they're given the chance.

CHAPTER 16

OUTSOURCING AND IMMIGRATION— HOW HAVE DEMOGRAPHICS TRANSFORMED THE WORLD ECONOMY?

A T PRESENT BIRTH rates, only a handful of developed countries will avoid seeing their populations decline significantly over the course of the 21st century. In the European Union, for example, not one member country has a fertility rate that ensures a growing population over the next decades.

In some countries, populations are declining drastically. In Russia, for example, the average life expectancy of Russian men has fallen below sixty, and birth rates have reached historic lows. It is estimated that Russia's ninety-million-member workforce will be reduced by fifteen million by the year 2020—due mainly to heart disease, smoking, and rampant alcoholic consumption, which has accounted for over a million deaths a year, primarily among working-age men. At the beginning of the 21st century, the probability of an eighteen-year-old Russian surviving until retirement age was only 50 percent. According to the World Health Organization, the death rate of working-age Russians— mainly because of chronic diseases such as heart disease, strokes, and diabetes—is more than 1 percent per year, a rate much higher than in any other country in the world economy, including relatively poor countries such as Tanzania, Nigeria, and Pakistan.

In Japan, a fertility rate of less than 1.3 has also created a demographic time bomb. Over the next decades, the Japanese population is expected to shrink at a pace unseen in any developed country during peacetime. The percentage of elderly, age sixty-five or over, has risen from less than 5 percent after the end of the Second World War to more than 20 percent by the beginning of the 21st century—and an estimated 40 percent by the year 2050.

In Italy, Germany, Spain, Hungary, and many other countries in Southern and Central Europe, the story is the same. Despite generous social welfare payments to promote childbirth, not one country in Europe has a fertility rate higher than 2.0. Among developed nations, only the United States has a significantly increasing population—due mainly to immigration. In fact, without immigration, no country in the developed world will be able to fill the jobs needed to keep their economies strong and healthy.

It has been estimated that the United States needs to bring in more than ten million immigrants per year just to keep the ratio of workers to retired people steady. Essentially, in the wealthy countries of the world millions of well-paying jobs will go unfilled over the course of the next decades—and without immigration, there will be no one available to fill them. The influence of immigrants on economic growth in host countries can, therefore, be substantial. In the U.S. Midwest, for example, immigrants have revitalized many stagnating towns and rural areas. It has been estimated that 40 percent of the growth in home ownership in the United States during the first years of the 21st century was due to purchases by immigrants.

Contrary to popular belief, immigrants usually do not put much of a burden on their host countries' economies. And in many cases, unskilled immigrants help the economy by doing the jobs most people in wealthy industrial countries refuse to do.

An eighteen-year-old British college student may not think it is "trendy" to work in an old-age home, but for someone from Africa or south Asia, going to London to work, even in a retirement home, could be a dream come true. In the United States, immigrants provide an increasingly important source of educated labor as well. The H1B visa program, among others, provides immigration visas to highly skilled and highly educated foreign workers. According to Microsoft founder Bill Gates, the U.S. lead in high technology would be "seriously disrupted" without a steady flow of talented science, technology, engineering, and math graduates from abroad.

Immigration has significantly contributed to economic growth in almost every country where it occurs, primarily because the vast majority of immigrants move to their host country for one purpose: to work. In Spain, for example, the arrival of more than three million immigrants, mostly from Spanish-speaking countries in Latin America, has contributed billions of dollars to Spain's economic growth, allowing it to outpace almost all other European countries during the first years of the 21st century. Since many of these immigrants worked as nannies and maids, many Spanish nationals were able to leave home and reenter the workforce, reducing unemployment significantly.

Switzerland, which for decades has allowed foreign workers to come and work for nine-month stints, has benefited enormously from the availability of a labor force willing to do work that most Swiss would shun. Even though it refused entry into the European Union, Switzerland has signed several bilateral agreements with EU members during the first years of the 21st century, allowing it to join in the freely flowing EU labor market—eventually including workers from the ten new member nations to the east. Some countries, such as Great Britain and

Ireland, have based much of their economic growth on the avail-ability of new labor forces—coming mainly from Poland and the other countries of Central and Eastern Europe.

The vast amount of labor available in the developing world has only begun to be tapped. Like the great migrations from Ire-land in the 1850s and Italy in the 1880s, large numbers of semi-skilled and low-skilled workers in countries around the world are moving to higher-paying jobs far from home. The question is how to reconcile political pressures to limit the number of immigrants with the economic pressures of jobs going unfilled in important industries because of a lack of qualified personnel.

Another important factor to consider is the positive effect of emigration on the home country's economy. The amount of money sent home by immigrant workers more than doubled during the first years of the 21st century, reaching more than $300 billion before the end of the century's first decade. These *remittances* make up a sizable percentage of many home coun-tries' economies—more than 10 percent of GDP in many cases—contributing greatly to economic and political stability. Without the influx of money earned by citizens abroad, many developing countries' economies would decline and poverty rates would soar.

• •

INFORMATIONAL TOOL:

What are **remittances**?

Think of an immigrant worker going to a Western Union office to transfer part of his or her salary to family members back home. All money sent home by workers abroad is called remittances. *Most remittances go to developing countries, providing an important source of aid. In many cases, the amount of money sent home by citizens working abroad exceeds the money provided by rich-country aid. India, China, and Mexico are the countries receiving the largest amount of remittances—even though Latin America is the region receiving the most money in total.*

• •

In order to facilitate immigration and assuage those afraid of being swamped by hordes of foreign workers, some countries have put limits on the amount of time immigrants can stay—stints often range from several months to several years—and others have prohibited family members from joining the foreign workers during their stay. The "guest workers," like Germany's *Gastarbeiters* of the 1950s and 1960s, would be expected to return to their home country after a fixed amount of time, with no path for citizenship.

But how can countries ensure that immigrants return home when their stay is up? One plan forces them to return to their home countries by blocking a part of their salaries, allowing them to be collected only when the immigrants have returned home. Other countries refuse to allow immigrants to bring their families with them—forcing them to live sometimes for years away from their spouses and children. Statistics show that migrant workers, alone and isolated, are much more prone to alcoholism, drug abuse, and behavior leading to HIV/AIDS, which can be spread further when the migrants return home to their cities and villages in the developing world.

Basically, as long as huge disparities in wealth and income exist in the world—and as long as hunger and poverty are allowed to exist in the developing world—immigration, legal or otherwise, will be always be part of the world economy. It is important for authorities, therefore, to devise equitable systems for managing the flow of workers from one country to another. One solution is to rely on international organizations such as the

Office of the United Nations High Commissioner for Refugees (UNHCR) or the International Organization for Migration (IOM). Both organizations are based in Geneva, Switzerland, with the UNHCR being more active dealing with migration issues during times of war and natural disasters. In Europe, the Schengen Agreement has created a zone stretching from the Atlantic to the Russian border. The idea was to strengthen controls on the zone's outer borders while dismantling border controls inside—allowing people to move between member countries without passport checks in most cases.

• •

INFORMATIONAL TOOL:

What is the Schengen Agreement?

Think of a "United States of Europe" with no border controls within the free-movement zone. With the exception of the United Kingdom and Ireland, the Schengen Agreement—signed in two phases in 1995 and 2000—established a "border-free" zone covering almost all Western and Central European countries. The idea was to allow free movement of people while at the same time strengthening external border controls via the Frontex agency, harmonizing entry rules and requiring closer cooperation between the members' police and judiciary. Schengen members include almost all twenty-five European Union states—with the U.K. and Ireland opting out of most accords—and four non-EU members: Iceland, Norway, Liechtenstein, and Switzerland.

• •

Illegal immigration, the illicit transfer of workers from one country to another, is on the rise in most developed countries around the world—including Europe, where hundreds of thousands are smuggled in from outside the Schengen zone's borders annually. In the United States, it is estimated that there were more than ten million illegal immigrants at the beginning of the 21st century, with an additional four to five million dependent children.

According to some estimates, more than thirty million people are smuggled across international borders each year. Sometimes entire villages in poor developing countries pool resources to have friends and family members smuggled into wealthy countries abroad, expecting to be repaid tenfold when the money starts flowing in from lucrative jobs in the developed world. Illegal immigration also occurs among developing countries—for both economic and political reasons. In Syria, for example, millions of refugees from the war in Iraq were housed in "temporary" camps with little possibility of getting work permits that would allow them to get jobs, even menial ones.

Unlike migrations of the past, when great hordes of people crossed borders en masse, modern illegal migration mainly occurs clandestinely. People cross porous borders such as the Rio Grande between Mexico and the United States, or the border between the European Union's easternmost members and their non-EU neighbors in a wide variety of ways—on foot, in boats, or hidden in the back of trucks. For example, several illegal Iraqi immigrants lost their lives just outside Venice in 2007 when the truck they were hiding in turned out to be a refrigerated vehicle—they froze to death. According to the International Organization for Migration, there are between twenty and forty million "irregular" immigrants in the rich countries of the world, and the problem is only getting worse.

But what can individual governments do? Taking its cue from the system used by U.S. immigration authorities, the European Union announced plans in 2007 to institute a *blue card*, like the U.S. green card, which would bring in skilled workers to fill vacant jobs. In Germany, where tens of thousands of engineering jobs were going unfilled at the beginning of the 21st century, the ramifications were felt throughout the economy. Since one employed engineer generates approximately 2.3 jobs in other areas of the economy, it is estimated that the value of economic activity lost from unfilled jobs is more than $4 billion in Germany alone.

Instead of bringing in the worker to fill the job, some companies and countries have embraced another option: sending the job to the worker. Despite being criticized by many politicians as giving away jobs, outsourcing often provides a valuable economic service. Instead of wasting valuable human capital doing jobs outside the scope of the company's core business—bookkeeping, for example, or software development—companies outsource these activities to third parties.

• •

INFORMATIONAL TOOL:

What is **offshoring**?

Think of sending your shirts out to be laundered instead of having them washed at a relatively expensive Laundromat around the corner. Offshoring is the practice of moving a job to a country where wage rates are lower. Even though the terms outsourcing *and* offshoring *are often used interchangeably, there is a difference. Outsourcing technically refers to any job that is shifted to an outside firm, wherever it is located. Offshoring refers to those outsourced jobs located in another country.*

• •

Contrary to popular belief, outsourcing is not limited to low-wage, low-skilled work. Law firms, for example, have found that lawyers in India are just as capable of reviewing basic contracts or updating cases as highly paid American lawyers.

Given that junior lawyers in India rarely earn more than $10,000 per year and New York lawyers earn ten to twenty times that much, it makes economic sense to give the routine work to someone in India and let the New York lawyers concentrate on the high-end work—that often generates high fees. Lawyers in India are frequently more interested in working for a foreign firm because of the wide range of international legal activities they are asked to be involved in—and the $10,000 per year they earn in an outsourced job may be double or triple what they would earn at a local law firm.

The variety of outsourced work is expanding exponentially in the 21st-century economy. Call centers, in addition to providing technical support and reservations services, can also be used to provide online tutoring or language training. A company in India called TutorVista, for example, provides unlimited tutoring to students around the world for a monthly fee. Tutors are available around the clock, and tutorials can be arranged with a few hours' notice. Because the work is done online, with virtual whiteboards used to share information just like a blackboard in a traditional classroom, language barriers do not pose a significant problem. And if students are interested in brushing up on their English or Mandarin, tutors can be arranged for that as well.

Outsourcing can also work in both directions. In 2007, an Indian outsourcing company announced plans to set up several call centers in Ohio and one in the U.K. to take advantage of access to highly trained IT personnel and to provide work that can be done only *onshore*, such as contracts with government entities. From Ohio and North Dakota to Bangalore and Bangkok, in the 21st century any region with affordable salary levels can create jobs by offering an economical alternative to expensive work being done in the high-wage centers of the new world economy.

CHAPTER 17.

WHAT IS THE GREEN ECONOMY?

EVEN THOUGH SCIENTISTS and environmental activists had been warning of the effects of global warming for decades, it was only in the first years of the 21st century that governments and citizens began to realize the magnitude of the problem. A devastating worldwide food crisis and the near destruction of New Orleans by Hurricane Katrina served as wake-up calls. If global warming is to be reduced, significant changes are going to have to be made in the way the world economy operates.

What causes global warming? Essentially, an excess of particles in the earth's atmosphere. The presence of some particles is actually beneficial to the environment; without them, the earth's temperature would sink below freezing. These particles—mainly water vapor, carbon dioxide, methane, nitrous oxide, and ozone—cause a *greenhouse effect*, trapping some of the sun's rays and warming the earth just as a greenhouse creates a healthy environment for plants to grow. Unfortunately, economic activity over the past years has increased the amount of particles in the atmosphere drastically, leading to an exponential growth in the amount of greenhouse gases. Al Gore's documentary, *An Inconvenient Truth*, put the situation in easy-to-understand terms: Never before in history has so much carbon dioxide been released into the earth's atmosphere as during the last decades.

INFORMATIONAL TOOL:

What is a **carbon footprint**?

Think of the trail a comet leaves as it flies by. A carbon footprint is the measure of the amount of greenhouse gas released by a specific action. Even though greenhouse gases can be anything from methane to water vapor, every greenhouse gas that you cause to be released into the atmosphere by your actions—driving a car to work, buying a Big Mac—is translated to its carbon dioxide equivalent. The carbon footprint of eating a hamburger, for example, includes not only the carbon dioxide released into the atmosphere by the truck that transported the burger from the warehouse, but also the extremely potent methane gas released by the cow as it digests in the field.

The main contributors to the increase in carbon dioxide in the atmosphere are deforestation and the burning of fossil fuels. But other activities such as livestock farming have led to massive amounts of methane and other gases being released into the atmosphere as well. The United Nations Food and Agriculture Organization has pointed out that the livestock industry is responsible for up to one-fifth of the greenhouse gas emissions being put into the atmosphere—contributing, in many countries, more to global warming than transportation activities, such as car, truck, and airline emissions.

Why do modern industrial economies pollute so much? Essentially, because it is more expensive to clean up the pollutants than it is to dump them into the environment. It's as simple as that. No one wants to pollute, but environmental protection, like all other economic decisions, involves an economic trade-off. Companies, countries, and consumers now need to decide how much they are ready to pay to keep the environment clean and healthy. And this decision is, essentially, an economic one.

Unfortunately, most industrial nations have often treated the world's resources as if they were disposable commodities. This ignores a basic economic concept: that all factors of production—whether land, labor, or clean air and water—are scarce commodities and have an intrinsic "price" that should be factored into every business and consumer decision. Clean air and water were once thought of as limitless, but in recent years have been depleted by burgeoning populations and widespread industrial development.

Although this depletion is occurring around the world, in rich countries as well as poor, the effects of global warming will be felt much more in the poor countries of the developing world. In many developing countries, large portions of the population are rural—and earn their living from agriculture. A minor disruption in the supply of water that is used to irrigate crops can kill millions. In Bangladesh, the low-lying regions would suffer catastrophic floods with only a small rise in the level of the ocean. Ironically, the countries that will suffer the most from climate change are those that have contributed the least to global warming—and often have the least amount of resources to deal with the harm when it comes.

What can be done? Basically, there are only two ways to get consumers and businesses to reduce environmentally harmful activities. One is the "stick" of economic sanctions. The other is the "carrot" of economic incentives.

Economic sanctions are often the most effective way to change environmentally unsound practices. When a company is forced to pay for its pollution, it will think twice before discharging industrial waste into the air and into the water. Forcing a government to include the depletion of its natural resources in the calculation of economic activity—creating an *environmental GDP*, for example—could have a significant effect on public policy. And if consumers were forced to pay an eco-tax, which added environmental costs to the goods and services they purchase, many would alter their spending habits drastically.

• •

INFORMATIONAL TOOL:

What is **environmental GDP**?

Think of a special scorecard for environmentally friendly economic behavior. Instead of just adding up all the traditional economic activity— summarized in the gross domestic product ('GDP') figure that tells us how many dollars, yen, yuan, or euros were spent in a given economy in a given year—Yale and Columbia universities have devised an environmental performance index (EPI) that tracks six additional economic areas: environmental health, air pollution, water resources, biodiversity and habitat, productive natural resources, and climate change. The idea is to add pollution control and natural-resource management to the normal economic figures, providing an environmental GDP that can be used to track a country's total economic activity, not just how many cars are produced or video games are sold in a given year. See www.epi.yale.edu for a summary of each country's EPI score.

• •

A major effort to deal with global warming was undertaken when the Kyoto Accord entered into force in 2005, providing a framework for reducing the amount of carbon dioxide being released into the atmosphere. However, widespread reluctance to respect the rules of the accord—and the outright refusal of some industrialized countries, such as the United States, and some rapidly developing countries, such as China, to implement it—has led to an overall increase in the rate of pollution rather than the decrease that had been projected by the Kyoto Protocol.

The problems posed by global warming are global in scope, and global solutions are required. For example, the main cause of the increase in greenhouse gas emissions worldwide has been the increased use of fossil fuels to power industrial production and transportation—mainly in the developing world. In China, where the use of highly polluting coal has played a major role in meeting growing energy needs, a new coal-fired power plant was being built every three days during the first years of the 21st century. No solution is possible unless all countries agree to work together.

But the developing countries say that they have just as much right to economic growth and concomitant pollution in the 21st century as the developed countries enjoyed during their boom years in the 20th century. In fact, the amount of energy consumed in the developing countries, when viewed on a per capita basis, is still small when compared to the per capita consumption of energy in countries like the United States and Canada. India, for example, contributes less than 5 percent of the world's greenhouse gases, even though its population constitutes 17 percent of the world's total—and the average carbon emission per person is estimated to be 1.2 tons per year, compared to a world average of four tons, and twenty tons per person in the United States.

What can be done on a global level to reduce greenhouse gas emissions? One solution would be to provide subsidies and other economic incentives to develop new technologies. Another would be to replace some of the taxes on employment and production with taxes on pollution—principally carbon dioxide. This would have the double effect of stimulating economic growth through lower taxes in one sector and modifying behavior in the other by providing an economic incentive for businesses and consumers to reduce their consumption of fossil fuels.

* *

INFORMATIONAL TOOL:

What is a **carbon tax**?

Think of it as a fine for polluting. The idea behind a carbon tax is to make polluters pay for the environmental damage they cause—and, hopefully, get them to change their environmentally unfriendly behavior. A gas tax is one example of a carbon tax, even though it's not perfect—someone with a lot of money may just pay more to drive a gas guzzler, rather than switching to a lower-pollution-per-mile-driven vehicle. The perfect carbon tax would be one that's based on the exact amount of carbon dioxide released by a specific action. Carbon taxes have been used in the Scandinavian countries since the 1990s—with mixed results. By the first years of the 21st century, the Danish carbon tax had gotten companies to reduce their carbon dioxide emissions by nearly 15 percent with a minimal loss of economic output. The success of this effort was due in part to the Danish government's efforts to provide alternative sources of energy, such as wind power, and reduce reliance on coal-fired power plants.

* *

It has been estimated by the Intergovernmental Panel on Climate Change that the cost of consuming carbon would have to be raised by only $20 to $50 per ton in order to stabilize carbon dioxide concentrations in the atmosphere by the years 2020–30. This is entirely manageable in the current economic environment. The extra costs would raise the price of gas in the United States, for example, by an average of 30 cents per gallon, and electricity prices by 25 percent. The effect of such a tax on the world economy would also not be catastrophic, a slight drop of 1.5 percent of world GDP by the year 2050.

Unfortunately, a carbon tax—mainly because it uses the word *tax*—would not be easily accepted by skeptical governments and populations. An alternative solution is to institute a

cap-and-trade system of carbon emissions that is already func-
tioning in some countries around the world. The way it works is
simple: Governments or governmental agencies stipulate the
amount of carbon dioxide that may be emitted during a given
year and then allow the companies and people to trade their
"rights" to pollute.

• •

INFORMATIONAL TOOL:

What are **pollution rights?**

*Think of a get-out-of-jail-free card that can be traded if not used. The key
to pollution-rights plans, also called emission-rights plans, is to induce
companies and other polluters to decrease their output of harmful
emissions in the most efficient way possible. This is done by capping the
amount of pollution that is being produced by the economy at large and
then allowing companies and industries to trade their rights to pollute
among themselves. If a factory wants to pump out more carbon dioxide
than it was allotted, it would have to buy pollution rights from other
players. These pollution rights can be traded on exchanges such as
the Chicago Climate Exchange in a way that encourages productivity
without increasing the total amount of pollutants released into the
atmosphere.*

• •

As strange as it may sound, the trading of pollution rights
has received overwhelming support from many environmental
groups because it solves two seemingly irreconcilable goals: economic growth and a clean environment. Instead of simply telling
everyone in an economy they have to pollute less—which has the
effect of giving everyone in the economy the right to pollute a certain amount, regardless of how useful they are to the economy at

large—cap-and-trade schemes try to differentiate between "good" polluters and "bad" polluters.

An efficiently run wheelchair factory, for example, usually produces much less pollution per wheelchair than an inefficient one. Under traditional antipollution plans, the government would have reduced production at both plants. But under a pollution-rights plan, the efficient wheelchair producer could buy pollution rights from the inefficient one and use those rights to produce many more wheelchairs for a given amount of pollution—making everyone in the economy better off, with no increase in total emissions.

Providing an economic incentive to reduce pollution could have immediate and far-reaching effects. Selling unused pollution rights, for example, provides the biggest incentive of all: cash in hand. Companies and individuals will want to do everything they can to reduce their output of carbon dioxide if they get enough cash for their "unused" output of greenhouse gas. With the right economic incentive, polluters will finally begin to invest in new technologies to reduce pollution. And with more economic incentives on the horizon, clean-energy businesses will begin to receive funding from venture capitalists and hedge funds, who will invest in pollution control just like any other cutting-edge industry.

Some companies have set up entirely new divisions to come up with new ways to grow without increasing pollution. And many corporations around the world have created sustainability directors who oversee the effort to reduce pollution and attract "green" investors. The *Carbon Disclosure Project*, for example, allows companies around the world to report their emissions—allowing for investors to see which companies are making the effort to do business in environmentally friendly ways and which ones aren't.

• •

INFORMATIONAL TOOL:

*What is the **Carbon Disclosure Project**?*

Think of a scorecard for companies and organizations that keeps track of the amount of pollution they put into the air and water. The Carbon Disclosure Project (CDP) works with corporations to encourage them, via stockholder pressure, to integrate an effective carbon emissions reduction strategy into their business plan. Thousands of major companies, from Wal-Mart to Cadbury Schweppes to Procter & Gamble, have already signed on.

• •

Groups of investors, organized in part by the Investor Network on Climate Risk, can use their financial clout to encourage companies to change their pollution patterns—by investing only in companies that make concerted efforts to reduce carbon dioxide emissions. Participants in this project include some of the world's biggest fund managers, such as CalPERS, the Californian public employees' pension fund, and CalSTERS, the Californian teachers' pension fund. These two alone have more than $4 trillion available to invest in environmentally friendly companies.

Many banks now offer funds that channel investment to corporations involved in sustainable development—investing in companies involved in the business of recycling, for example, or companies that make wind-power generators or catalytic converters. Many of these funds have equaled—and, in some cases, exceeded—the returns from more traditional investment funds.

Another economically advantageous way to reduce carbon emissions is for companies in the rich world to earn emission-reducing credits for investing in energy-efficient projects in the developing world. This has led to the creation of a world market for carbon credits—in parallel to the cap-and-trade pollution credit market. The basic idea of this Clean Development Mechanism (CDM), developed under the Kyoto Accord, is to stimulate companies in wealthy countries to pay for carbon-reduction schemes at companies found in low-cost countries. The result is a significant drop in carbon dioxide being released into the atmosphere, at a much lower cost than if the wealthy country had to reduce the emissions itself.

Dollar for dollar, money invested in greenhouse gas reduction accomplishes far more if used to improve the efficiency of power plants in poor countries than if spent in wealthy countries like the United States, Japan, or the European Union members. It may sound like exploitation to some, but many companies in poor countries have made considerable profit by investing in relatively low-cost greenhouse gas reduction schemes—reducing smokestack emissions in China or India, for example. In the end, companies on both sides profit, and the world breathes a bit easier.

Another option is for companies and individuals to pay for green projects in parts of the world where the return—lower carbon dioxide emissions, for example—comes at a relatively cheap price. By paying for the reforestation of an entire island in Hungary, for example, the Vatican was able to entirely offset its carbon emissions in 2007 and become "carbon neutral." Following the Vatican's example, companies such as Dell and several European governments paid for trees to be planted in the same project. It is difficult to determine the exact contribution a tree provides in the fight against carbon dioxide production, although it is clear that young, growing trees provide much-needed oxygen and soak up large quantities of carbon dioxide—which can then be used to offset carbon dioxide production from sponsors' operations in other parts of the planet.

Tropical rain forests, an important source of oxygen production and carbon dioxide absorption, can also be protected via economic incentives. Many countries in the developing world lack the funds to prevent the destruction of tropical forests. In Brazil, for example, farmers in search of new land are often able to burn down large areas of the rain forest with relative impunity. And rain forests in other parts of the world are being felled to make way for timber and mining operations, cattle ranches, and sugar and palm oil plantations—mainly because there is no economic incentive to keep the forests intact.

With the European Union emissions-trading scheme requiring companies that have reached their carbon limits to purchase the right to emit more—at the rate of more than $20 a ton in some years—it sometimes becomes economically viable for them to pay countries like Madagascar to preserve tropical rain forests, providing much more of a return. In many cases a living tropical forest that is supported by purchases of pollution rights provides the owner with significantly more income per hectare than other uses such as farming or cattle ranching.

In Brazil, where the Amazon rain forest has been decimated by rampant burning—mainly by ranchers looking for new land on which to graze their cattle—an international program was set up to promote environmentally friendly economic development. This plan called for a combination of ecotourism, more sustainable cutting—such as cutting down only selected trees—and economically viable uses for the rain forest as a living entity. One plan encouraged local people to go into the forests to pick guaraná berries, a natural stimulant used in popular soft drinks. Harvesting the fruit of the trees, and not the trees themselves, ensured that the forests were kept alive for future generations—in addition to providing jobs for thousands of local inhabitants. Once it can be shown that precious wildlife and trees are worth more alive than dead, people can often be convinced to change their environmentally and economically destructive behavior.

Carbon sequestration is another valuable tool for reducing the amount of carbon dioxide entering the atmosphere. Most coal-fired plants—still the major source of energy for many countries—emit enormous amounts of carbon dioxide that can be trapped relatively easily. The question is, What to do with the trapped greenhouse gas? Some Danish and Australian coal-fired plants have found it relatively easily to store trapped carbon dioxide in unused oil fields or in limestone or sandstone cavities left empty by the extraction of natural gas. When stored properly, the trapped gases remain underground for millennia—or longer. The idea is that when they finally are released into the atmosphere, they won't cause the same damaging effect as they would today.

Another powerful economic incentive to reduce auto use and subsequent carbon dioxide emissions—at least in urban areas—is road pricing. Supported by the Sierra Club and many other environmental groups, road pricing consists of charging a fee for road use, with different prices for different times of the day and different pollution levels. By charging more to use roads during rush hour, for example, road pricing reduces congestion and delays and, in the end, reduces pollution.

• •

INFORMATIONAL TOOL:

What is **congestion pricing**?

Think of a parking meter for the open road. The idea behind congestion fees is to charge drivers to use public roads and highways. Since congestion has an economic cost—it is estimated that the seventy-two hours every driver in Los Angeles wastes in traffic jams annually cost the local economy

more than $9 billion per year—it seems only natural that an economic
solution be found. In London, for example, there is a congestion charge for
all cars that enter the city center. After the charge was instituted, there was
an immediate drop of seventy thousand cars a day in the affected zone—
and traffic congestion fell by 20 percent. Similar plans have been adopted
in Singapore, San Diego, and Stockholm.

• •

What can individuals do to reduce global warming? Basically, we all have to reduce our carbon footprint—the amount of carbon dioxide and other greenhouse gases that our everyday activities release into the environment. Beyond the obvious small steps—replacing incandescent lightbulbs with carbon fluorescent bulbs, for example, or reducing our consumption of fossil fuels—there are a number of major steps that every citizen can take, must take, to affect climate change.

Biofuels can provide an important alternative to fossil fuels and thus reduce carbon emissions, but the way they are produced has to be chosen very carefully. The production of ethanol in Brazil, for example, is a relatively eco-friendly way of producing fuel to power automobiles, since sugarcane is a relatively efficient vehicle for transforming the sun's energy into glucose. The production of biofuel in the United States, however, was based mainly on making ethanol out of corn—a relatively inefficient way of creating fuel.

In order to make the production of biofuels in the United States viable, the government has had to spend billions of dollars on subsidies. This not only led farmers to drain valuable aquifers for the water-intensive production of corn-based biofuel, it kept them from growing crops that could have been used to feed the world's hungry masses. United Nations representative Jean Ziegler has called the diversion of resources for the production of biofuel a "crime against humanity." Indeed, the skyrocketing prices of foodstuffs—going up more than 100 percent per year in some cases—has led to a worldwide outcry to reconsider the consequences of efforts to reduce carbon emissions and make America less dependent on foreign oil.

Basically, all the decisions we make in the 21st-century economy, even ones that affect global warming, have pluses and minuses. There is no absolute good—or absolute evil. We need to weigh the costs and benefits, and our own personal preferences, carefully. If we're told that becoming a vegetarian reduces as much greenhouse gas emissions as switching to a hybrid car—mainly because of the enormous amount of methane and other gases that are released into the atmosphere during the production of meat—which do we choose? If we don't have the money to spend on a new car, or if we're not inclined to become a vegetarian, we may have to look for other alternatives to reduce our carbon footprint.

In addition to being conscientious consumers, we'll have to be clever as well. It's not easy keeping track of all the pluses and minuses that our activities generate. If we switch from plastic to paper or cloth bags at the grocery store, for example, we'll definitely reduce oil consumption—by millions of gallons a year, if all consumers followed our lead. But the use of paper or cloth also has an environmental cost, although the environmental cost of cutting down trees that were planted specifically for cellulose production may not be as destructive as we assume.

Transportation costs also have to be taken into consideration in everything we do in the new global economy. As counterintuitive as it may seem, a bottle of Bordeaux shipped from France to New York City puts less carbon into the atmosphere than a bottle of wine trucked in from California—mainly because of the high efficiency of oceangoing transport. And a rose grown in Kenya has a smaller carbon footprint than a rose grown in Holland, even when sent by plane to a London or Paris florist—mainly because of the enormous environmental cost of heating and lighting Dutch greenhouses.

How do we, as consumers, best keep track of our green economy activity? One helpful tool is the use of carbon-footprint labels, provided by organizations like the U.K.-based Carbon Trust, that show us exactly how much carbon was released during every stage of the production process—including packaging, getting it to the store, and even disposing of it once we're finished using it. Such tools allow us to make environmentally smart economic decisions that may seem counterintuitive. For example, we may think we're doing the right thing by buying locally produced food at the supermarket. But it may be worth taking a second look at the carbon footprint, which could be greater than the footprint for more traditional food—especially if the locally produced food is transported to market by farmers using a lot of small vehicles, which end up emitting more carbon dioxide into the atmosphere, per item transported, than more traditional forms of transportation such as ships or trucks.

A healthy environment is not necessarily incompatible with a prosperous economy. Indeed, some of the world's worst pollution occurs in poor countries, such as those in the former Soviet bloc in Eastern Europe. Some of the world's cleanest air and water can be found in the richest economies—such as Canada, Denmark, and Sweden. By looking at the environment from an economic perspective, it becomes clear that protecting the earth and its air and seas is not only good for human health, it will also allow the world economy to achieve sustainable—and healthy—growth during the years to come.

CHAPTER 18

HEALTH, DEVELOPMENT, AND GLOBAL PANDEMICS—HOW HAS PUBLIC HEALTH BECOME A MAJOR FACTOR IN THE GLOBAL ECONOMY?

IMPROVING PUBLIC HEALTH used to be seen by world leaders as a desirable by-product of economic development, something achieved only after many long years of economic growth. But by working actively to improve public health— mainly by fighting the diseases that do the greatest harm, such as AIDS, tuberculosis, and malaria—the leaders of many developing countries have been able to greatly increase economic growth as well.

Reducing the number of sick people and reducing death rates around the world have allowed millions to reenter the work-force, take better care of their families, and lead more productive lives. But in many countries around the world where HIV has infected large segments of the population, whole economies are imploding. Because AIDS weakens and kills people in the prime of their working years, in many countries where AIDS is prevalent there are simply not enough working adults to make the economy function properly. And not only are the wage earners in many families absent, spouses and other family members are increasingly required to take time off from work to take care of the children left behind when one of the parents dies. In addition, when both parents die—unfortunately, the case of many families stricken by HIV/AIDS—many children are forced to drop out of school to help out at home. This causes severe economic repercussions, because without education and skills, they are unable to become productive members of society when they become adults—assuming they live that long. According to the World Health Organization, losses due to HIV/AIDS in sub-Saharan Africa are estimated to be at least 12 percent of the annual GNP. And economic development in malaria-free zones is at least 1 percent per year higher than in areas where malaria is endemic.

• •

INFORMATIONAL TOOL:

What are **chronic diseases**?

Think of the proverbial monkey on your back. You can live with chronic diseases your whole life—even though, if not treated properly, many can kill you. Major chronic diseases include heart disease, cancer, diabetes, and respiratory diseases such as asthma. According to the World Health Organization, chronic diseases account for more than half of all deaths worldwide—even though many of them could be prevented with proper care. The two other main categories of death are injuries such as those caused by violence and accidents, and communicable diseases such as HIV/AIDS, tuberculosis, and malaria. Although, with proper care, even AIDS can become a chronic disease—allowing patients to live long and relatively healthy lives.

• •

Although few countries spend as much as the United States does on health care—health-related expenditures in the United States had risen to 16 percent of total economic output during the first years of the 21st century—every country in the world economy has found that even small investments in health care can bring enormous, economically quantifiable results. For example, a few months after the government began providing antiretroviral treatment for AIDS patients in Kenya, more than 20 percent were back at their jobs. In India, where the states are in charge of health care, those that have spent significant funds on fighting HIV/AIDS have seen a sharp decline in infection rates. In Churachandpur, for example, health care and prevention programs have been able to reduce the percentage of pregnant women testing positive for HIV by half during the first years of the 21st century. In the eastern state of Manipur, however, HIV infection rates have risen during the same period, primarily because of needle swapping among drug users—the state borders Myanmar and the Golden Triangle opium-growing region—and because the state spends so little on education and prevention.

Worms and other neglected tropical diseases such as elephantiasis, dengue fever, and trachoma kill more than five hundred thousand people in the world every year. The majority can be treated for less than a dollar per person per year, but most countries where these diseases are prevalent, mainly in sub-Saharan Africa, just don't have the money or infrastructure to deal with them. This neglect brings severe economic consequences. For example, it has been determined that chronic hookworm infections in childhood reduce future earnings by 40 percent in those infected. In many countries, school attendance would increase significantly if children were simply given worm medications regularly.

With the World Health Organization estimating that every 10 percent improvement in life expectancy brings an approximate increase in economic growth of 0.3 to 0.4 percent per year, improving public care has become one of the major efforts of governments and international organizations in the 21st century. The

United Nations' Millennium Development Goals, for example, call for major improvements in child health care, longevity, and a dramatic reduction in deaths due to infectious diseases by the year 2015.

In response, many governmental and nongovernmental agencies have begun funding expensive campaigns to improve public health worldwide. The Global Fund to Fight AIDS, Tuberculosis, and Malaria, for example, has been funded with multibillion-dollar contributions from many governments around the world—including the United States, Japan, and almost all European Union countries. The number of people saved from early death by the Global Fund's efforts has been estimated to be in the millions, and increasing by one hundred thousand every month of the fund's existence.

Private efforts to improve public health—such as those funded by the Bill & Melinda Gates Foundation—have also made significant contributions to improving world health. The Gates Foundation has invested billions of dollars into the effort to prevent, and possibly eradicate, malaria—one of the biggest killers of children in the developing world. It is estimated that it would take up to $10 billion to pay for an effective eradication effort, including the cost of developing vaccines and paying for the purchase and distribution of the drugs and equipment, such as nets impregnated with insecticide. It has been discovered that when 80 percent or more of a village has nets, a barrier is created by the insecticide, which drives off mosquitoes for everyone. And if the disease isn't eradicated, it will cost an estimated $3 billion per year just to contain it.

Progress is being made. The United Nations Children's Fund (UNICEF) has determined that the number of deaths among children has recently fallen below ten million a year, the lowest rate since record keeping began. The improvement was attributed mainly to campaigns against malaria, measles, and bottle-feeding in developing countries without access to clean water. A big factor was the improving economies of many countries, such as China and India, where improved living conditions and more opportunities for economic advancement have led to decreased child mortality, of girls especially. Under the one-child policy in China, for example, girls began receiving health care and education equivalent to boys—giving them the wherewithal to marry later, have fewer children, and make sure more of them survive.

• •

INFORMATIONAL TOOL:

What is the **World Health Organization (WHO)**?

Think of a world doctor, taking care of global public health from a fancy office in Geneva. The World Health Organization, the public health arm of the United Nations, is based in Geneva, Switzerland, but has offices around the world, promoting public health in its 193 member countries. Its primary mandate is to provide public health assistance to member countries and help them attain their "highest possible level of health." One of the WHO's greatest successes was the eradication of the smallpox virus in the 1970s. Its primary focus in the 21st century is to strengthen health systems to be able to provide better care worldwide as well as preventing outbreaks of global pandemics such as HIV/AIDS, severe acute respiratory syndrome (SARS), and avian flu.

• •

Because of the increasing interconnectedness of the 21st-century economy, infectious diseases are spreading at a much faster rate—as well as becoming much more deadly. When the WHO issued its first report on infectious diseases in 1960, people still traveled by ship, and the number of diseases was small. Most of the diseases prevalent at that time—cholera, smallpox, typhus, yellow fever, etc.—were easily contained by quarantining the person or persons carrying the disease. Today, many of those 20th-century diseases are rare or are preventable by vaccines. Most diseases of the 21st century, however, are transmitted by people traveling in airplanes, with more than two billion passengers crisscrossing the globe every year. Consequently, the new pathogens are appearing and spreading at a much faster rate than at any other time in human history.

One of the biggest problems in combating global pandemics is the lack of cooperation among countries. When the SARS respiratory disease epidemic struck China in 2002, for example, local authorities didn't report the full extent of the disease immediately for fear of alarming the population and hurting the tourism industry. And in 2006, during a serious avian flu epidemic in Indonesia, authorities refused to share samples of the virus in an effort to develop a vaccine on their own—and earn considerable amounts of money from future worldwide sales.

In order to prevent competition among countries in developing vaccines, various international initiatives have been attempted to encourage more global health cooperation between countries. One such initiative is advance market commitments (AMCs), which provide guarantees, paid for by wealthy nations and private donors, to subsidize future purchases of vaccines developed to fight diseases in developing countries. In addition, an international treaty to encourage cooperation and improve reporting of epidemics was signed in 2007 under the auspices of the World Health Organization. These new International Health Regulations obliged governments to report any outbreak of infectious diseases at once and required them to share all information. The WHO was empowered by the new regulations to get information on outbreaks outside the normal channels—such as using the Internet or monitoring the local press or other nongovernmental sources—which allowed it to act proactively to stop infectious diseases from spreading and not rely on requests for action from governments in the affected countries. To oversee these efforts, a large control room was established at the World Health Organization headquarters in Geneva, with electronic screens and global satellite links—allowing it to monitor global public health events on a twenty-four-hour basis, and respond to new outbreaks of infectious diseases when they occur.

Economic incentives can also be valuable in encouraging countries and companies to work together to find solutions to global public health problems. Unfortunately, many pharmaceutical companies—faced with the difficulties of selling drugs and vaccines in poor developing countries—have not made much effort to find solutions to disease occurring in parts of the world where money is scarce, patents are not respected, and generic production is allowed.

Some public health advocates have actually encouraged countries to develop more generic drugs, even if they override patents—including those guaranteed by international agreements such as the Agreement on Trade-Related Aspects of Intellectual Property Rights (TRIPS). The drug companies point out, however, that unless they are allowed to make a profit from the drugs they develop, there will be a significant decline in research and development, reducing the number of lifesaving drugs that will be available to future generations.

One solution is for donors, such as wealthy countries or well-funded foundations, to purchase the patented drugs on the open market and distribute them for free to people in poor countries who can't afford them. Another solution is to use innovative funding—such as government-backed bonds or sur-charges on airline tickets—to fund vaccine research and vaccine distribution. Part of the airline surcharges applied in Chile, France, and Norway, for example, are used to fund UNITAID, a nongovernmental organization that purchases bulk quantities of vaccines and drugs and distributes them in developing countries. UNITAID's ability to purchase large volumes of drugs and diagnostics allows them to get lower prices—and as manufacturers increase their production, improving economies of scale, they may be more willing to offer drugs and diagnostics to the whole world at reduced prices.

• •

INFORMATIONAL TOOL:

*How are financial securities used to fund **immunization** in developing countries?*

Several innovative financial mechanisms, such as that of the Global Alliance for Vaccines and Immunization (GAVI Alliance), have been set up to fund vaccine research and immunization in the poor countries of the world. One system works like this: Rich-country governments provide financial commitments to GAVI's financing arm, the International Finance Facility for Immunization (IFFIm). These commitments are then used as collateral to facilitate borrowing on the international capital markets—mainly by issuing long-term bonds. Based on the legally binding commitments from rich donor countries such as Norway, the United States, and the other G7 countries, bonds issued by IFFIm have a relatively low rate of interest. And the funds they raise are used solely for vaccine research and distribution. The initial plan was to raise and distribute $4 billion between 2006 and 2016—more than the health budgets of all the world's poorest countries combined.

• •

Often dubbed *maladies of affluence*, chronic diseases such as heart disease and diabetes are no longer limited to rich countries. The number of deaths from chronic diseases in poor developing countries is already more than deaths from infectious diseases, and this number is climbing as the developing countries' expanding economies provide more disposable income. In Bangladesh and Indonesia, for example, the percentage of men who smoke was more than 50 percent at the beginning of the 21st century, exceeded only by the percentage of men who smoke in China—and in Egypt and Russia, people were spending more than 5 percent of their household income on cigarettes. In Mexico, increased access to sugar-filled drinks and processed food has led to the highest level of obesity in the developing world—exceeded in global terms only by its neighbor to the north. Four-fifths of all deaths in China are now from chronic diseases.

The rapid rise of chronic diseases has severe economic ramifications as well. The death rate for working-age people in developing countries—such as India, Russia, and Brazil—is three times higher than in wealthy countries. And since chronic diseases are, by definition, diseases that are not "cured" but are managed—often for the patient's entire life—the economic burden is enormous. Families in poor countries often spend their life savings looking after chronically ill family members, and children are often pulled out of school to help out.

The macroeconomic effect of global health has become a major issue of the 21st-century economy. GDP growth in some countries has been drastically reduced because of the toll of pandemics and chronic diseases. According to the World Health Organization, the annual reduction in world economic output just from heart disease, stroke, and diabetes will rise to hundreds of billions of dollars during the second decade of the 21st century. In Russia, the loss is expected to remove more than 5 percent from the country's gross domestic product. And in Botswana, where up to 40 percent of the adult population has HIV/AIDS, life expectancy is expected to drop to the mid-twenties in the coming years.

Basically, the failure to improve public health can have serious consequences for any country, rich or poor. And just like other global crises, such as global warming, currency melt-downs, and trade wars, the economic consequences of public health crises can be enormous—not only for the people stricken with sickness or disease, but for their families, their communities, and future generations as well.

EPILOGUE

AS I WRITE the last pages of this book, I'm sitting on the front porch of a farm in the interior of the state of São Paulo. It's a sultry summer evening and a vast, verdant landscape stretches out before me. Orange trees, fields of sugarcane and soy, grasslands and pastures extend virtually uninterrupted up to the Amazon forest, approximately a thousand miles to the north.

Unfortunately, the distance to the Amazon forest's edge is growing. Cattle farmers and loggers—some acting legally, some not—are clearing vast swaths of the rain forest. The farmers say they need new pastureland for their cows to graze in, their previous pastures having been put to other uses. As in many countries around the world, prime agricultural land in Brazil is now being turned over to grow crops that will be used to produce biofuels, ostensibly to prevent global warming—the same global warming that is being caused, in part, by the destruction of the rain forest.

Beyond this idyllic landscape, the world seems headed for chaos. In addition to the fallout from the global financial meltdown, more than thirty countries have put restrictions on agricultural exports after there were riots in many countries—mainly in Africa, the Caribbean, and Asia—over increasingly scarce supplies of food. Meanwhile airlines in North America have been widening seats to accommodate a population that is more than 50 percent obese or seriously overweight. All that extra weight being flown around has been estimated to cost the airlines hundreds of millions of dollars annually in additional fuel.

What can we do to make things right? It's a tough question. While some see globalization as the cause of the world's woes, I see it as the most effective solution to the world's array of serious problems: pollution, poverty, disease, malnutrition, and—increasingly—starvation. More than a billion people around the world lack access to clean water—the water in our toilets that we don't even let our pets drink is, in fact, cleaner than the water in many parts of the world.

Unfortunately, it's no longer an option to do nothing. Problems are not going to fix themselves on their own. One of the difficulties in approaching the complex economic issues of our day is that many effective solutions—reducing the use of automobiles, opening borders to trade, or improving chronic health care, for example—have been around so long that we tend to discount them as being flawed, at best, or simply irrelevant.

It has been widely reported that while a frog placed in a pot of boiling water will jump out, one that has been placed in cool water that is slowly heated will end up boiling to death. When confronted with the important economic issues of our day, it's important that we not sit idly by like frogs in incrementally warming water. The world economy has become so interconnected that no one can remain impassive when the financial world is imploding around us.

When banks and insurance companies in New York fail, the U.S. government is forced to turn to central banks around the globe—from Frankfurt to London to Zurich to Tokyo—to provide the liquidity to keep the world economy from collapsing.

In today's fusion economy, no single economy is immune to what happens in other parts of the world. A major financial institution in the United States that goes bankrupt because of investments in subprime mortgage securities can have enormous, unforeseen consequences for people everywhere. And often, it's not the politicians and business leaders who suffer the most when a company goes under. Consumers and investors can lose their savings, their jobs—and even their homes—when economies fall.

The converging global economy has made all of us participants and players—whether we want to admit it or not. And as we move into the heart of this turbulent 21st century, we're going to have to find a way to ensure economic health and economic growth without losing our souls or destroying the environment.

Perhaps by using the tools presented in this book, and by approaching the world's problems and opportunities from entirely new perspectives, we can find new ways to preserve this beautiful landscape stretched out before me and still make the world a better place to live—for ourselves and for the billions of new members of the expanding global economy.

Why not give it a try? What have we got to lose?

GLOSSARY

The media is bombarding us with a plethora of economic terms: "Subprime Mortgage Crunch Leads to Global Credit Crisis," "Growth Stocks Outpace Tech Sector," "Carbon Footprints Increasing in Developing World," "G8 to Meet Tomorrow, Riots Expected." The jargon of the world economy fills our newspapers, magazines, Web sites, radio and TV programs—even our water-cooler conversations. If we are going to be effective consumers, businesspeople, and voters, we're going to need to be fluent in the language of the 21st-century economy. This glossary provides a list of the most commonly used terms. More detailed descriptions of the major terms can be found in the 101 Informational Tools scattered throughout the book. Like the items in the glossary, they can be referred to periodically to refresh your memory.

401(k). Many governments allow individuals to set aside some income for retirement—tax free. In the United States, this deferred income is put in special tax-free accounts called 401(k)s. In the U.K., it's referred to as a Self-Invested Personal Pension (SIPP), and in Switzerland it's referred to as the *Dritte Säule*, or "third pillar." All of these plans are meant to supplement retirement funds coming from the government or from company-financed plans.

Acquisition. In the mergers-and-acquisitions game, a company can acquire another in two ways: by using its own stock and merging the two companies' assets, or by using cash or borrowed money to acquire the company by buying enough stock to give the investor control. An acquisition is often referred to as a *takeover* and can occur as a friendly takeover, one that takes place with the acquired company's approval, or as a hostile takeover, where the acquired company is taken over by an investor buying enough of the company's shares—usually against the wishes of the acquired company's board of directors.

Affiliate. A company that is related to, but not necessarily controlled by, another is referred to as an affiliate. In the world of e-commerce, the word *affiliate* is often used to describe a broad range of relationships among entities—such as companies that arrange their Web sites to link to another in an effort to generate more business. If an affiliate is owned or controlled by another company it is referred to as a *subsidiary*.

Algorithmic Trading. In a few milliseconds large preprogrammed computers use algorithmic trading programs to buy or sell stocks before the market has had a chance to react to new events. This allows them to take advantage of discrepancies in the market caused by unexpected world events and fluctuations in the markets. By the beginning of the 21st century algorithmic trading was responsible for 30 to 50 percent of all trades on America's stock exchanges.

Alpha. *Alpha* is the term used to describe the extra return that fund managers are perceived to provide to their clients. When compared to standard market indexes such as the Dow Jones Industrial Average and the S&P 500, many fund managers do provide higher returns, but many do not. In any event, fund managers insist on receiving, in many cases, several percentage points in fees for the extra alpha they provide to investors.

American Depositary Receipt (ADR). ADRs are repackaged shares from foreign stock markets, sold in the United States as dollar-denominated securities. The idea is that investors in North America can invest in foreign-currency stocks in the same way they buy domestic ones. Even the dividends are paid in U.S. dollars.

Appreciation. A rise in an asset's value. Appreciation is the opposite of *depreciation*, which describes the decline in an asset's value over time and is accounted for as a loss in the company's books. Appreciation is accounted for as income or *capital gain* (see **depreciation** and **capital gain**).

Arbitrage, Arbitrageur. An arbitrageur attempts to spot discrepancies in world markets, and then acts quickly to buy where a product is sold cheaply and sell where prices are higher. Unlike *speculators*, who take risks (see **speculator**), an arbitrageur tries to avoid risk by buying and selling at the same time, operating in markets around the world where small discrepancies temporarily exist.

Asset. Like gold, cash, or a valuable building, on a company's balance sheet assets are seen as positive—as opposed to liabilities, such as debt, which are seen as negative. The assets of most companies are divided into financial assets such as cash and securities, fixed assets such as buildings and computers, and intangible assets such as goodwill and patents.

Asset Stripping. Asset strippers acquire an undervalued company and sell off its assets, such as real estate or undervalued subsidiaries, often making more money than it took to acquire the company to start with. Asset stripping often allows takeover artists to generate the cash that is needed to pay off the debt incurred to acquire the company.

Audit. In accounting, an audit is meant to guarantee the fairness and accuracy of a company's financial statements. In the 21st-century economy, audits are becoming broader in scope. An environmental audit provides an overview of a company's environmental performance—certifying compliance, for example, with accepted standards for limiting pollution and reducing the firm's carbon footprint.

B2B, B2C. Transactions on the Web limited to businesses (a car supplier selling mufflers to a Tennessee automaker, for example) are referred to as B2B—business-to-business transactions. A transaction involving a consumer buying over the Web (an individual buying a book at Amazon.com, for example) is referred to as a B2C—business-to-consumer—transaction.

Balance of Payments. The sum of a country's international trade and investment is called its balance of payments. This measure includes all of the country's transfers of goods, services, and money. It is called a balance because purchases and sales of goods and services to and from other countries are always compensated by transfers of money flowing in the opposite direction. This measure is often confused with *balance of trade*, which is not the same—the trade balance measures only the trade in goods, not services or investments (see **merchandise trade balance**).

Balance Sheet. A balance sheet is a "snapshot" of a company's financial situation at a given point in time. A typical balance sheet has two sides, with assets—what the company owns—on the left and liabilities—what the company owes—on the right. Whatever's left after subtracting liabilities from assets is called *shareholder's equity*, the extra value of a company that belongs to the company's owners.

Bank for International Settlements (BIS). Based in Basel, Switzerland, the Bank for International Settlements is often referred to as the central banks' central bank. It serves as a clearinghouse for transactions between the world's central banks in addition to regulating the international banking system.

Bankruptcy. A company that can't pay its debts on time is said to be bankrupt. In many countries, bankrupt companies are given an opportunity to try to pay off their creditors. This is called Chapter Eleven in the United States. If the company can find no other solution to its problems, it goes into liquidation (Chapter Seven in the United States), and its assets are sold to pay off the debts.

Barter. Exchanging one good for another, bartering allows businesses or consumers to avoid problems posed by inconvertible or hard-to-exchange currencies. Although a bit of an anachronism in modern times—where money-based commerce is ubiquitous—

bartering still exists—especially with Web-based exchanges offering new opportunities to trade goods over the Internet. In addition, some countries tax income from barter differently than that derived from money-based exchanges, providing an advantage to trading rather than buying and selling.

Basis Point. A hundred of these make up a percentage point. Financial markets have become so finely tuned that it is no longer enough to talk about interest rates changing one-quarter or one-sixteenth of a percent. They now move by as little as one-hundredth of a percent, or one basis point. Using this system, a half of a percent rise in a bond's yield, 0.5 percent, would be fifty basis points.

Bear Market/Bull Market. A bear market, like the proverbial grouchy ursine, is said to be headed down. A bull market, roaring ahead, is used to describe a market headed up. A market experiencing more than a 20 percent decline in value is usually defined as a bear market.

Bearer Bond. Like a cashier's check, a bearer bond is the payment of choice for villains in James Bond movies, because it, in theory, will be cashed with no questions asked—there is no owner's name or registration required for a bearer bond. The holder of the bond owns the right to receive the full value of the bond, plus interest payments.

Big Bang. In Japan, the term *big bang* was used to refer to a package of financial reforms undertaken in 1998. The earlier deregulation of London's securities markets was also referred to as the big bang, which led to an explosion in banking and financial services that let many international banks and trading houses move to the city to take advantage of the opportunity to trade large blocks of international securities with no restrictions or taxes imposed by local authorities.

Bilateral Trade Agreements. Two countries agreeing to liberate, or reduce, the trade in goods and/or services (see also **multilateral trade agreements**).

Black Market. Whenever a desired good or service is prohibited by law, black markets tend to spring up to satisfy frustrated consumer demand. In some countries, currency exchange is prohibited, so black markets—sometimes called *parallel markets*—are set up to take over the normal role of banks or currency traders. The black-market economy consists of all those underground transactions, such as prostitution, illegal drugs, pornography, and gambling, that, because of their illegality, are out of the control of local officials.

Blue Chip. AAA, top-of-the-line. A blue-chip stock is one that is considered the best in its field. The term originated in the game of poker, where the most expensive chips are usually the blue ones.

Blue Collar/White Collar. Workers who perform manual labor and earn an hourly wage are generally referred to as blue collar in reference to the color of shirt many manual laborers used to wear. White-collar workers, professionals earning a salary, have higher levels of education and are usually higher-paid than blue-collar workers.

Bond. The ultimate IOU. A bond is a piece of paper that says, "I, the borrower, promise to pay you, the bond owner, a certain amount of money in the future." Originally bonds had little slips of paper attached to them, called coupons, that gave the owners the right to periodic interest payments. Bonds around the world are now traded on electronic exchanges, but the payments of interest are still often referred to as *coupon payments*.

Botnet. A shortened form of the words *robot network*, the term *botnet* is used to describe a network of hijacked "zombie" computers that are joined together to send waves of unwanted mail, swamping the target's site and bringing online business to a standstill.

Brady Bond. Named after the former U.S. treasury secretary Nicholas F. Brady, Brady bonds were repackaged debt from developing countries, mainly in Latin America, that had fallen on hard times. The advantage of Brady bonds was that they had the backing of U.S. Treasury securities, which made them more attractive to international investors.

BRIC. The term BRIC, first used by the U.S. bank Goldman Sachs, is an acronym for the four largest developing countries of the 21st-century economy: Brazil, Russia, India, and China.

Bridge Loan. Like a bridge over troubled waters, bridge loans are meant to cover short-term borrowing needs. The idea is to allow the borrower to arrange more long-lasting financing. The International Monetary Fund and the Bank for International Settlements in Basel often provide bridge loans to poorer countries trying to arrange bailouts with the World Bank or other long-term lenders.

Broker/Dealer. Just as a real estate broker brings together buyers and sellers for a nice commission, a securities broker acts as a go-between in financial transactions. Most brokers—stockbrokers, for example—receive a fee that is based on the volume of securities traded. A securities dealer, like a car dealer, has an inventory of securities that can be sold to investors for a fixed price. Some investment bankers fill both roles and are called, not surprisingly, broker/dealers.

Bubble. Economic bubbles, also referred to as *market bubbles*, are defined by hugely overpriced stocks or other items of value. Bubble economies have existed since the beginning of markets. In Holland, during its golden age in the seventeenth century, there was the tulip bubble, and in America in the late 1990s there was the dot-com bubble. Even the Great Depression of the 1930s was partly the result of the crash of greatly overpriced shares in 1929. The housing bubble in the United States and other countries at the beginning of the 21st century led to sharp losses, especially in subprime mortgages when the bubble burst (see **irrational exuberance**).

Budget Deficit. A country runs a budget deficit when revenues, usually in the form of taxes, are exceeded by spending. Just like anyone spending more than they earn, a country running a budget deficit has to make up the difference by borrowing money. In the case of the United States and other creditworthy countries, deficit spending is allowed to go on virtually unchecked—as long as there are enough domestic and foreign investors willing to subsidize the nations' spendthrift ways by buying government debt.

C2C. Transactions on the Web between consumers. Consumer-to-consumer transactions—like buying and selling DVDs or football tickets on eBay—may involve paying a fee to the Web site but are essentially limited to transactions between individuals, not businesses (see **B2B, B2C**). The ultimate C2C market can be found on no-fee sites, such as Craigslist, Loquo, or Kijiji.

Call Option. A call option gives the holder the right to buy something at a certain price. Like other options, a call option can usually be exercised only for a certain length of time. An investor who thinks the price of an asset will go up will want to buy call options—as the underlying security goes up in price, so does the call option. Investors can buy *put* and call options (see **put options**) on such diverse instruments as stocks, commodities, and foreign currencies.

Capital. Capital and labor are the two main inputs into economic production. Capital is generally defined as equipment, such as machines or roots, but capital can also include managerial expertise, corporate culture, infrastructure, and the firm's capacity for innovation.

Capital Account. All international flows of money-related investment are grouped together in a country's capital account. Capital accounts typically include *foreign direct investment* and portfolio investments such as purchases and sales of stocks and bonds. The capital account and the *current account* (see **current account**), when added together, determine the country's total international economic activity, referred to as *balance of payments* (see **balance of payments**).

Capital Gain. When securities or real estate are sold at a profit, the difference between the sale price and the original purchase price is called a capital gain. Capital gains are usually taxed at different rates from other income such as interest and dividend payments.

Capitalism. The economic system that lets people and the markets make the decisions on how much to produce and at what price. Capitalism is based on the idea of private ownership, as opposed to *command* or *communist* economies, where the assets are in the hands of the state.

Capital Market. Where investors go to buy or sell securities. A capital market is an exchange or a group of exchanges where bonds and other debt instruments are traded. Most capital-market trading is done on trading floors in banks scattered around the world and connected electronically to form one big international market.

Carbon Footprint. The amount of greenhouse gases, translated into their carbon dioxide equivalent, released by a specific action or series of actions is referred to as a carbon footprint. Even though they may include emissions of other greenhouse gases such as methane or sulfur dioxide, most carbon-footprint calculations translate emissions to their carbon dioxide equivalent— in order to make it easier for us to understand and compare. Concerned citizens of the world economy can calculate their carbon footprint by going to Web-based carbon footprint calculators, such as that provided by the Conservation Fund, an environmental organization based in Arlington, Virginia.

Carry Trade. The practice of borrowing money in one currency, where interest rates are low, and investing it in another currency, where interest rates are high. The idea is to earn money on the *spread*, the differential between the two interest rates.

Cartel. A group of companies or countries that band together to control production and prices. The most famous example of a cartel in the global economy is the *Organization of the Petroleum Exporting Countries* that was set up in the 1960s to coordinate the production of oil—thus allowing them to better control the market.

Cash Cow. A company or a stock that generates a continuous flow of cash is often called a cash cow. Cash-cow industries or products usually don't need any marketing or special attention—they just keep churning out the profits.

Cash Crops/Food Crops. In many developing countries, a food crop is often used just for feeding the farmer's family. If there is a surplus, it can be sold for cash—hence the name *cash crop*. This surplus can provide income that allows the family to buy clothing, shelter, and other items necessary for survival.

Cash Flow. A quick measure of the money coming into and going out of a company. Cash flow tells investors what the company has done over a specific period of time without accounting tricks such as depreciation and other write-offs.

CD. See **certificate of deposit**.

CEO. The big cheese. The chief executive officer is the person who runs the company. The CEO reports to the board of directors, who are chosen, in theory, to look after the stockholders' best interests. In many European countries, there are two types of boards: the executive board, overseen by the CEO, and the supervisory board, elected directly by the shareholders.

Centrally Planned Economy, Planned Economy. Where the bureaucrats get to make the decisions. In a centrally planned economy, the state has the authority to decide who produces what and at what price it will be sold. Resource allocation is also decided by the central decision-making bodies. Centrally planned economies are also called *command economies* or *planned economies*.

Certificate of Deposit (CD). Certificates of deposit are similar to normal savings accounts in that they are insured (by the FDIC in the United States, for example) and offer a fixed rate of interest. They are usually issued for a fixed term, however—from three months to five years in most cases. Investors are expected to hold CDs until maturity, when they are paid back and the money can be invested again.

CFO. The chief financial officer is in charge of the money coming into and going out of a company. The CFO usually reports directly to the CEO.

Chaebol. In South Korea, many companies are grouped together in conglomerates, or *chaebols*, that sometimes become quasi-monopolies. After the economic crisis of the late 1990s the Korean government moved to dismantle them.

Chairman, Chairperson. The person in charge of overseeing what a company's management does. The chairman/chairperson and the board of directors are supposed to look after the best interests of the company's shareholders, who appoint them for fixed terms—and pay them a yearly fee.

Chapter Seven, Chapter Eleven. The two most important concepts in the book of *bankruptcy* (see **bankruptcy**). In the United States, Chapter Eleven (called *administration* in Britain) allows a bankrupt company to try to work out its troubles. Chapter Seven (called *receivership* in Britain) is when the struggling company is liquidated—the assets are sold off to pay as many of the company's debts as possible.

Collateralized Debt Obligation (CDO). Collateralized Debt Obligations are loans with an asset or a bundle of assets attached to them. The assets can be anything from a flow of money—from mortgage payments, for example—to a flow of goods, such as a farmer's future crops or an orange juice factory's future production. The loan and the assets are usually grouped together and sold as a single instrument. A CDO can also be based on a wide variety of assets, such as a series of different mortgages with different levels of risk.

Command Economy. An economy where the government calls all the shots, from how much is produced to how much consumers are allowed to purchase (see also **centrally planned economy**).

Commercial Bank. A bank that takes deposits and makes loans is commonly referred to as a commercial bank. Although commercial banks—at least in Japan and the United States—have traditionally been prohibited from getting involved in investment banking activities such as selling stocks or underwriting new issues of securities (see **IPO**), by the beginning of the 21st century, they were allowed to do almost everything their investment-banking brethren do (see **merchant bank, investment bank**).

Commercial Paper. Short-term securities issued by banks, corporations, and other commercial entities. Commercial paper is a relatively safe investment because of the short-term nature of the risk. Commercial paper is normally used not to finance long-term investments, but for short-term uses, such as financing the purchase of inventory or to increase working capital. Commercial paper can consist of promissory notes, drafts, checks, or certificates of deposit.

Commodity. Raw materials, such as oil, gas, or orange juice, are referred to as commodities. Most commodities are easily traded on the world markets because they are relatively homogeneous: Gold from Siberia is basically the same as gold from Nevada. Commodities can be traded in many ways: in spot transactions, for immediate delivery; or in the futures market, where they are traded at a fixed price that will be effective at some later date. Other commodities include corn, silver, tin, beef, wheat—and the proverbial pork bellies.

Common Market. The former name of the European Union (see **EU**). The idea, at the time of the EU's founding, was to allow goods and money to flow, unrestricted, across member countries' borders. When the original European Economic Community became a political as well as an economic entity, it was decided to change its name to the more generic European Union.

Communism. Communism's goal is to create a society with total equality. This utopian idea, developed during the 19th century by economic philosophers such as Friedrich Engels and Karl Marx, was based on the desire to remedy the abuses of the capitalist system—especially egregious during the early years of the Industrial Revolution, when child labor, unsanitary work conditions, and abuse of workers were rampant.

Comparative Advantage. The law of comparative advantage is based on the synergies produced when each country in the world is allowed to produce and export the goods and services it produces most efficiently. In the end, the theory goes, everyone will be better off.

Constant Proportion Debt Obligation (CPDO). First created in

2006, constant proportion debt obligations are structured-finance investment vehicles that are somewhat similar to *mortgage-backed securities* in that their value depends on the creditworthiness of borrowers. CPDOs' values, however, are based not on the creditworthiness of mortgage holders but on the creditworthiness of major corporations. Even though they were rated AAA by major ratings agencies, CPDOs crumbled in value during the financial meltdown in 2008.

Consumer Price Index (CPI). The index of prices in the U.S. economy. Referred to as the *retail price index* in Britain, the CPI summarizes the prices of a basket of goods and services that a typical citizen would buy over the course of a given year.

Convention on International Trade in Endangered Species of Wild Fauna and Flora (CITES). Along with the United Nations Environment Programme (UNEP), the CITES organization regulates the trade in endangered species of fauna and flora. By controlling the sale of ivory, for example, CITES is able to reduce poaching. CITES makes a distinction between animals that need to be protected by a total ban on trade and hunting, called Appendix I, and those species that can be "harvested" in sustainable numbers, called Appendix II.

Convergence. Individual countries often have divergent economic needs in different areas, so governments try to homogenize the economy as a whole by converging economic policy. Just as it's hard for the Fed to balance the needs of each region of the United States—California could be booming, for example, while the Midwest stagnates—it is extremely difficult for the European Central Bank to accommodate the needs of the various countries of the European Union. Central banks try, therefore, to make the different economies converge as much as possible, especially in the areas of inflation, growth, and unemployment.

Convertible Bond. To make bonds or other securities more attractive to investors, companies sometimes make them convertible, allowing investors to exchange them for something else of value, usually the issuing company's shares. A convertible bond is often comparable to a stock option: The owner has the right, but not the obligation, to trade the bond into a company's shares at any time.

COO. The chief operating officer is the person who's in charge of overseeing a company's operations, usually second in command to the CEO.

Core Inflation. *Core inflation* refers to the rise in prices over time of the most relevant components of economic behavior, such as consumer goods and housing prices. It excludes the more volatile components, such as food and energy (see **headline inflation**).

Corporate Finance. When companies or governments need to borrow large amounts of money, they usually turn to investment banks to help them find financing at an attractive price. The goal of a corporate finance adviser is to find the right mix of bonds, equity, swaps, or other forms of financing that allow the borrower to secure funding at the lowest possible cost.

Corporate Governance. The rules that govern the way corporations are managed and controlled are referred to as corporate governance. It basically refers to the relationship among the company's stakeholders—shareholders, management, and the board of directors—but may include the company's relationship with customers, employees, suppliers, banks, regulators, and the community at large.

Corporate Social Responsibility. See **socially conscious investing**.

Correction. A temporary market drop. As opposed to a *crash*, which is expected to last over a longer period of time, a *market correction* is the way economists describe a short-term decline in the value of stocks or bonds.

CPI. See **consumer price index**.

Creative Destruction. New technologies tend to push out old ones. Joseph Schumpeter's theories, developed back in the 1930s, foresaw the 21st-century New Economy revolution. Schumpeter believed that economies grew by leaps, and if businesses didn't adapt to new technologies, new products, and new ways of producing and distributing goods, they would be destroyed—or, more mildly put, go out of business.

Credit Crisis, Credit Crunch, Liquidity Crisis. A credit crisis occurs when banks and other financial institutions refuse to lend money—even for short periods—to otherwise creditworthy borrowers. Although most credit crises have resulted from central bank restrictions on lending, the credit crisis, or "credit crunch," of 2008 occurred when bank lending froze up during the global economic meltdown.

Credit Default Swap. A credit default swap is a derivative that works basically like an insurance policy. The seller agrees to indemnify the buyer if a specified bond defaults or if a specified financial institution goes bankrupt. At the beginning of the 21st century, large investors, such as college pension funds, bought trillions of dollars' worth of credit default swaps, assuming that they were buying a guarantee that their investments wouldn't disappear in the event of a financial meltdown. When the markets crashed in 2008, however, some insurance companies that had issued CDSs had to be bailed out—or be declared bankrupt themselves.

Cum. In Latin, *cum* means "with." A bond with a warrant still attached to it is referred to in the markets as *cum*. A stock sold with the dividend still to be paid is traded as *cum dividend*.

Currency. A euro, a yen, a buck, or a pound—printed money is the currency of all advanced economies. Currencies are printed by central banks and monetary authority backed by nothing more than the good faith of the issuing authority. In the United States, the treasury used to provide the option of exchanging dollar bills for gold. Since 1971, this is no longer the case. Nowadays, most major currencies are worth only what other people or businesses are willing to pay or trade for them.

Current Account. The measure of a country's international trade in goods and services over a given period of time. Current accounts measure *visible trade*, such as rice and television sets, as well as *invisible trade*, such as banking services and movies. The current account also includes financial transfers, such as money sent home by citizens working abroad and interest paid on foreign debt. The current account is balanced by the country's *capital account*, which adds up all international purchases and sales of financial assets such as stocks or bonds.

Datsu-sara. The Japanese had to invent a new word to describe the once rare event of a manager who left a company to go work somewhere else. With today's global economy, however, an employee is not expected to be a *sarariman*, working for the same company forever. *Datsu-sara* literally means "corporate dropout."

Davos. See **World Economic Forum.**

Dealer. See **broker/dealer.**

Debenture. A debenture is a bond backed only by the good credit of the company issuing it. The purchaser relies on the full faith of the issuer to be paid back, which means that they are paid off only after other, more senior debt has been paid off. *Subordinated debentures* naturally provide a higher rate of interest to reward investors for the higher risk.

Debt/Equity Ratio, Debt Ratio. A good way to judge a company's health is to look at how much it owes and how much it owns. The basic idea of a debt ratio is that if a company owes too much money to creditors it will have a hard time staying afloat in troubled times. In many New Economy companies, debt ratios are extremely high, often because assets and income (in the beginning, at least) are relatively low. A start-up company often needs many years to begin showing a profit.

Debt Glut. During the meltdown of the credit markets following the subprime mortgage defaults of 2007 and 2008, many banks were faced with a glut of *commercial paper* that investors refused to buy. Some banks took this debt onto their own balance sheets, in effect buying the short-term bonds and other instruments that they had issued on behalf of corporations and other entities.

Default. When a company—or a country—is unable to pay its creditors on time, it is said to be in default. Interest payments on notes and bonds are usually the first to be stopped by a cash-strapped borrower. If no solution is found, the borrower is forced to declare bankruptcy. A country in default sees its credit rating plummet and often finds it difficult to get more money from international investors.

Deficit, Deficit Spending. Almost too good to be true, deficit spending allows you to spend more than you earn. In the world economy, there are two kinds of deficits: *budget deficits* and *trade deficits*. A government is said to run a budget deficit when tax revenues are not enough to cover spending. To overcome this, governments issue debt—such as treasury bonds—to provide the funds they need to continue their profligate ways. In a worst-case scenario, a government can simply print up more money. A trade deficit occurs when a country spends more on imports than it earns from exports.

Deflation. The opposite of *inflation*. Deflation occurs when an economy slows down to the point that prices—usually measured by a basket of goods and services—decline. It is an extremely rare event, because most producers are reluctant to lower prices. Japan is one of the few countries during recent years to suffer from deflation.

Demand. Demand is an important aspect of economics, relating primarily to consumption. Essentially, demand tells us what consumers or businesses will buy at a given price. Economists use supply-and-demand curves to explain the concept that when producers raise prices, consumers lower their purchases—demand falls. Conversely, when prices are reduced, demand increases.

Depreciation. Accountants refer to the reduction of an asset's value over time as depreciation. For example, as a car or computer loses its value, its value is depreciated in the company's books. Tax authorities often allow companies to treat depreciation as a cost of doing business, thus reducing taxable income. Therefore, companies prefer to depreciate as much as they can, as early as they can, to take advantage of the opportunity to reduce their tax bill.

Depression. A prolonged economic slowdown is defined as a *depression* if it lasts for more than two or three quarters. A depression is usually marked by a steep decline in production and demand. As a result, stock markets drop, companies go bankrupt, and unemployment usually rises. Governments try to avoid depressions by providing economic stimuli, such as increasing government spending or allowing the money supply to rise. The Great Depression of the 1930s, caused in part by trade wars, made it clear—even then—how interconnected the world economy is.

Deregulation. *Qué será, será*—Whatever will be, will be. When governments want to encourage competition and make economies more productive, they often deregulate, removing restrictions on companies' behavior. After deregulation, previously state-owned companies such as airlines or cable-service providers are allowed to make their own decisions on prices and markets, regardless of the effect on consumers.

Derivative. A financial instrument that gets its value from other financial instruments. A derivative such as a call option will increase in value whenever the value of the underlying security on which it is based goes up. It may sound like a house of cards, but derivatives allow people to invest in profitable ways. Basically, derivative investors get more bang for the buck when the underlying instrument changes value, but they can lose big if the market turns against them (see also **stock option**).

Devaluation/Revaluation. The decision to raise or lower a currency's value is usually not taken lightly. Governments usually prefer to use open-market purchases and sales or alter interest rates to regulate their currency's value on the international markets. However, when speculators and other international investors begin dumping a currency they perceive to be weak, a government is sometimes forced to devalue, letting the currency fall to a new, more sustainable level. Devaluations have occurred everywhere over the past years, from Argentina to China, and from Turkey to Thailand. China was actually encouraged to revalue its currency in the early years of the 21st century—the yuan was priced too low, according to many experts, leading to excessive trade surpluses and angry trading partners.

Diminishing Returns. Consumers and producers tend to pay a lot for their first purchase—the first iPhone, for example, or a new tool for the factory. But the law of diminishing returns shows how subsequent purchases need to be encouraged by ever-declining prices in order to keep sales up. Offices and factories are also subject to the laws of diminishing returns. When the first new machine is installed, productivity increases rapidly—just imagine the result of installing the first computer in an office that previously used hand calculators—when additional machines are installed, however, productivity still increases, but not as significantly.

Dirty Float. See **managed float.**

Discount Rate. The interest rate that the U.S. Federal Reserve, America's central bank, charges on loans to member banks. This rate is set periodically by the Fed in an attempt to influence interest rates throughout the economy, thus allowing the Fed to control economic growth. The discount rate is often confused with the Fed funds rate, although only the first is directly determined by the Fed (see **Fed funds**).

Disinflation. A bit of an oxymoron, *disinflation* refers to a slowdown in the rate of inflation, which is a rise in the prices of a basket of goods and services. Basically, under disinflation prices still rise, but not as quickly. Not to be confused with *deflation*, which is a decline in prices.

Dividend. A payment to the company's shareholders. A dividend occurs when a company has made a profit and, instead of investing the money back into the company, it decides to pay it out to the company's shareholders.

Division of Labor. A butcher, a baker, a candlestick maker—when an economy divides up work, letting each worker do what they do best, things usually get done more efficiently. The same concept can be applied to the world economy, letting some countries excel at making one thing and others at something else (see **comparative advantage**).

Doha Round. The World Trade Organization's attempt to organize a global trade agreement was initiated in Doha, Qatar, in 2001. The primary purpose was to get the rich industrialized countries in Europe and North America, along with Japan, to remove barriers to trade in agriculture, and the developing countries to remove barriers to trade in manufactured goods.

Dormant Account. An inactive bank account. In most countries, after a few years, dormant accounts are closed and the money is handed over to a government agency. In Switzerland, however, many accounts left dormant after World War II were inactive, earning little or no interest until the 1990s, when international pressure forced the Swiss banks to reveal that thousands of these accounts were still around. The Swiss banks made a billion-dollar settlement with international authorities to get part of the money to Holocaust survivors and their heirs.

Double Deficit. When a government overspends it is said to run a *budget deficit*. A *trade deficit* occurs when a country "spends" more than it "earns" on the international marketplace. A double deficit occurs when a country runs both deficits simultaneously. Double deficits are also referred to as *twin deficits*.

Dow Jones Industrial Average (DJIA). The Dow Jones index is one of the most watched market indexes in the world. Even though it tracks the prices of only thirty or so stocks, it is seen as one of the best indicators of how the market as a whole is doing. It used to include only "old economy" stocks from the New York Stock Exchange. Then it began to add NASDAQ New Economy shares, such as Intel and Microsoft. The Dow Jones group also produces indexes for many other types of stocks, including transportation and utilities.

Downsizing. The term *downsizing* was first used in the 1970s to describe the practice of companies of laying off large numbers of employees, usually in an effort to reduce costs and, consequently, increase profits. Unfortunately, it doesn't always work. Losing experienced employees often leads to decreased productivity, and lower morale often leads to losses instead of profits.

Dumping. The sale of goods or services at a price below cost. Dumping doesn't really hurt anyone, since the consumers buying the product are certainly happy to pay less than they normally would. But when a foreign producer is found to be engaged in dumping, local producers cry foul and usually get the government to provide sanctions (see **tariffs**) to get the offending country's producers to stop selling products abroad too cheaply. The American government, despite its claims to be a leader in trade liberalization, has often used dumping as an excuse for high tariffs on everything from steel to ethanol.

Earnings. A company's proverbial bottom line. Earnings are what is left after subtracting all expenses from revenue. Earnings are sometimes also referred to as *net income* or, more simply, *profit*.

ECB. See **European Central Bank**.

Econometrics. The scientific use of statistics and mathematical formulas to develop and test economic theories. Econometricians use complex models to simulate real-life situations and test the effects on economic behavior of a wide range of variables, such as interest rates, taxes, and investment incentives.

Economic Fundamentals. See **fundamentals**.

Economy of Scale. "Many hands make light work." *Economy of scale* describes the benefit of making a lot of something at one time. Essentially, the average cost per unit goes down as you produce in larger numbers. The Industrial Revolution was based on the idea of producing in large numbers, which meant that the costs of producing something were spread out over a large number of products or services (see **division of labor and comparative advantage**).

ECU. The European Currency Unit (ECU) was created by the countries of the European Union (before the establishment of the euro) to facilitate accounting between member states. It was based on a basket of currencies from each of the EU member countries. (see **euro**). The ecu was also the name of a gold coin used in France during the Middle Ages.

EFTA (European Free Trade Association). The four Western European holdouts to the European Union—Switzerland, Liechtenstein, Iceland, and Norway—decided to form their own free-trade union and take a wait-and-see policy on joining the EU, choosing to take advantage of access to the EU market through separate trade agreements.

Elasticity, Elasticity of Demand, Elasticity of Supply. The economic term that refers to the propensity of a behavior to change, or *stretch*, over a given period of time. *Elasticity of demand*, for example, describes how much the demand for a given product will change if there is a change in the product's price. A shopper with a high elasticity of demand would tend to rush out and buy a product as soon as it goes on sale. A shopper with a low elasticity of demand tends to keep buying the same products at the same store—even when they could be had at a lower price in another store down the street.

Emerging Economies. See **developing economies**.

Emissions Trading. The basic idea of emissions trading is to provide economic incentives to reduce carbon dioxide and other greenhouse gas emissions—the major cause of global warming. The idea behind emissions trading is to *cap and trade*, which means setting limits on the amount of greenhouse gases that can be emitted by a sector or the total economy—and then allowing individual players to trade their "pollution rights," achieving a rational and economically viable approach to reducing pollution.

Equilibrium. Economics is based on the theory that all forces in an economy move toward equilibrium. When the price of a product is too high, for example, people tend to reduce their purchases. In order to sell more inventory, therefore, producers have to lower the price until demand and supply match each other. Equilibrium exists for most economic concepts, such as savings, investment, and employment.

Equity. *Equity* means ownership. On a company's balance sheet, equity refers to the part of a company that belongs to the shareholders—after all the liabilities have been subtracted, of course. A company's *net worth* is also referred to as *stockholders' equity*.

EU (European Union). The European Union—previously called the European Economic Community, European Community, or Common Market—began as a simple customs union in the 1950s. The original idea was to do away with barriers to trade between the member countries. Eventually, this community evolved into a broader union, with common political, social, and economic policies.

Euro. The euro was created by the European Union on January 1, 1999, when eleven countries fixed their currencies to a totally new unit of exchange. From that point on, the national currencies of Germany, France, Italy, Spain, Portugal, Ireland, Austria, Finland, Belgium, Luxembourg, and the Netherlands existed no more. Euro notes and coins were put into circulation. Britain, Denmark, and Sweden opted to retain their own currencies. Since then, Greece, Slovenia, and Malta have joined the *euro zone*.

Eurodollar. A currency abroad. Eurodollars are U.S. dollars that are held in bank accounts outside the United States. The prefix *euro*- is used to describe any currency held outside its country of origin, even if the country isn't in Europe. Japanese yen held in Singapore, for example, are referred to as *euroyen*, just as British pounds held in Canada are called *europounds*. And what do you call a euro that is held outside Europe? A *euroeuro*, of course.

Euromarket. The restriction-free market for securities trading, centered mainly in London, is referred to as a euromarket. The Eurobond market, for example, allows issuers and investors to buy and sell a wide variety of securities—free from the restrictions and taxes of local authorities.

European Central Bank (ECB). Based in Frankfurt, the European Central Bank was set up when the euro was created in the late 1990s. Its mission is to oversee economic and monetary policy in the countries that have adopted the euro. The ECB has supplanted most of the activities of the various countries' central banks (such as the Bundesbank and the Banque de France). It was clear that without a common interest rate and monetary policy, the individual member states would all tend to go their own way in charting economic policy, and the new common currency would have little chance of success. The head of the ECB is appointed by the various countries that make up the *euro zone* (see **euro zone**).

Euro Zone. The euro zone is made up of the fifteen countries that use the euro: Austria, Belgium, Cyprus, Finland, France, Germany, Greece, Ireland, Italy, Luxembourg, Malta, the Netherlands, Portugal, Slovenia, and Spain. Montenegro and Kosovo decided to use the euro as their primary currency, even before becoming members of the European Union.

Ex. The Latin term meaning "from" is used to describe bonds or other securities that have had their warrants removed. A stock that is sold *ex* is one that has already had its dividend distributed to a previous owner (see **cum**).

Exchange Rates. The value of currencies worldwide is determined by their exchange rates. Since currencies have no value other than what they're worth in terms of other currencies, the exchange rate tells you what each currency is worth at a given point in time. A Norwegian krone, for example, is worth a fixed amount of euros—or dollars or yen. Exchange rates are constantly readjusted to keep them in line with the other currencies' values.

External Debt. See **foreign debt**.

Fair Labor Association (FLA). One of the many human-rights organizations active on college campuses, the FLA attempts to build coalitions of companies, consumers, and social activists to find solutions to the sweatshop conditions in factories in many developing countries. The idea is to get consumers to support the group's efforts to establish rules governing such areas as freedom of association, minimum wages, maximum working hours, sanitation, and worker safety.

Fairtrade, Fairtrade Labeling Organization (FLO). Fairtrade Certification, provided by the nongovernmental organization FLO-CERT, identifies products that meet previously agreed-upon environmental and labor standards. FLO-CERT uses independent auditors to ensure that producers of everything from bananas to sugar and tea are produced according to standards set by a sister organization, FLO International.

Fannie Mae, Freddie Mac. The Federal National Mortgage Association (Fannie Mae) and Federal Home Loan Mortgage Corporation (Freddie Mac) were set up by the United States government to provide banks with a way of passing on outstanding home mortgages—freeing up cash to be loaned to other homebuyers. Although both institutions are nominally private, with shareholders just like any other privately owned company, they have the implicit backing of the U.S. government—which means that they can rely on the government bailing them out if things go badly. During the subprime mortgage crisis in the United States, the outstanding loans on Fannie Mae's and Freddie Mac's books were devastated by rapidly declining home prices. The money loaned out was in many cases more than the home was actually worth, called *negative equity*, which led the U.S. government to step in and cover the losses.

FDI. See **foreign direct investment.**

Fed, Federal Reserve Bank. The United States' central bank, the Federal Reserve manages the money supply, regulates the banking system, and acts as a lender of last resort to banks in trouble. The Fed is meant to be relatively independent: It answers to no one, except in periodic reports to Congress. The seven members of the Federal Reserve Board are appointed by the president.

Fed Funds. The interest that banks in the United States charge on money loaned overnight to other banks. It's called the Fed funds rate because the money being loaned between banks is usually kept at the Federal Reserve. When a bank has excess reserves at the Fed, it can loan this money to other banks that may need it to meet the Federal Reserve's strict reserve requirement. The Fed funds rate is often confused with the *discount rate*, which is, in fact, set by the Fed. Although heavily influenced by the Fed's policies, the Fed funds rate is actually set by the banks themselves.

Federal Open Market Committee (FOMC). U.S. economic and monetary policy is controlled, in large part, by a small group of Federal Reserve board members who meet on a regular basis to chart the course of the nation's—and often the world's—economic growth. The FOMC sets certain growth targets, including money supply, inflation, unemployment, etc. The minutes of FOMC meetings are released to the public on a regular basis.

Financial Action Task Force (FATF). Based in Paris, the Financial Action Task Force is an independent organization that examines tax havens around the world and issues regular reports on which countries are cooperating in the fight against money laundering. It is an arm of the *Organisation for Economic Co-operation and Development.*

Financial Stability Forum. Based in Basel, Switzerland, the Financial Stability Forum was set up by the *G7* to promote financial stability and other matters of concern to the international markets. One of their tasks is to keep an eye on money laundering worldwide.

Fiscal Policy. In contrast to monetary policy, which is mainly in the hands of central bankers around the world, fiscal policy is in the hands of each country's government, which gets to decide how much to tax, how much to spend, and how much to borrow (see **monetary policy**).

Flextime, Flexitime. Instead of requiring fixed eight-hour days—

from nine to five, for example—some companies allow employees to choose their hours. Often they are required to be at work during a "core" period in order to facilitate interaction with other employees, but are otherwise free to come and go as they please. The term *flextime* was derived from the German *Gleitzeit*, which means "sliding time."

Flight Capital. Fearing impending economic turmoil or government policies that may threaten savings, citizens and companies often send money to financial havens outside a country in times of crisis. This flight capital sometimes amounts to a large percentage of a country's total wealth. Latin American citizens, for example, during times of high inflation, have bought U.S. dollars and euros and sent them to bank accounts abroad—sometimes in defiance of currency-exchange laws. Attempts by governments to limit the transfer of money abroad often end up encouraging capital flight—exactly what they are trying to avoid.

Floating-Rate Note (FRN). Just like a home loan with an adjustable interest rate, a floating-rate note is a security that has its interest rate adjusted periodically, usually reflecting changes in interest rates in the economy at large. Most floating-rate notes use LIBOR, the London Interbank Offered Rate, as a reference for determining the interest rate to be paid to the holder. Adjustable-rate home loans usually are tied to the prevailing corporate loan rate (called the *prime rate* in the United States). Banks and investors prefer the price stability of floating-rate notes because during periods of widely fluctuating interest rates the interest rates on FRNs change accordingly, keeping the price—or total value of the loan—stable.

Flotation, Listing. A *listing*, or *flotation*, refers to a company's shares being quoted or listed on the "board" of stocks that are officially traded at a stock exchange. The purpose of an *IPO* is to float all or part of a company's shares on a public exchange—and receive a big payment from the sale of the new company's shares.

FOMC. See **Federal Open Market Committee.**

Foreign Debt. Sometimes called *external debt*, a country's foreign debt consists of all money that is owed to creditors abroad. This debt can be owed by individuals, companies, or even the government. The International Monetary Fund provides guidelines on how to calculate foreign debt, defining what gets included and what doesn't. Debt owed by residents to nonresident creditors is included, for example, but only if the creditor's center of economic interest is located abroad.

Foreign Direct Investment (FDI). When a foreign firm buys a domestic one, or even a controlling share of the company's stocks, it is accounted for as foreign direct investment. FDI often provides needed capital to companies and countries that is more long-lasting than *hot-money* investments, which come in and go out at a moment's notice. FDI can often provide needed foreign expertise and new business practices. In some countries FDI accounts for up to half of all company ownership.

Foreign Exchange, F/X, Forex. Currencies are traded on a twenty-four-hour-a-day basis on forex exchanges, usually located on bank floors in major financial capitals around the world. Foreign exchange trading is unique in that there is no intrinsic value for the items being bought and sold. Each currency is quoted in terms of other currencies. A dollar, for example, is quoted in terms of how many euros or yen or pounds or yuan it is worth (see **currency**).

Foreign Reserves. Foreign exchange reserves, or *forex reserves*, are the foreign currency and other reserves such as gold and *standard drawing rights* held by a country's central bank. Traditionally, most countries have held the bulk of their foreign reserves in U.S. dollars that were used to back the liabilities, such as local currency issued or reserves put on deposit by financial institutions or the country's government. Since the beginning of the 21st century, however, many central banks have diversified their foreign reserves positions to include large portions of euros, yen, and other international currencies.

Forest Stewardship Council (FSC). The watchdog of the world's forests. The Forest Stewardship Council was set up by the *World Wildlife Fund* to provide consumers and businesses with an official seal of approval for purchasing tropical woods. The FSC seal certifies that wood or wood products have been harvested in ways that ensure sustainability. Instead of clear-cutting, for example, the FSC encourages selected harvesting, cutting only selected trees in a forest to keep the forest—and the surrounding biosphere—intact.

Forward Markets, Forward Trading. A *forward contract* fixes the price of a transaction to be executed at a specific date in the future. A wheat farmer, for example, can sell next year's harvest by going to the forward markets to find someone who will agree to set a price today. Unlike futures contracts (see **future trading**), which are traded on exchanges with fixed prices and dates, forward contracts are tailor made to accommodate the needs of both the buyer and the seller.

Freddie Mac. See **Fannie Mae**.

Free-Market Economy. Where the decisions are made by the market, not the government. The idea of a free-market economy is to provide consumers and businesses with the best products at the best prices. In contrast to centrally planned economies, where decisions on how much to produce and how to distribute that production are made by the government (see **centrally planned economy**), a free-market economy lets the markets decide everything, from prices to production.

Free Trade Area of the Americas (FTAA). In 1994, Western Hemisphere leaders decided to join together all of the disparate economies and trading groups, from the Yukon to Tierra del Fuego, and create a Free Trade Area of the Americas, which would eventually encompass all of the free-market economies of North, Central, and South America. Unfortunately, political infighting and entrenched special interests have kept the venture from becoming much more than an idea.

Friction. *Friction* refers to impediments that may keep consumers or businesses from buying a particular good or service. Basically, less friction leads to higher demand. Online music sales, for example, languished for many years because the songs purchased were subject to restrictions such as DRM, digital rights management, which limited the number of times consumers could recopy them or share them with their friends. When these restrictions were done away with, sales soared.

Friedman, Milton. The best-known free-market economist. Milton Friedman, Nobel Prize winner and University of Chicago economist, did more than almost anyone to promote the idea that free markets are the best way to make difficult economic decisions. The freedom to choose is the goal of Friedmanian economics: If consumers are allowed to buy what they want and producers are free to sell what they want, the world will be made a better place for (almost) all.

FTAA. See **Free Trade Area of the Americas.**

Future Contract, Future Trading. A future is a security that can be bought or sold, just like a stock or bond. It is, essentially, a contract to buy or sell a commodity or a financial instrument at a fixed price and at a fixed time in the future. Futures are unlike *forward contracts* in that their terms are standardized. Because the time and date on future contracts correspond to other contracts, they can be traded on exchanges around the world.

G7, G8, G20. The first group of nations set up to coordinate economic strategy was the Group of Seven, or G7, which included Canada, the United States, Japan, France, Germany, Italy, and the United Kingdom. The leaders of the seven countries meet regularly to discuss a wide range of political and economic issues. When Russia joined the ranks of capitalist economies, it was invited to become an associate member of the G7, leading to the formation of the G8. Not to be outdone, developing nations set up a forum to group together the major economies of the developing world into a similar organization called the G20, consisting of a varying number of members—the name came from the date it was founded, August 20, 2003. The core leadership of the G20 consists of four of the largest countries: Brazil, China, India, and South Africa, which are sometimes referred to as the G4. Another completely separate G20 consists of nineteen relatively rich countries plus one, the European Union representative. It was set up in 1999 to promote sustainable growth in the global economy.

GDP, GNP. See **gross domestic product.**

Gearing. Gearing gets you more bang for your buck—allowing companies to borrow money to supplement their funds provided in the form of share capital. Gearing is also referred to as the *debt ratio.*

Global Warming. The effect of a drastic increase in greenhouse gases in the atmosphere has led to an increase in the amount of the sun's rays being trapped in the earth's atmosphere, leading to increasing temperatures in many parts of the world. Transportation, industrial production, and agricultural activities have all contributed to the increase in particles in the earth's atmosphere and subsequent global warming. The economic effect of global warming, when catastrophes such as hurricanes and floods are included, is expected to reach into the trillions of dollars.

Gold Standard. It used to be that a currency's value was either fixed by the government or linked to some other item of value— such as gold. In the United States, for example, before 1971 you could convert U.S. dollars into gold at a fixed exchange rate. The gold standard was meant to ensure that the currency would always have a minimum value. Most currencies now use a system of floating exchange rates that lets the market decide what each currency is worth.

Golden Parachute. Fearing hostile takeovers, many top managers incorporate huge guaranteed bonuses into their severance packages to ensure that they'll land on their feet, with their pockets full of money, should they ever be forced out of their jobs. Golden parachutes have become common ingredients in pay packages for most executives in the 21st-century economy. Not all golden-parachute agreements are respected, however. When the U.S. government had to bail out the semiprivate Federal National Mortgage Association (see **Fannie Mae, Freddie Mac**) after it suffered unprecedented losses, political pressure forced the CEO out, with his multimillion-dollar golden parachute drastically reduced.

Goodwill. The part of the company that can't be attributed to tangible assets and liabilities is referred to as goodwill, even though it may have nothing to do with the company's benevolent intentions. A typical example of goodwill is a brand name. Since many 21st-century companies, such as dot-com start-ups or Web sites, have no *tangible value*, their goodwill is said to be worth millions—if not billions.

Green GDP. The attempt to evaluate the effect of economic activity on the environment and the cost of resources is referred to as green GDP. If goods are produced in an environmentally friendly way—using renewable energy such as wind or hydroelectricity, for example—the economic activity is accounted for differently from those that use nonrenewable resources such as oil or gas. The idea is to deduct the value of depleted raw materials or lost resources such as clean air or water and provide a more complete picture of a country's total economic activity.

Greenhouse Gas. Without some particles in the atmosphere, the earth's temperature would sink below freezing. The presence of certain particles—mainly water vapor, carbon dioxide, methane, nitrous oxide, and ozone—cause a "greenhouse" effect, trapping some of the sun's rays and warming the earth just as a greenhouse creates a healthy environment for plants to grow. Unfortunately, man-made pollution has been increasing rapidly, leading to exponential growth in the amount of greenhouse gases in the atmosphere and increased global warming.

Greenmail. In a hostile takeover or leveraged buyout, companies sometimes get opponents to change their minds—and course of action—by offering them huge financial incentives. One of the most common forms of this greenmail is to offer to buy their shares at above-market prices.

Gross Domestic Product, Gross National Product (GDP, GNP). Gross domestic product and gross national product both measure economic activity. While gross domestic product adds up all the goods and services produced within an economy over the course of the year, GNP adds some international components, such as income from foreign operations. Neither GDP nor GNP tells the whole story, however. Many economies have considerable unreported activities—including unpaid housework, volunteer work, and illegal activities such as drug sales and prostitution. Another word for GDP/GNP is *output*.

Guevara, Che. Antiglobalization activists have adopted Che Guevara, the Argentinean guerrilla fighter, as one of the symbols in their fight against the established global order, citing Che's revolutionary activities across Latin America. After taking up arms with Cuba's Fidel Castro and leading the Communist revolution there—Cuban schoolchildren still begin their day by chanting, "We will be like Che"—he fought anticapitalist battles as far away as the Congo and Bolivia, where he was killed at age thirty-nine. As minister of industries in Cuba, Che oversaw the expropriation of virtually all privately owned assets.

Headline Inflation. Because inflation figures can be disproportionately affected by sudden spikes in prices of certain components, such as food or energy, economists have devised two ways of defining it: headline inflation and *core inflation*. Headline inflation figures include all price increases in an economy over a given period of time, while core inflation factors out the volatile components such as the price of wheat, soy, beef, natural gas, or gasoline.

Hedge. A hedge provides protection from an uncertain event in the future. Homeowners, for example, feel safer during inflationary times, knowing that their house's value will probably also increase in value, hedging other eventual losses. An owner of a stock portfolio can hedge by buying put options, which give the right to sell the shares at a relatively high price should the market drop precipitously.

Hedge Fund. Only remotely related to the original practice of hedging, hedge funds are large investment funds run by savvy managers for a highly sophisticated clientele. They have been mainly associated with risky bets, investing clients' money in speculative instruments such as derivatives and securitized loans (see **algorithmic trading**). Some hedge funds, however, have been quite successful in providing high returns for their clients—which include many college endowments and pension funds.

High-Net-Worth Individual. The kind of client most banks dream about. A high-net-worth individual is one who has a lot of disposable assets and few liabilities. Banks around the world have discovered that having this type of client can be a lucrative business. Operations catering to the needs of high-net-worth individuals can be found all around the world: in New York, London, Paris, Geneva, Luxembourg, Tokyo, São Paulo, Singapore, and Zurich.

Hot Money. Money invested internationally for very short periods of time is often referred to as hot money. In developing countries, billions of dollars often come flooding in, in search of high returns. But when economic fundamentals change, or a world financial crisis occurs, the money can flow out at a moment's notice. Nobel Prize winner James Tobin once proposed a tax on hot-money transfers, called the Tobin Tax, to reduce the unrestricted flow of money into—and out of—developing-world economies.

Human Development Index (HDI). Economic statistics usually tell only part of the story. The United Nations Development Programme, therefore, has set up a human development index to track member countries' progress in improving the standard of living of their citizens. They examine such factors as infant mortality, average age, literacy, and death rates.

Hyperinflation. Prices rising out of control. Hyperinflation usually occurs in countries with severe economic and political problems, such as Germany in the 1920s and Argentina in the 1990s. In some hyperinflationary countries, prices can rise by more than 1,000 percent per year.

ICANN (Internet Corporation for Assigned Names and Numbers). ICANN oversees the system of domain names on the Web, including those ending in .com, .org, .gov, etc. Some of the ICANN directors are chosen by Internet service providers, and some are elected by "netizens," ordinary Web users from around the world.

IMF. See **International Monetary Fund.**

Import Substitution. Governments sometimes use protective tariffs or quotas to force businesses and consumers to substitute locally produced goods and services for imported ones. This policy of import substitution is often used in developing countries in an effort to avoid spending precious foreign currency reserves—as well as stimulating local economic development. The problem is that many countries can't produce all goods at the same level of quality as imported goods. When a government forces farmers to buy poorly made domestic tractors, for example, it reduces crop yields, and everyone suffers.

Incomes Policy. Incomes policy is an inflation-control plan that countries use to reduce consumers' real disposable income. Freezing wages is one way of accomplishing this: By reducing spending, it is hoped that the economy will slow down and inflation will be brought under control.

Industrial Revolution. The rapid industrialization in Britain during the late 18th and early 19th centuries, when steam power allowed the previously agricultural economy to expand and grow enormously, is referred to as the Industrial Revolution. The changes soon spread throughout the world, referred to as simply industrialization.

Inflation. Inflation is, simply put, the percentage increase in prices. It is usually given as an annual figure, although sometimes it is difficult to tell if the figures announced refer to the annual rise in prices or the rise over a quarter or an even shorter period of time. Since the 1970s inflation has become the biggest concern of central banks—stimulating growth without unduly increasing prices is the goal but is not always realized. In most economies, inflation is measured by an index of consumer prices that measures a basket of goods and services (see **consumer price index**).

Initial Public Offering. See **IPO**.

Insider Trading. A company's insiders are those who have access to the company's financial statements or other company secrets. Normally, insiders are the company's top managers. The activities of insiders are carefully watched—by the markets and by financial oversight authorities. Insider trading is illegal in most countries. TV celebrity Martha Stewart, for example, had to serve time in prison for trading on insider information.

Institutional Investor. Unlike small "retail" investors, institutional investors invest large amounts of money—billions of dollars or yen, pounds, or pesos—in the world markets every day. Typical institutional investors include insurance companies, banks, pension funds, hedge funds, and *sovereign funds*.

Interbank Market. The interbank rate that banks charge for loans to other banks is usually the lowest interest rate in the market. These interbank rates are then used as a benchmark, or standard, for other lending.

International Development Association (IDA). The arm of the World Bank that lends to the world's developing countries. The IDA provides loans at generous interest rates and under generous conditions—using money provided by wealthy World Bank member nations.

International Labour Organization (ILO). Based in Geneva, the ILO is responsible for overseeing all aspects of the world economy that relate to labor. One of the major goals of the ILO is to make sure that workers in developing countries are provided minimum workplace standards.

International Monetary Fund (IMF). The International Monetary Fund was established in 1945, at the same time as the *World Bank*. Its first job was to regulate the world's exchange rates. It has now assumed a leading role in restructuring debtor countries' economies and providing short-term loans to economies in need.

International Standards Organization (ISO). Although it defines itself as a nongovernmental organization, the Geneva-based International Standards Organization sets industrial and commercial standards that often become law in most countries in the world economy. The ISO 9000 family of standards, for example, defines how companies produce and deliver goods and services.

Investment. Economists use the word *investment* to refer to the part of economic production that is not saved or consumed. Accountants, on the other hand, use the word to refer to a company's purchase of productive assets, such as factory buildings, equipment, vehicles, and computers.

Investment Bank, Investment Banking. As opposed to *commercial banks*, which take deposits and loan out the money to earn income, investment banks are primarily occupied with issuing and trading securities and providing financial advice to companies. In some countries, investment banks are referred to as *merchant banks*. During the financial meltdown in 2008, most U.S. investment banks ceased to exist, the survivors becoming commercial banks to take advantage of Federal Reserve oversight and support.

Investor Relations. The area of corporate communications related to a company's relationship with its investors is referred to as investor relations. The idea is to communicate effectively with the investment community at large, presenting a positive image for the company and, hopefully, encouraging new investment.

Invisible Hand. The idea of an "invisible hand" of the marketplace, guiding consumers and businesses to make the right economic decisions, was developed by the economic philosopher Adam Smith in the 18th century. His theory was that markets, if left to themselves, would find the most efficient way of doing things.

Invisible Trade. Exports and imports of services—such as banking, insurance, and media—are referred to as invisible by economists because they aren't actually shipped abroad. Invisible trade can be anything from sales of movies to consulting services to online music downloads. In many economies, invisible trade has become more profitable than trade of visible goods like commodities and automobiles.

IPO (Initial Public Offering). When a company goes public, its shares are allowed to be sold and traded on a recognized exchange. This allows the company to have access to a large investor pool and provides the original owners with a lot of money when they sell their shares to the new investors. An IPO has become a rite of passage for many start-up companies.

Irrational Exuberance. Originally used by former U.S. Federal Reserve chairman Alan Greenspan, the expression *irrational exuberance* is used to describe any overvalued market—in comparison to traditional prices, at least. The first bubble to burst after Greenspan's words was the dot-com bubble, which had valued companies with no profit and no assets—only promise for future earnings—at levels that ranked them alongside some of the biggest and most important companies in the world. Paper millionaires can become paupers overnight when their shares or holdings of companies are reduced to more realistic levels (see **bubble**).

ISO. See **International Standards Organization.**

Joint Venture. Two or more businesses joining forces in order to get a competitive advantage in a particular market. Joint ventures are particularly useful in foreign countries, where partnering with a local company allows a foreigner to take advantage of the partner's local knowledge and skills.

Junk Bonds. Companies with low credit ratings—usually below BBB (see **rating**)—often have to issue bonds with high interest rates in order to get needed capital for expansion or takeovers. These lower-than-investment-grade bonds are usually referred to as junk bonds, but the companies that issue them—along with their investment advisers—prefer to call them high-yield securities.

Kereitsu. Another way of saying "Japan, Inc." *Kereitsu* describes the tightly organized system of interlocking companies in the Japanese economy. It involves multiple layers of businesses, banks, wholesalers, distributors, and brand-loyal retailers that group together, often limiting the penetration of foreign companies and brands in local markets.

Keynesian Economics. British economist John Maynard Keynes was one of the most influential economic thinkers of the twentieth century. Keynes's ideas on using government spending (see **fiscal policy**) to combat economic recession revolutionized modern economic science. Basically, Keynesian economics calls for overspending, or *deficit spending*, during an economic slowdown, and underspending, or running budget surpluses, during times of too-rapid economic expansion. Most politicians are easily convinced to use deficit spending to stimulate the economy, but are decidedly un-Keynesian when it comes to spending less during periods of rapid economic growth.

Kyoto Protocol, Kyoto Agreement. Once derided by George W. Bush as "unnecessary," the Kyoto Protocol was eventually ratified by almost every nation in the world. The purpose of the agreement, signed in the Japanese city of Kyoto, was to find ways to limit the production of carbon dioxide and thereby reduce *global warming*. Critics said that the complex rules for reducing pollution would stifle economic growth. Others said that it was an important first step in finding a way to reduce the amount of greenhouse gases entering the earth's atmosphere.

Laffer Curve. Rumor has it that an American economist, Arthur Laffer, drew a curve on a restaurant napkin to show that a reduction in taxes would lead to more taxes coming in, not less. His idea was that if a government reduced taxes, it would free up money that people would use more efficiently than the government, thereby stimulating the economy. This new economic activity would then bring in even more taxes than before. The curve headed down at the beginning, showing lower taxes in the short term, but rose toward the end, showing the expected positive effects of reduced taxes.

Lagging Economic Indicators. Unemployment and GDP growth are called lagging economic indicators because they tend to tell you where the economy has been, as opposed to information like new home starts (see **leading economic indicators**) that tend to tell you where the economy is going.

Laissez-Faire. The French term *laissez-faire* means, literally, "let them do it." It is used to describe a government policy that lets the markets decide what is best. Consumers and producers, in theory, will usually come to the right decisions if they are left to decide on their own.

LBO. See **leveraged buyout.**

Leading Economic Indicators. Statistics that help economic and political leaders plot the future course of the economy. Leading economic indicators include such things as retail sales, spending on new plants and machinery, and housing starts. These indicators tell us where the economy is headed, not where it's been (see **lagging economic indicators**).

Letter of Credit. In international trade, importers often are required to prove that funds are available to pay for an incoming shipment of goods. This letter of credit is usually provided by a bank that guarantees to the seller that the import will be paid for once it arrives.

Leveraged Buyout (LBO). A leveraged buyout uses borrowed money to take over a company. The buyer puts up a certain amount of capital and borrows the rest—in the form of either bank loans or high-yield securities (see **junk bonds**) that give the investor the leverage to acquire the desired company.

Liability. On a balance sheet, liabilities are listed on the right of the assets. Liabilities typically include debt or other anticipated obligations—money that the company has to pay back sometime in the future. Current liabilities are those that have to be paid off in twelve months or less. Longer-term liabilities are referred to as long-term debt.

Liquidity. In the corporate world, *liquidity* describes a company having enough cash on hand to meet debt payments, but in the world of trade and finance, *liquidity* refers to the ability to buy and sell with ease. Essentially, it means that there are enough buyers and sellers in the market to guarantee a seamless flow of trades. During the credit crunch of 2008, when banks were reluctant to lend to one another, even overnight, the lack of liquidity brought much economic activity to a halt.

Liquidity Crisis. See **credit crisis**.

Listing. See **flotation**.

Lombard Rate. The interest that central banks in many European countries charge on collateralized loans is called the Lombard rate. The banks borrowing the money usually have to put up top-rated government bonds as collateral to receive the preferential Lombard rates. The name is based on Europe's early bankers, who often came from Lombardia, the northern Italian region where Milan is located.

M&A. See **mergers and acquisitions**.

Macroeconomics. The big picture. Macroeconomics is the study of an economy's aggregate factors, such as unemployment, growth, inflation, and government spending. The other side of the economy, called *microeconomics*, looks at the more detailed aspects of an economy, primarily related to the behavior of businesses and consumers.

Managed Float, Dirty Float. As opposed to a free-float currency regime, many developing countries use a managed float, or dirty float, to "peg" their currencies—keeping their value stable, relative to a chosen reference currency or basket of currencies. For example, Hong Kong, China, and Saudi Arabia have traditionally kept their currencies pegged to the dollar, while many Eastern European countries—including Hungary, Lithuania, Estonia, and Bulgaria—have kept their currencies pegged to the euro. At the beginning of the 21st century, more than one hundred countries in the world economy used some form of managed float to keep their currency exchange rates stable.

Margin. When investors are allowed to leverage their securities purchases. Margin trading is a way of getting more bang for your buck. In a margin account, banks or brokers loan money to investors so they can buy more stocks and bonds. The client puts up some of the money: The bank puts up the rest. Essentially, the client uses what's already in the account as collateral to borrow money to buy more securities. The reward to the client is huge, if the market goes up. But when markets go down, the client can lose a lot as well. If the market drops too much, the bank gives the client a margin call—asking for extra money or more collateral. If margin calls are not met, the securities the client holds are sold immediately, before the market has a chance of going down any further.

Marginal Analysis. The study of economic behavior "at the edge." Marginal analysis examines how people or firms behave when given the option of having or producing "one more" of something. The additional "one thin wafer" is not so appetizing if it follows a big meal. Marginal consumption, for example, describes what it would take, in terms of lower prices, to get a consumer to buy just one more.

Market Capitalization, Market Value. A publicly traded company's market capitalization is derived by multiplying the number of shares outstanding by the share price. The market cap figure gives us an idea of the company's relative size—allowing us to compare companies across borders and across market segments.

Market Economy. See **free-market economy**.

Market Maker. A market maker is a professional trader who makes a two-way price for an item of value. The price that a market maker is willing to pay, the bid price, is always lower than the offer price. By buying low and selling high all day long, the market maker ends up making a lot of money.

Marx, Karl. The father of Communism. The German economic philosopher and sociologist Karl Marx wrote *Das Kapital*, the first major work outlining the principles of the communist economic model. In it, he predicted the demise of capitalism and called for the creation of a socialist economic system based on the following principle: "From each according to his abilities, to each according to his needs" (see **communism**).

MBA (Master of Business Administration). The main way to break into the world of business and management. Most universities around the world now offer MBAs to allow their students to learn the skills to manage organizations.

Mean, Median. Although both words describe the concept of *average*, they use different calculations—which means they provide different types of information to investors and market observers. The mean is the simple average, which is determined by adding up all the numbers in a list and dividing by the number of items listed. This is used in most economic calculations, such as average per capita income, or average unemployment rate. Sometimes, however, it is useful to be aware of the way economic figures are distributed. Median income, for example, tells us the point at which half the members of a population are above and half below. The median is the point at which 50 percent of the numbers in a list are higher and 50 percent are lower.

Mercantilism. The economic policy of using a consistent trade surplus to accumulate wealth and power. A mercantilist economy emphasizes exports over imports. Consumers in the home country suffer, but businesses and government amass enormous wealth from foreign exchange receipts that can be used for saving and investment.

Merchandise Trade Balance. The narrowest measure of a country's trade, the merchandise trade balance counts only visible goods such as wine and laptops—not services. This measure is often referred to in the press as the *trade balance* or *trade surplus*, even though a country's total trade figure should include all trade, such as financial services and income from foreign investment (see **current account**).

Merchant Banking. The term *merchant banking* refers to the practice of a bank or securities house investing in its clients' businesses. In some countries, an *investment bank* is also referred to as a merchant bank.

Merger, Mergers and Acquisitions (M&A). Buying or selling companies, or working to bring them together, is referred to in international banking circles as M&A, or mergers and acquisitions. Many mergers are fueled by the desire of companies to reap the benefits of increased synergy—taking advantage of each party's strengths and reducing redundant costs.

Metcalf's Law. The more the merrier. Metcalfe's Law postulates that the more organizations—or people—participate in a network, the more effective it becomes. This is particularly relevant in the New Economy, where Web sites and online exchanges tend to work better when more participants are involved. Metcalfe's Law is based on the postulation that the value of a network increases in a square: When the number of participants increases by two, for example, the value of the network will increase by four.

Microcredit. *Microcredit financing* refers to the practice of providing small loans, or microloans, to poor-country entrepreneurs who are not able to get money from traditional banks, used mainly to set up a business. Because they lack collateral, steady employment, or verifiable credit history, many people in developing countries cannot meet even the most minimal qualifications to gain access to traditional credit.

Microeconomics. The study of an economy's individuals and firms is called microeconomics. It is the opposite of *macroeconomics*, which looks at the big picture, like unemployment and GDP growth. Microeconomics, like a microscope, looks at the economic behavior of individuals and how firms make decisions under various economic conditions.

Minimum Wage. The lowest hourly wage permitted in an economy. Minimum wage laws exist in most but not all modern industrial economies. Some politicians and many economists criticize minimum wage laws as counterproductive—by setting minimum wages too high, the laws hurt small businesses and discourage them from hiring new employees.

Monetarism. The economic theory based on the belief that changes in the *money supply* control economic growth. Monetarists believe that inflation can best be controlled by limiting the money supply.

Monetary Policy. In contrast to *fiscal policy,* which is determined by government decisions related to taxes and spending, monetary policy is decided by central banks, such as the U.S. Federal Reserve and the European Central Bank. By regulating the money supply and interest rates, monetary authorities can pretty much control economic growth—and, hopefully, the rate of inflation.

Money Laundering. The idea of money laundering is to take illegally earned money and pass it through a legitimate business operation, such as an offshore company, with little financial oversight. In the end, the money looks like it's been earned legally and can then be spent without arousing suspicion.

Money Market. The market that brings together short-term borrowers and lenders is referred to as the money market. Most short-term investments (such as treasury bills or fiduciary deposits and CDs) are traded on electronic exchanges and special floors set up in banks and securities houses scattered around the world. In the United States, a money market deposit account is one that provides a higher rate of interest than a normal savings account—and with a relatively low penalty for early withdrawal.

Money Supply. A country's money supply has several different components, ranging from coins and banknotes to deposits in savings and checking accounts. The money supply most often referred to in the news is M1, which consists of all currency in

circulation as well as money in easy-to-access bank accounts—
not long-term deposits (see **monetarism**).

Monopoly. Complete control of one sector of production within an
economy is referred to as a monopoly. A sole producer of a good
can, in theory, raise prices without limit. Monopolistic behavior
is illegal in most advanced industrial economies.

Moody's. One of the biggest credit rating agencies in the world.
Moody's, like Standard & Poor's, provides up-to-date analysis of
the financial health of countries, companies, and other borrowers
in the world economy. Moody's stamp of top quality, AAA, is
awarded only to the world's most creditworthy borrowers.

Moral Hazard. Cited as a major reason for financial failures during
troubled economic times, *moral hazard* refers to the propensity
for players in the global economy to take unnecessary risks.
Assured by explicit or implicit guarantees that governments
won't allow certain institutions to fail, managers tend to take on
many more risks than they normally would. Some blame the
subprime crisis on moral hazard, whereby banks and finance
companies made unwise loans because they assumed—rightly—
that if the mortgage failed, someone else would end up paying
for it.

Mortgage-Backed Security. A mortgage-backed security is backed
by payments from mortgages. Instead of keeping the money that
is expected to flow in over the future, the banks and finance companies that issued the mortgages hand over this money flow to be
repackaged into securities that can be sold to other investors. The
advantage for banks and mortgage companies is that they get
their money up front, and don't have to worry about the borrowers going bankrupt. The problem for the investors is that they
may end up owning worthless pieces of paper if enough of the
borrowers stop making their mortgage payments.

Most Favored Nation (MFN). A preferred status for trading partners. The United States used to give this status to selected
nations, implying special access to the domestic market in goods

and services, but in an age of burgeoning trade, trading partners are now given the more anodyne title *permanent normal trade relations*.

Multilateral Trade Agreements. An agreement between three or more trading partners to liberate, or reduce, trade in goods and/or services. Regional and global trade agreements are by far the best way to make sure that countries reap the advantage of comparative advantage, letting each produce what it does best. By the beginning of the 21st century most multilateral trade agreements had stalled, mainly because of the reluctance of governments to dismantle semipermanent barriers to trade, such as agricultural subsidies and protective tariffs on imports of manufactured goods. Most countries found it easier to establish trade agreements on an ad hoc basis (called *bilateral trade agreements*) and settled for a one-step-at-a-time approach to liberalizing trade.

Mutual Fund. A mutual fund is a collection of bonds or stocks sold as a single investment. The advantage of a mutual fund is that investors are able to diversify risk over a wide range of securities within a single investment vehicle. Most investment funds available in the market are mutual funds—very few investors would use a fund to invest in a single stock or bond. Mutual funds are especially appropriate for people wishing to invest internationally: Funds make it easy to avoid mistakes in markets where information on individual companies is not easily accessible.

N11. See **Next Eleven**.

NAFTA. See **North American Free Trade Agreement**.

NASDAQ. The National Association of Securities Dealers Automated Quotations system was the world's first major electronic stock exchange. NASDAQ trades many New Economy stocks, such as Microsoft, Amazon.com, and Intel. Its goal is to become a global trading powerhouse, merging with or acquiring electronic trading exchanges in many other countries around the world. In addition to providing domestic market indexes such as the NASDAQ Composite Index, NASDAQ provides several global market summaries, including the NASDAQ Global Select Market and NASDAQ Global Market indexes.

Nationalization. The government taking ownership of previously privately owned enterprises is called nationalization. Nationalizations are common under socialist or communist regimes that prefer to have all means of production in the hands of the government. But even in free-market bastions, such as the United Kingdom, banks were nationalized during the credit crisis to keep them from failing. Expropriation is a nationalization that doesn't pay the previous owners for their assets. The opposite of nationalization is *privatization*.

Net Assets. What a company really owns. A company's net assets, or *net profit*, are what's left after deducting all of the costs or liabilities of doing business. Basically, net assets are what is left over when a company's debts are subtracted from its assets. Stockholders consider this to be the part of the company that belongs to them. Net assets are also referred to as *stockholders' equity* or *shareholder's equity*.

Net Asset Value (NAV). In order to calculate the true value of shares in mutual funds or open-end funds, it is necessary to add up all the fund's assets—such as securities and cash—and subtract all the liabilities. This figure is then divided by the total number of shares outstanding to give investors an idea of what each share in the fund is worth.

Net Income. Another way of saying *profit*. Net income is determined by subtracting all expenses from a company's total revenue. It tells us what a company has earned over a given period of time (see **earnings**).

Net Profit. See **net assets**.

Net Worth. An individual's net worth is calculated by adding up the monetary value of all assets—including house, car, and bank accounts—and subtracting all the liabilities, such as mortgages and credit card bills. Another term for net worth is *net assets*.

Newly Industrialized Countries (NICs). The select group of developing countries that are on their way to joining the ranks of advanced industrialized economies. Even though most countries in the booming 21st-century economy could be included in the list of newly industrialized countries, the countries most often mentioned include Brazil, Chile, China, India, Mexico, Singapore, South Africa, South Korea, Taiwan, and Thailand.

Next Eleven (N11). In addition to the BRIC group of developing economies, comprising Brazil, Russia, India, and China, a second tier groups together eleven countries that have particularly promising outlooks for investment and future growth. This group is usually referred to as the Next Eleven, or N11, and consists of Bangladesh, Egypt, Indonesia, Iran, Mexico, Nigeria, Pakistan, the Philippines, South Korea, Turkey, and Vietnam.

NGO. See **nongovernmental organization.**

Nongovernmental Organization (NGO). International nonprofit organizations that are not directly controlled by national governments are referred to as NGOs (Nongovernmental Organizations). Doctors Without Borders, the World Wildlife Fund, the Sierra Club, and the Red Cross are all examples of NGOs.

North American Free Trade Agreement (NAFTA). The agreement to open up the borders of Canada, the United States, and Mexico to trade in goods and services was not an easy sell. Opponents predicted a "sucking sound" of jobs being lost south of the border. But, in the end, workers in all three countries benefited (on the whole) when all three economies expanded, aided by the benefits of increased trade with their neighbors. Unlike other trade groups, such as the European Union, NAFTA didn't allow barriers to be erected to countries outside the trading bloc—it simply removed barriers to trade among the three NAFTA members.

OECD. See **Organisation for Economic Co-operation and Development.**

Offshore, Offshore Companies. A company that does little or no business in its home country is referred to as a nonresident or offshore company. Many countries treat offshore companies' profits differently from normal companies—they tax them, usually, at a lower rate.

OPEC (Organization of the Petroleum Exporting Countries). OPEC was set up in the 1960s to coordinate the production of oil—allowing member nations to better control the market. The thirteen OPEC members consist of Iran, Venezuela, and the major Arab oil producers of the Middle East.

Open-Market Operation. Central banks use open-market operations to control economic growth. By buying and selling securities on the open market, the U.S. Federal Reserve and other central banks are able to inject money into the financial system—or remove it, if that's what they desire. Since money held at central banks is not considered to be part of the money supply, any purchase of securities by the Fed increases the U.S. money supply by the amount paid. Alternatively, when the Fed sells securities on the open market, the U.S. money supply is reduced by the amount paid by the purchaser and placed in the central bank's vaults. Most of the securities bought or sold in open-market operations are government bonds.

Option. An option gives the holder the right to buy or sell something at a certain price in the future. A stock option, for example, is a *call option* that gives the holder the right to buy a certain number of shares, called underlying shares, at a certain price in the future. The opposite, the right to sell the underlying share or other asset, is called a *put* (see **stock option**).

Organisation for Economic Co-operation and Development (OECD). The OECD, based in Paris, France, groups together the world's major economies. In addition to providing statistics and documenting all aspects of the member countries' economies, the OECD serves as a forum for discussion and coordination of economic policy. It includes the United States, Canada, Mexico, Japan, South Korea, Australia, New Zealand, and most of the European Union members, including France, Germany, and Spain.

Output. Another word for gross domestic product (see **GDP/ GNP**). Output is the total amount of goods and services sold in an economy during a given period of time.

Outsourcing. Taking advantage of advances in telecommunication and computer capabilities, many companies in rich countries have decided to send many low-skill operations abroad. By the beginning of the 21st century, operations ranged from call centers in India to back-office bookkeeping operations in Eastern Europe. The idea is to take advantage of lower salaries abroad. Even online tutoring allows students with broadband access to interact with low-cost tutors usually based in developing countries to get online help in subjects ranging from languages to mathematics.

Over-the-Counter (OTC). Over-the-counter shares are not traded on established stock exchanges, but are traded electronically, reducing overhead—and oversight. Most OTC stock sales are for small companies that don't meet the strict financial requirements necessary for listing the shares on major exchanges such as the NYSE or NASDAQ.

Par. When a bond sells at 100 percent of its face value (nominal value), it's said to trade at par. For most bonds in the dollar-denominated sector, the face value is $1,000. The price of most bonds does not stay at par for long. Once issued, whenever interest rates rise or fall in the market, the bond's price is adjusted, rising above or falling below par, to make the bond's return competitive with other securities in the marketplace.

Paradigm. The rules of the game. In economics, you shift the paradigm by changing the rules governing how the economy is perceived and consequently how it works. The Internet, for example, has changed the paradigm of how economies produce and sell goods and services. Based on the concept of *Weltanschauung*, or worldview, a paradigm consists of the sum total of beliefs and values that make up a society or economic system.

Patent. The exclusive right to market a specific product or service in a given market. Patents are usually issued by government authorities, such as the U.S. Patent Office. Without patent protection, companies would never invest as much as they do into research and development. In some developing countries, patents—on lifesaving drugs, for example—are often ignored because the patented product is often too expensive for people on low incomes to afford.

Per Capita. Often translated as "per person." Putting a per capita value on an economic statistic is often the best way to understand the number's true effect on the economy's inhabitants. Per capita spending, for example, helps us understand the "real" effect of something like health care or education. It allows us to put the numbers on a more human scale.

Perestroika. Russian for "economic restructuring," *perestroika* was the buzzword for Mikhail Gorbachev's daring plan to reform the Soviet Union in the 1980s. Coupled with the word *glasnost*, which called for political openness, perestroika's goal was to make the economy more efficient by decentralizing decision making (see **centrally planned economy**).

Permanent Normal Trade Relations (PNTR). The latest word in accommodating trade. The United States used to give most favored nation status to selected nations it wanted to encourage trade with—allowing special access to the domestic market in goods and services. Now it's referred to as PNTR, even though, in theory, with a global trade agreement being promoted by the United States and other nations, *all* nations should have permanent normal trade relations.

Phillips Curve. The economic principle that inflation is linked to unemployment is shown by a curve, usually referred to as the Phillips curve in honor of the economist who "discovered" it, A. W. Phillips. The curve shows that low inflation is usually accompanied by high unemployment, and, conversely, that high inflation is accompanied by low employment. During times of low unemployment, there usually aren't enough people around to take all the available jobs and employees will ask for—and probably get—higher salaries. This leads to inflation, a rise in prices. In the New Economy, however, some economies are able to take advantage of advances in technology to keep from having to hire more employees, reducing the demand for higher wages, reducing the need to raise wages and prices.

Planned Economy. See **centrally planned economy.**

Plaza Accord. On September 22, 1985, an agreement was reached at the Plaza Hotel in New York City to devalue the dollar—particularly against the German mark and Japanese yen—through coordinated intervention in the international currency markets. The goal was to make U.S. industries and farmers more competitive on the international markets. The agreement was signed by five nations: France, West Germany, Japan, the United States, and the United Kingdom.

Poison Pill. When a company wants to defend itself against a hostile takeover, it may attempt to render itself unattractive through certain "unhealthy" financial maneuvers. A poison-pill defense may involve a drastic increase in debt, or selling off valuable pieces of the company, in order to ward off evil takeover artists. Unfortunately, even if a poison-pill defense succeeds in keeping the company in the hands of the original owners, it often ends up irreparably harming the company—and managers—it was meant to protect.

Pollution Rights. See **emissions trading.**

Preferred Stock. Stocks that pay a fixed dividend are called preferred stocks. In some ways, a preferred stock is like a bond in that its fixed dividend resembles an interest payment. Preferred stock is usually considered to be senior to common stock—which means that in the event of a bankruptcy, holders of the preferred stock are paid before those holding common stock. However, owners of preferred stock—like bond owners—usually have no voting rights.

Primary Market. When new stocks and bonds are issued, they are often traded in a primary market before they are allowed to join the ranks of seasoned securities on the world's markets. A primary market for bonds, for example, usually exists until the payment date, when interest payments start being calculated and the life of the bond really begins. Primary market trading normally takes place among banks and securities dealers, not on established exchanges.

Prime Rate. The prime rate is the interest rate that U.S. banks charge their best corporate customers. Like the London Interbank Offered Rate, the prime rate is often used as a guideline for determining other interest rates that banks charge on loans to riskier customers. Following the guideline of "low risk, low reward," a bank's prime corporate customers are usually able to pay the lowest interest rates in the market.

Principal. Anyone making a loan wants to get paid back at some time—and earn a little interest along the way. The amount of a loan that has to be returned to the lender is called its principal. A bond's principal is often referred to as its face value.

Private Placement. A new issue of stocks or bonds that is too small to be treated as a full public placement—such as a large IPO or a full-fledged bond issue—is referred to as a private placement. The securities issued in a private placement are often sold to a small group of *institutional investors*. Usually, there are fewer reporting requirements on private placements, and the securities are usually not traded on the open market once they have been placed in the hands of the investors.

Privatization. Privatization is the selling off of state-owned companies to improve efficiency and bring more money into the government's coffers. Countries burdened by the debt and losses of poorly run public companies often turn to privatization to improve efficiency and get more cash into public coffers. The opposite of privatization is *nationalization*.

Productivity. Productivity is defined as the amount of goods or services produced by a given unit of labor, capital, land, etc. One of the hallmarks of the 21st-century economy has been a marked increase in productivity as new technologies have allowed people to produce much more than before for a given amount of time spent.

Profit. The proverbial carrot that balances the stick of bankruptcy. A company's profit is its revenue minus expenses. Profit is the driving force behind most economic activity in free-market economies. In accounting, a company's profit is often referred to as *net income*, or *earnings* (see **earnings**).

Profit and Loss Statement (P&L). The financial overview of a company's activities over a given period of time is called an income statement or, more commonly, a profit and loss statement. A typical P&L starts with income, called revenue, then deducts all the cost and expenses of doing business to arrive at the bottom line: *net income*, which is what's left after deducting taxes and other fees from the profit.

Program Trading. Instead of buying stocks as an investment to hold and cherish for years, program traders try to take advantage of discrepancies in the markets, buying large amounts of stocks—or options, or bonds, or futures—in a market where prices are slightly out of line with prices in other markets in other parts of the world. Program traders use computers to track the prices of a wide variety of securities in markets around the world—and use that information to buy where it's cheap and sell where prices are slightly higher.

Producer Prices, Producer Price Index. Measured "at the factory gate," producer price indexes track the price of goods before they enter the retail chain. These figures provide early warning signals of inflation, allowing central bankers to adjust the economy before the price rises show up in the more commonly watched CPI (see **consumer price index**).

Purchasing Power Parity (PPP). Unlike currency exchange rates, which are determined by the market, PPP looks at what your money actually buys in each country—calculating, in a sense, its purchasing power. PPP looks at the prices of a basket of goods and services—including everything from housing to haircuts, from bread to movie tickets—to arrive at a real-world exchange rate. Purchasing power parity is often used to compare the size of economies around the world when traditional exchange rates don't tell the whole picture. China, for example, where prices are much lower than in Europe or the United States (if you use official exchange rates to make the comparison), would be ranked much higher if you used equivalent prices for the goods and services produced there.

Put Option. A put option gives the holder the right to sell something at a certain price over a certain period of time. It's the opposite of a *call option*, which gives the buyer the right to buy something at a certain price over a certain period of time (see **call option**). An investor who thinks the price of something will go down in the future will buy a put option—hoping to profit if the market moves in the expected direction. As the price of the underlying asset goes down, the price of the option will go up. The price at which a put option allows you to sell the underlying security is called its striking price.

Quota. In international trade, a quota is a limit on the quantity of a good that may be imported into a country over a certain period of time. It is one of the three main tools governments use to limit imports (see also **subsidy** and **tariff**).

Rating. Bonds and stocks often are given a rating by specialized agencies, such as Moody's and Standard & Poor's, which allows investors to easily compare them without going into all the financial details. AAA is usually the best rating. Having a triple-A rating means a company or government can get the best terms for loans and other debt. Other investment-grade ratings include AA, A, and BBB (or Baa). Anything below that is said to be speculative. Or in the case of C ratings, very risky.

Rational Expectations. Much of modern economic theory is based on the concept of rational expectations: that people, when armed with all available information, will make rational decisions. Lower prices, for example, will always get people to buy an equivalent product. Unfortunately, consumers and business-people don't always act rationally—they often buy the product they like even though it may not be in their best economic interest. *Errare humanum est*, "to err is human," even in the world of economics.

Real. It's usually much more important, especially in high-inflation times, to look at real figures—those that take into account the effect of inflation. Real income, for example, may go down, even if the nominal amount goes up—as long as inflation is high enough to offset any gains made from the higher salary. Any values that have been adjusted for inflation are referred to as real.

Real Estate Investment Trust (REIT). Instead of buying a piece of property and holding on to it for years before selling it through a real estate broker, a REIT investor buys a security, a piece of paper that represents ownership in a "basket" of real estate investments such as shopping centers and apartment houses. The advantage of real estate investment trusts, besides certain tax benefits, is that the investor can buy and sell their share like any stock or bond—on a quoted market—and not have to worry about mowing the lawn or repairing the roof.

Receivables. Counting your chickens before they're hatched. On a balance sheet, something that's owed to the company can be treated as an asset—even before it's been received. These receivable assets can actually be sold or packaged into securities to trade on the open market. Receivables become *current assets* once they've been paid in.

Recession. A recession is a prolonged economic slowdown. Normally, a recession is "official" if an economy stops growing for two consecutive quarters. When an economy is seen to be heading into a recession, central banks usually lower interest rates to stimulate purchase of goods and services and business investment—the goal is to spur economic growth returns and reduce unemployment. Unfortunately, this doesn't always happen.

During the first years of the 21st century, some countries reduced interest rates to zero, a d their economies still languished.

REIT. See **real estate investment trust.**

Repurchase Agreements, Repos. The purchase of securities with the agreement to sell them back at a certain price and at a certain time in the future is called a repurchase agreement. Repos are essentially a loan, or a form of short-term investment. Central banks, such as the Federal Reserve or the Bank of Japan, often use repurchase agreements to inject money into—or remove it from—the economy at large. When traders hear that the Fed is doing repos they often act accordingly, buying or selling on their own, expecting the Fed's action to lead to a rise or decline in interest rates.

Rescheduling. It is said that when a customer owes a bank a small amount of money and can't pay, the customer is in trouble, but when the customer owes the bank a large amount of money and can't pay, the bank is in trouble. Confronted with problem borrowers who can't repay their loans, creditor banks—or creditor nations—often reschedule the loans, essentially giving the debtors more time to come up with the money. If a country has no hope of growth without additional funds—such as many African countries during the first years of the 21st century—the loans are forgiven, removed from the creditors' books.

Retained Earnings. When a company makes a profit it can choose to distribute its net income to the company's shareholders in the form of dividends or keep it for future use. What doesn't get distributed remains on the company's books as retained earnings.

Return on Equity (ROE). Return on equity is the relationship between net income and the price of the company's stock. It is calculated by adding up a company's profits over the course of a year and dividing them by the net assets the company uses to create those profits. It shows how efficiently the investors' money is being used to generate income. In the world of personal finance, investors use the expression *return on investment (ROI)* to describe the ratio of total return (or profit) relative to the amount of money invested.

Road Pricing. In order to reduce pollution and overcrowding of public roads, cities sometimes set up a system of electronic devices to monitor and charge for the roads' use. From San Diego to London, road pricing has helped to drastically reduce the amount of cars coming into the city center. By charging more for cars to use roads at certain times of the day, road pricing can be a powerful economic incentive to reduce traffic jams. It gets commuters to make more efficient use of roads—or even switch to less polluting ways to get to work, such as carpools or the use of public transportation.

ROE. See **return on equity**.

Sarbanes-Oxley Act. The United States Congress passed the Sarbanes-Oxley Act in 2002 in response to corporate abuses—particularly the bankruptcies of Enron and WorldCom. Officially called the Public Company Accounting Reform and Investor Protection Act of 2002, Sarbox, as it is commonly called, established new standards for the way publicly traded companies conduct business, particularly how company boards, management, and accounting firms are allowed to function.

Savings. In any economy, income that is not spent is referred to as savings. A high savings rate means that the economy has more money for businesses to invest—mainly because most savings are kept in banks, where they can be loaned out for other uses.

Savings and Loan (S&L). Savings and loans are financial institutions that take depositors' money and make loans, primarily to finance clients' real estate purchases. In England, savings-and-loan-style banks are usually called building societies.

Securities and Exchange Commission (SEC). The SEC is a federal agency that oversees and regulates financial markets and securities trading in the United States. The primary goal of the SEC is to protect the public from malpractice and fraudulent behavior in the securities industry. The closest thing the world economy has to an SEC is the BIS (see **Bank for International Settlements**), based in Basel, Switzerland.

Security, Securitization. A security is any financial instrument that represents something of value. A security can be anything from a stock to a pollution right to a savings bond. Even an IOU is a security because it is a promise to give to the holder something of value, usually money. Banks sometimes securitize their assets— mortgages or credit card debt, for example—by grouping them in blocks and selling them, as bonds or other securities, to investors.

Share. See **stock**.

Short Sale. In most of the world's stock markets, investors are allowed to sell stock they don't own—as long as they agree to provide the securities at some time in the future. The reason for selling short is the investor's belief that the stock's price will go down and his desire to benefit from the future fall in prices. By selling in advance, investors get to take advantage of the higher price. When they "cover" their short position by buying the securities at a later date, they pocket the difference in prices. The opposite of going short is the more traditional investment strategy of going long, buying securities to keep in the hope that the price will rise at some point in the future.

Sierra Club. One of the world's largest environmental groups, the Sierra Club has taken a leading role in finding economic incentives—such as road pricing—to reduce pollution and environmental destruction. The Sierra Club was founded in 1892 by the outdoorsman and preservationist John Muir.

Smith, Adam. The father of modern economics. Adam Smith was an enlightened 18th-century Scotsman who believed that the markets worked best when left to take care of themselves. He introduced to the world such terms as *invisible hand of the marketplace* and *division of labor*. His book *The Wealth of Nations* provided the foundation for the modern capitalist economic system.

Smoot-Hawley. The Smoot-Hawley Tariff Act of 1930 raised tariffs on thousands of imports to the United States economy. The idea was to stimulate the economy by encouraging local production. The result was somewhat different. When other countries retaliated by raising tariffs of their own, U.S. exports plummeted, resulting in job losses and a significantly worsened depression.

Socialism. The basic idea of socialism is that an economy should ensure an equitable distribution of wealth. Sometimes confused with communism, the socialist model allows for some private control of the means of production. There are many free-market socialist economies. Paris, for example, didn't stop being a thriving, elegant capital when the French elected a socialist government. Sweden and other Nordic countries are often cited as models of how capitalism and socialism can coexist to everyone's benefit.

Socially Conscious Investing, Socially Responsible Investing, Corporate Social Responsibility (CSR). Socially conscious investors, such as college endowment funds, make an effort to invest their money in companies or funds that correspond to a specific view of how the world should be run. Many socially conscious equity funds, for example, invest only in companies that have proven corporate social responsibility by treating their workers well, for example, or using sustainable resources, such as planting a tree for every one they cut down.

Sovereign Debt Rating. Sovereign debt consists mainly of bonds or other securities issued by central governments. As opposed to companies, sovereign debt is backed by the full faith and security of the government and is, therefore, considered to be the most unlikely to go unpaid in times of crisis. If sovereign debt is issued in the country's own currency, it is virtually impossible to default: All the government would have to do is issue currency to back the debt. The most highly rated sovereign debt is from the wealthy countries of Europe, North America, and Asia. U.S. treasury bonds, British gilts, and Swiss government bonds, for example, have all been rated AAA—the best rating available.

Sovereign Fund. Instead of investing excess reserves in bonds or overnight deposits, many countries and states have set up sovereign funds to make equity investments abroad, buying companies or shares of companies from around the world.

Special Drawing Right (SDR). A "money" that was created by the International Monetary Fund to provide an alternative to gold or other currencies. SDRs are mainly used as an accounting tool to keep track of funds and make payments within the *International Monetary Fund* system. Essentially, SDRs are a form of IOU that gives the holder the right to claim the "real" currency held by the IMF members. The exact makeup of SDRs has changed over time, but consists mainly of U.S. dollars, euros, British pounds, and Japanese yen. SDRs give countries or businesses the possibility to denominate transactions in a sort of virtual currency that isn't subject to the same fluctuations and uncertainties of any one individual currency in the world economy. Many countries use SDRs as a reserve currency.

Special Economic Zone. When a government wants to attract foreign investment and trade to a specific region, it sometimes sets up a special economic zone that provides incentives such as low taxes or reduced import and export barriers. The idea is to stimulate economic activity to create jobs and improve the standard of people within the zone. One of the most successful special economic zones has been Shenzhen, in the People's Republic of China. Other special economic zones include Manaus in Brazil, Subic Bay in the Philippines, and the Aqaba Special Economic Zone in Jordan.

Speculator. A speculator buys or sells something for one reason only: to profit from the investment's subsequent rise in price. In contrast to *hedgers* and *arbitrageurs*—who take advantage of market discrepancies to make money—speculators think they know something that the other investors in the market haven't figured out—and they act on it by buying or selling in the marketplace.

Spot Market. A trade executed for immediate delivery and payment is called a spot trade. The alternative to spot trading is buying or selling on the *forward* or *futures markets*, where trades are executed at fixed prices for delivery or payment at some future date.

Spread. The difference between the purchase price and the sale price. When you buy or sell foreign currency, for example, the price changes, depending on whether you're selling or buying. If the difference between the bid price and the offer price is big enough, the exchange can make a lot of money on the spread.

Stagflation. Where economic stagnation meets inflation. Stagflation occurs in an economy with high inflation and low growth. This phenomenon rarely occurs because inflation is usually the product of an overheated economy, not a stagnating one. Stagflation is a worst-case scenario for central bankers, where inflationary pressures are so strong that even an economic downturn isn't enough to quell the pressure toward rising prices.

Standard & Poor's (S&P). One of the world's biggest ratings agencies, Standard & Poor's looks through a company's books—or those of another entity, such as a country or a securitized loan—and makes a judgment about how creditworthy the country, company, or entity is. This judgment is usually given in the form of letters. AAA, for example, is used to describe the most creditworthy debtors.

Standard Drawing Rights (SDR). In an effort to create a sort of "world currency," the *International Monetary Fund* uses a unit of account called SDRs or Standard Drawing Rights. The value of SDRs is based on a basket of international currencies. By the beginning of the 21st century, the currencies used to calculate the value of SDRs were U.S. dollars, euros, Japanese yen, and British pounds, with the relative value of each currency being revised every five years by the IMF Executive Board. SDRs can be used for everything from foreign reserves in cental bank vaults to calculating how much airlines have to pay you when they lose your luggage. The idea is to have a "paper gold" that can be used to replace individual currencies in international accounts and transactions.

Stock. Stock is ownership in a company. This ownership is usually represented by pieces of paper—or electronic bookkeeping entries—called stock or shares. Stockholders (also called shareholders or shareowners) have a claim to the earnings and assets of the company. If the company makes a profit, anyone holding the company's stock can share in the benefits, usually paid out as dividends. If earnings are retained within the company, stockholders can still benefit—positive news and increased cash usually lead to a rise in the price of a company's shares.

Stockholders' Equity. Sometimes referred to as *net worth*, stockholders' equity is determined by subtracting a company's liabilities from its assets. It is also sometimes called shareholders' equity. Theoretically, if a company were to use all its assets to pay off all its liabilities, whatever is left belongs to the shareholders.

Stock Index. A stock index tracks the prices of a group of representative stocks to give investors an idea how the market as a whole is doing. Most indexes are weighted, giving more importance to shares of big companies, but the Dow Jones Industrial Average is technically just an average because each share, whatever its price and value of shares traded, is given equal weight in estimating the market's movement on any given day.

Stock Index Future. A stock index future allows investors to benefit from the rise (or fall) of a stock index, such as the Hang Seng Index in Hong Kong or the S&P 500 in New York. Buying or selling a stock index future is like buying or selling individual shares in the index. If the index goes up in value, the buyer of the stock index future profits handsomely. If it goes down, whoever sold the stock index future would come out ahead (see **short sale**).

Stock Option. A stock call option gives the holder the right to buy a certain number of shares, called underlying shares, at a certain price in the future. The opposite, the right to sell the underlying share or other asset, is called a *put*. Many companies provide employees with call options that allow them to profit when the share's price goes up. The holder of a stock option, like any other *option*, has no risk in the sense that if the market doesn't move enough to make it worthwhile to exercise the option, the option is simply allowed to expire.

Stock Split. A stock split increases the number of shares in publicly traded companies. It does nothing to change the company's total market capitalization. The only thing that changes is the price of the individual shares. A $100 share, for example, would usually be split into two $50 shares to facilitate trading.

Stock Swap. When a company uses its shares to acquire another, a common tactic in the *mergers-and-acquisitions* game, the operation is referred to as a stock swap, or equity swap. Shareholders of the acquired company receive shares of the company's new owner. In the world of high finance, the word *swap* is also used to refer to an operation that exchanges one asset for another—such as income flows, currencies, or assets with different interest rates, such as *floating-rate* or *fixed-rate bonds* (see **swap**).

Structural Change. An economy is said to undergo structural change when factors of production—such as labor markets or investment policy—are radically altered. In the 21st-century economy, technological advances and the use of the Internet have allowed economies to grow and produce well beyond normal levels.

Structured Investment Vehicle (SIV). A sort of virtual bank, a structured investment vehicle allows investors to use short-term funding—usually *commercial paper*—to finance purchases of long-term securities. Since short-term interest rates are lower than long-term rates, most SIVs make money on the *spread*, or difference in interest rates between the two types of securities.

Subprime Debt, Subprime Mortgage Securities. Subprime loans are those issued to borrowers with less than perfect, or prime, credit ratings. Subprime debt usually requires a higher interest rate to compensate for the higher risk of the borrowers. This debt is sometimes repackaged into securities—called *mortgage-backed securities*—that, in theory, have a lower risk of failure (see **collateralized debt obligation**).

Subsidiary. A company that is controlled by another is referred to as a subsidiary. The controlling company or corporation is referred to as the subsidiary's parent and acquires control by owning enough shares to determine the composition of the subsidiary company's board of directors. For accounting purposes, a subsidiary is treated as a separate entity, paying its own taxes and subject to separate regulation by authorities. A company that is totally integrated into the parent company is referred to as a division. A wholly owned subsidiary, where all the shares are owned by the parent company, is also referred to as a branch.

Subsidy. Subsidies are government payments to businesses, ostensibly to help them through economic hard times. Most subsidies are criticized as being a waste of the taxpayers' money, because they often end up rewarding inefficiency: In many economies, badly managed and inefficient industries would not survive if they didn't receive generous government subsidies. Examples include shipbuilding, steelmaking, and some areas of agribusiness, such as sugar and cotton producers.

Supply and Demand. All free-market economies work on the principle that the supply of any good or service is limited. The less there is of it—gasoline or wheat, for example—the more expensive it will be. Application of the law of supply and demand allows consumers and businesses to decide how to allocate their resources—hopefully in the most economically rational way possible.

Supply-Side Economics. Based on the view that producers and consumers can stimulate economic growth better than governments, the idea of supply-side economics is to reduce taxes—taking the money from the government and putting it in the more productive hands of companies and individuals. In this way, money is supposedly freed up for saving and investing by consumers and businesses—stimulating the economy more efficiently than if the money were pumped into the economy through increased government spending (see **Laffer curve**).

Surplus. A surplus occurs whenever there is more coming in than going out. A trade surplus, for example, occurs when a country sells more abroad than it imports, increasing the inflow of foreign exchange. A government budget surplus occurs when tax receipts exceed expenditures.

Swap. A swap is a trade agreement between two or more counterparties, such as banks, to exchange different assets or liabilities. A swap allows both parties to obtain the right mix of assets and cash flows. A bank, for example, might swap floating-rate loans for fixed-rate loans to reduce risk.

Synergy. Synergy occurs when two or more parties combine their particular skills or assets for mutual gain. In foreign trade, synergy refers to the comparative advantage of letting each country produce and export those goods and services that it produces more efficiently. In the end, the theory goes, when each country is allowed to do what it does best, everyone is better off.

Takeover. Anyone can take over a company if they own or control enough of the company's shares. In a hostile takeover, for example, outside investors usually borrow large amounts of money to buy enough shares to acquire the company. This allows them to restructure the company as they see fit, often selling assets to pay off the acquired debt. Management, in many cases, tries to avoid hostile takeovers by restructuring the company in a way that makes it difficult for the new investors to make a profit (see **poison pill**).

Tangible Net Worth. The real-world view of a company. Tangible net worth is an accounting tool that evaluates a company by looking only at its tangible assets and liabilities, which include everything from cars and cash to bank deposits and loans. What gets left out are intangible assets, such as brand names and goodwill, which have no quantifiable value.

Tariff. A tariff is a tax on imports. In most cases tariffs are a percentage "penalty" to the importer and can range from a few percent to more than 100 percent of the declared value. The money is pocketed by the government—in an effort to discourage the import of goods that could compete with those in the local market. As far as trade barriers are concerned (see **subsidy** and **quota**), tariffs are, in fact, the least difficult to get around—as long as you have enough money to pay the extra cost of importing the product. The goal of most free-trade agreements is to eliminate quotas and reduce tariffs and subsidies.

TARP. See **Troubled Asset Relief Program.**

Tax Haven. A country that offers extremely low tax rates to individuals or companies is referred to as a tax haven. By reducing or eliminating taxes on profit or income, tax havens—such as small islands in the Caribbean or Pacific—are able to attract business and large amounts of private wealth. Some countries, such as Monaco and Switzerland, are considered to be tax havens even though their tax rates aren't as low as many offshore islands'; they're just lower than their neighbors'.

Third World. The developing countries are sometimes referred to as the Third World because the world was once divided into three distinct economic areas: the First World of developed capitalist countries, the Second World of communist or Soviet nations, and the emerging economies of the third part of the world. By the beginning of the 21st century, however, the term had come to lose a lot of its original meaning. The Soviet "second" world had collapsed, and many emerging economies, such as Chile, Singapore, and Korea, had reached a level of development that surpassed some of the more developed countries of the First World.

Tobin Tax. See **hot money.**

Trade Balance. A country's trade balance sums up all international purchases and sales of goods and services—plus all international financial transfers, such as interest payments on foreign debt.

This balance gives us an idea of who's running a trade deficit and who's running a trade surplus. Many people erroneously call the *current account* the trade balance, but they're not exactly the same thing. The current account, in addition to adding up all trade in goods and services, also includes income from investments abroad, such as interest or dividend payments.

Transparency International (TI). A Berlin-based international organization, Transparency International aims to fight corruption and bribery in the world economy by working with other international organizations such as the OECD to expose, investigate, and unmask corruption throughout the world. One of its most effective tools is to publish lists of countries and companies that encourage and condone corrupt business practices.

Troubled Asset Relief Program (TARP). The $700 billion relief package passed by the United States Congress in 2008 created a government entity, called the Office of Financial Stability, to buy up the troubled assets of major U.S. banks. These assets, mainly mortgage-backed securities, had plummeted in value when the housing market declined and their lack of liquidity was preventing banks from selling them—even at fire-sale prices—and getting back to their primary business of taking deposits and loaning money. When the economic crisis continued to worsen, the law was used to inject funds directly into the banks—mainly by purchasing equity stakes and acquiring outstanding mortgages—allowing the banks to provide new funds to homeowners, consumers, and companies in the economy at large.

Twin Deficit. See **double deficit.**

UNCTAD (United Nations Conference on Trade and Development). The principal organ of the UN General Assembly dealing with trade, investment, and development issues, UNCTAD brings rich and poor countries together in periodic forums to solve problems related to international trade and development.

Underemployment. Economists define the *underemployed* as people who are working only part-time or are working at a level that is significantly below their training and qualifications. Normal unemployment rates don't usually include the underemployed because they're not actively looking for a new job.

UNDP. The United Nations Development Programme was set up to promote sustainable development around the world. Its goal is to help developing countries create jobs, protect the environment, and, in the end, hopefully, eliminate poverty. Based in New York City, the UNDP is the third-highest-ranking entity in the UN system and is funded through voluntary contributions from UN member countries.

Unemployment. The percentage of a market's labor force looking for a job, unemployment is one of the most watched statistics in any economy. It tells politicians and economists how well an economy is working and, therefore, how it should be regulated. When unemployment gets too high the economy needs to be stimulated; when it gets too low, the economy needs to be slowed down or inflation may rear its ugly head (see **Phillips curve**). A certain amount of unemployment is considered good for an economy—there have to be some people looking for work to keep the economy running smoothly.

Unilateral Trade Barrier. Like one hand clapping in the dark, unilateral trade barriers are imposed by one country acting on its own to limit imports. These barriers are usually set up to protect local producers from foreign competition—in theory, giving them time to improve their productivity and efficiency. The problem is that local producers, once given the comfort of a protected market, rarely make the sacrifices to improve their products or lower their prices. In addition, unilateral trade barriers often also cause other countries to erect barriers of their own.

Value-Added Tax (VAT). A tax applied at each stage of production is called a value-added tax because every time a product's value is increased, the person or company adding the value has to pay additional tax. The idea is to make taxation progressive and to distribute the tax burden more evenly between producers and consumers. In contrast to a sales tax, which is paid only at the moment of the final sale, a value-added tax is paid by each party in the production process. VAT is used in almost every modern industrial economy—except the United States.

Velocity. Economists use the word *velocity* to describe how quickly an economy grows in relation to available money. The "speed" of money tells us what an economy can do with the money supply at its disposal. When a country produces a large GDP (see **gross domestic product**) with a relatively small money supply, it is said to have a high velocity of circulation.

Venture Capital. Money that is invested in new companies, usually not showing a profit but having a lot of potential for growth, is called venture capital. The idea of venture capitalists is to get in early. When the company finally takes off and begins showing a profit—leading to skyrocketing stock prices—the venture capitalists and others who invested early can reap huge rewards.

Victim of Trafficking (VOT). The United Nations agency overseeing migration, the International Office of Migration (IOM), defines trafficking victims as those who are coerced into moving abroad, usually through fraud or misrepresentation. Many end up working as slaves or prostitutes and are allowed to return home only once their "debts" to the traffickers are paid off.

Volatility. The movement of a price over time is referred to as volatility. A stock, for example, is said to be highly volatile if its price changes a lot—and changes often. Essentially, volatility measures both the frequency of movement as well as the magnitude. Most investors don't like volatility, so it becomes a factor in determining the price of a stock—or any other security with fluctuating prices.

Wage-Price Spiral. The inflationary wage-price spiral involves rapid price rises followed by equally rapid demands for higher wages, which result in more price rises. Like the proverbial chicken-or-the-egg scenario, no one knows which comes first, the rise in wages or the rise in prices, but the end result is summed up in two words: uncontrolled inflation.

Wall Street, the City, Bahnhofstrasse, Kabuto-cho. The part of a financial capital where trading is done is often referred to by a major street or district—and this name becomes synonymous with the market as a whole. For example, in London most of the banks and trading houses are located in the City of London (as opposed to other areas such as Knightsbridge, Soho, or Chelsea). The New York financial center is called Wall Street, in Zurich it's the Bahnhofstrasse, and in Tokyo it's the Kabuto-cho. Back in the Middle Ages, when Venice was the center of the world economy, the banks and money traders were clustered around the Rialto Bridge. Hence, Shylock's famous line in Shakespeare's *The Merchant of Venice*: "What news on the Rialto?"

Warrant. A warrant gives its holder a right, but not the obligation, to buy a stock or other security at a certain price during a certain amount of time. It's like an option (see **call option**), but a warrant usually isn't traded on open exchanges. Warrants are often attached to bonds, to make the bond more attractive, and allowing the issuer to pay less interest.

Web 2.0. Coined by Tim O'Reilly, a technological conference promoter and book publisher, *Web 2.0* refers to the second wave of the Internet. According to Mr. O'Reilly, "Web 2.0 is the business revolution in the computer industry caused by the move to the Internet as platform, and an attempt to understand the rules for success on that new platform."

Welfare State. A country where the government takes primary responsibility for the health and well-being of its citizens is referred to as a welfare state—as opposed to a state where the individual is expected to take care of everything. Many modern economies are built on the welfare-state model, where cradle-to-grave education, health care, and even job creation are taken care of by the central government.

White Collar. See **blue collar**.

White Knight. In business, a white knight is a company or person who steps in to help out. In the takeover game, a white knight can be someone who helps management thwart an unwanted buyout by agreeing to purchase enough shares to block the takeover bid.

WIPO. See **World Intellectual Property Organization**.

Withholding Tax. A tax deducted at the time a dividend or other form of income is received is called a withholding tax. In most countries, interest payments on bonds and stock dividends are subject to a withholding tax—thus allowing the tax authorities to receive their money before it goes into the pocket of the investor.

World Bank. Founded at the same time as the International Monetary Fund, the World Bank loans billions of dollars every year to developing countries mainly for long-term projects to fight poverty and encourage economic growth. Unlike the IMF (see **International Monetary Fund**), which provides short-term lending and assistance, the World Bank looks for long-term solutions to the problems in the world's poor countries. The World Bank gets most of its money from rich-country contributions and by borrowing on the international capital markets.

World Economic Forum. The World Economic Forum is held every year in the Swiss ski resort of Davos. These meetings bring together business leaders and politicians in an informal setting to discuss and direct the world's major social and economic problems.

World Intellectual Property Organization (WIPO). Based in Geneva, Switzerland, the World Intellectual Property Organization, as its name implies, promotes the protection of intellectual property in the world economy. The United Nations organization provides an international forum to solve difficult intellectual property issues, such as the validity of pharmaceutical patents and music copyrights.

World Social Forum. Held every year, the World Social Forum brings together socially conscious leaders to discuss world issues in a less capitalist setting than that of the WWF forum in Davos. The two meetings usually coincide (see **World Economic Forum**).

World Trade Organization (WTO). Based in Geneva, Switzerland, the WTO provides a forum where disputing countries can meet to remove or rectify barriers to trade. When the WTO makes a ruling, the "guilty" country is supposed to remove the illegal trade barrier. If it doesn't, the country that has suffered from it is allowed to erect trade barriers of its own, usually in the form of tariffs.

World Wildlife Fund (WWF), World Wide Fund for Nature. Based in Gland, Switzerland, the World Wide Fund for Nature is the world's premier organization for protecting endangered species. In the United States and Canada it is still referred to by its original name, World Wildlife Fund.

WTO. See **World Trade Organization.**

WWF. See **World Wildlife Fund.**

Yield. "Many happy returns." Yield, the return on an investment, is usually calculated in terms of percentage. When a bond, for example, is said to be yielding 8 percent, the purchaser can count on receiving an average of 8 percent per year until the bond is redeemed. Yields can be applied to almost any investment in the world economy: from real estate to stocks and mutual funds.

Zero Coupon Bond. A bond that pays no interest obviously has to provide something extra to make it attractive to investors. Zero coupon bonds are always sold at a discount. The buyer pays less than the bond's face value, knowing that, at a determined point in the future, the bond will be repaid in full. The difference between purchase price and redemption price gives a "kicker" to the investor to forgo the interest payments normally provided on most bonds.

Zero-Sum Game. A zero-sum game is based on the concept that one side's loss is equal to the other side's gain. This concept was developed in the context of game theory, where economic and political decisions are made rationally, producing clear winners and losers. In the real world, however, there are few true zero-sum games. Inventing a better mousetrap doesn't hurt anyone except a few inefficient mousetrap makers—and, of course, the mice.